WHAT MAKES THIS BOOK SO GREAT

Jo Walton won the John W. Campbell Award for Best New Writer in 2002 and the World Fantasy Award for her novel *Tooth and Claw* in 2004. Her several other novels include the acclaimed Small Change alternate-history trilogy, comprising *Farthing*, *Ha'Penny* and *Half a Crown*. Her novel *Among Others* won the Hugo and Nebula Awards in 2012. Her most recent novel is *My Real Children*. She comes from Wales but lives in Montreal, Canada. She writes science fiction and fantasy, reads a lot, talks about books and eats great food. It worries her slightly that this is exactly what she wanted to do when she grew up.

Also by Jo Walton

The King's Peace
The King's Name
The Prize in the Game
Tooth and Claw
Farthing
Ha'penny
Half a Crown
Lifelode
Among Others
My Real Children

WHAT MAKES THIS BOOK SO GREAT

JO WALTON

corsair

CORSAIR

First published in the US by Tor Books, a registered trademark of
Tom Doherty Associates, LLC, 2014.

1 3 5 7 9 10 8 6 4 2

First published in Great Britain in 2014 by Corsair.
This paperback edition published in 2015.

A CIP catalogue record for this book
is available from the British Library.

ISBN 978-1-47211-161-6 (paperback)
ISBN: 978-1-47211-162-3 (ebook)

Typeset in Great Britain by SX Composing DTP, Rayleigh Essex
Printed in Great Britain by CPI Group (UK) Ltd., Croydon, CR0 4YY

Corsair
is an imprint of
Constable & Robinson Ltd
100 Victoria Embankment
London EC4Y 0DY

An Hachette UK Company
www.hachette.co.uk

www.constablerobinson.com

THIS IS FOR PAM ADAMS, AND STEVEN HALTER,
AND THE OTHER WONDERFUL PEOPLE I HAVE MET
THROUGH THEIR COMMENTS ON TOR.COM.

Contents

1. Introduction   1
2. Why I Re-read   3
3. *A Deepness in the Sky*, the Tragical History of Pham Nuwen   8
4. The Singularity Problem and Non-Problem   11
5. *Random Acts of Senseless Violence:* Why isn't it a classic of the field?   14
6. rom Herring to Marmalade: the perfect plot of *Dirk Gently's Holistic Detective Agency*   17
7. "That's just scenery": What do we mean by "mainstream"?   20
8. Re-reading long series   23
9. The Dystopic Earths of Heinlein's Juveniles   27
10. Happiness, Meaning and Significance: Karl Schroeder's *Lady of Mazes*   30
11. The Weirdest Book in the World   33
12. The Poetry of Deep Time: Arthur C. Clarke's *Against the Fall of Night*   36
13. Clarke reimagined in hot pink: Tanith Lee's *Biting the Sun*   39
14. Something rich and strange: Candas Jane Dorsey's *Black Wine*   43
15. To Trace Impunity: Greg Egan's *Permutation City*   47
16. Black and white and read a million times: Jerry Pournelle's *Janissaries*   50
17. College as Magic Garden: Why Pamela Dean's *Tam Lin* is a book you'll either love or hate   52
18. Making the future work: Maureen McHugh's *China Mountain Zhang*   55
19. *Anathem:* What does it gain from not being our world?   58
20. A happy ending depends on when you stop: *Heavy Time, Hellburner* and C. J. Cherryh's Alliance-Union universe   60
21. Knights Who Say "Fuck": Swearing in Genre Fiction   63
22. "Earth is one world": C. J. Cherryh's *Downbelow Station*   66
23. "Space is wide and good friends are too few": Cherryh's Merchanter novels   69
24. "A need to deal wounds": Rape of men in Cherryh's Union-Alliance novels   72
25. How to talk to writers   75

26. "Give me back the Berlin Wall": Ken MacLeod's
    The Sky Road   78

27. What a pity she couldn't have single-handedly invented
    science fiction! George Eliot's *Middlemarch*   82

28. The beauty of lists: Angelica Gorodischer's *Kalpa Imperial*   86

29. Like pop rocks for the brain: Samuel R. Delany's *Stars in
    My Pocket Like Grains of Sand*   89

30. Between Two Worlds: S. P. Somtow's *Jasmine Nights*   95

31. Lots of reasons to love these: Daniel Abraham's Long
    Price books   99

32. Maori Fantasy: Keri Hulme's *The Bone People*   102

33. Better to have loved and lost? Series that go downhill   106

34. More questions than answers: Robert A. Heinlein's
    The Stone Pillow   110

35. Weeping for her enemies: Lois McMaster Bujold's
    Shards of Honor   113

36. Forward Momentum: Lois McMaster Bujold's
    The Warrior's Apprentice   117

37. Quest for Ovaries: Lois McMaster Bujold's *Ethan of Athos*   120

38. Why he must not fail: Lois McMaster Bujold's
    Borders of Infinity   123

39. What have you done with your baby brother?
    Lois McMaster Bujold's *Brothers in Arms*   126

40. Hard on his superiors: Lois McMaster Bujold's *The Vor Game*   129

41. One birth, one death, and all the acts of pain and
    will between: Lois McMaster Bujold's *Barrayar*   133

42. All true wealth is biological: Lois McMaster Bujold's
    Mirror Dance   137

43. Luck is something you make for yourself: Lois McMaster
    Bujold's *Cetaganda*   143

44. This is my old identity, actually: Lois McMaster
    Bujold's *Memory*   147

45. But I'm Vor: Lois McMaster Bujold's *Komarr*   152

46. She's getting away! Lois McMaster Bujold's
    A Civil Campaign   156

47. Just my job: Lois McMaster Bujold's *Diplomatic Immunity*   161

48. Every day is a gift: Lois McMaster Bujold's "Winterfair Gifts"   164

49. Choose again, and change: Lois McMaster Bujold's
    Vorkosigan saga   167

50. So, what sort of series do you like?   171

51. Time travel and slavery: Octavia Butler's *Kindred*   175

52. America the Beautiful: Terry Bisson's *Fire on the Mountain*   178

53. Susan Palwick's *Shelter*   182

54. Scintillations of a sensory syrynx: Samuel Delany's *Nova*   186

55. You may not know it, but you want to read this: Francis
     Spufford's *Backroom Boys: The Secret Return of the British Boffin*   190

56. Faster Than Light at any speed   194

57. Gender and glaciers: Ursula K. Le Guin's
     The Left Hand of Darkness   197

58. Licensed to sell weasels and jade earrings:
     The short stories of Lord Dunsany   202

59. The Net of a Million Lies: Vernor Vinge's *A Fire Upon
     the Deep*   207

60. The worst book I love: Robert A. Heinlein's *Friday*   211

61. India's superheroes: Salman Rushdie's *Midnight's Children*   214

62. A funny book with a lot of death in it: Iain Banks's
     The Crow Road   218

63. More dimensions than you'd expect:
     Samuel Delany's *Babel-17*   221

64. Bad, but good: David Feintuch's *Midshipman's Hope*   224

65. Subtly twisted history: John M. Ford's *The Dragon Waiting*   228

66. A very long poem: Alan Garner's *Red Shift*   231

67. Beautiful, poetic and experimental: Roger Zelazny's
     Doorways in the Sand   236

68. Waking the Dragon: George R. R. Martin's A Song of
     Ice and Fire   240

69. Who reads cosy catastrophes?   243

70. Stalinism vs Champagne at the opera: Constantine
     Fitzgibbon's *When the Kissing Had To Stop*   247

71. The future of the Commonwealth: Nevil Shute's
     In the Wet   252

72. Twists of the Godgame: John Fowles's *The Magus*   260

73. Playing the angles on a world: Steven Brust's Dragaera   264

74. Jhereg feeds on others' kills: Steven Brust's *Jhereg*   268

75. Yendi coils and strikes unseen: Steven Brust's *Yendi*   272

76. A coachman's tale: Steven Brust's *Brokedown Palace*   275

77. Frightened teckla hides in grass: Steven Brust's *Teckla*   278

78. How can you tell? Steven Brust's *Taltos*   281

79. Phoenix rise from ashes grey: Steven Brust's *Phoenix*   283

80. I have been asking for nothing else for an hour:
     Steven Brust's *The Phoenix Guards*   286

81. Athyra rules minds' interplay: Steven Brust's *Athyra*   289

82. What, is there more? Steven Brust's *Five Hundred*
    Years After   292
83. Orca circles, hard and lean: Steven Brust's *Orca*   295
84. Haughty dragon yearns to slay: Steven Brust's *Dragon*   297
85. Issola strikes from courtly bow: Steven Brust's *Issola*   300
86. What has gone before?   303
87. The time about which I have the honor to write:
    Steven Brust's *The Viscount of Adrilankha*   305
88. Dzur stalks and blends with night: Steven Brust's *Dzur*   308
89. Jhegaala shifts as moments pass: Steven Brust's *Jhegaala*   311
90. Quiet iorich won't forget: Steven Brust's *Iorich*   315
91. Quakers in Space: Molly Gloss's *The Dazzle of Day*   318
92. Locked in our separate skulls: Raphael Carter's
    The Fortunate Fall   320
93. Saving both worlds: Katherine Blake (Dorothy Heydt)'s
    The Interior Life   324
94. Yearning for the unattainable: James Tiptree Jr.'s short stories   327
95. SF reading protocols   331
96. Incredibly readable: Robert A. Heinlein's *The Door*
    into Summer   337
97. Nasty, but brilliant: John Barnes's *Kaleidoscope Century*   342
98. Growing up in a space dystopia: John Barnes's *Orbital Resonance*   345
99. The joy of an unfinished series   349
100. Fantasy and the need to remake our origin stories   352
101. The mind, the heart, sex, class, feminism, true love,
    intrigue, not your everyday ho-hum detective story:
    Dorothy Sayers's *Gaudy Night*   357
102. Three short Hainish novels: Ursula K. Le Guin's
    Rocannon's World, Planet of Exile and *City of Illusions*   363
103. On reflection, not very dangerous: Harlan Ellison's
    The Last Dangerous Visions   369
104. Why do I re-read things I don't like?   373
105. Yakking about who's civilised and who's not:
    H. Beam Piper's *Space Viking*   376
106. Feast or famine?   379
107. *Bellona, Destroyer of Cities,* Jay Scheib's play of Samuel
    Delany's *Dhalgren*   383
108. Not much changes on the street, only the faces:
    George Alec Effinger's *When Gravity Fails*   386
109. History inside out: Howard Waldrop's *Them Bones*   389

110. I'd love this book if I didn't loathe the protagonist: Harry Turtledove and Judith Tarr's *Household Gods*   392

111. Screwball-comedy time travel: John Kessel's *Corrupting Dr. Nice*   396

112. Academic Time Travel: Connie Willis's *To Say Nothing of the Dog*   399

113. The Society of Time: John Brunner's *Times Without Number*   402

114. Five Short Stories with Useless Time Travel   404

115. Time Control: Isaac Asimov's *The End of Eternity*   407

116. Texan Ghost Fantasy: Sean Stewart's *Perfect Circle*   410

117. The language of stones: Terri Windling's *The Wood Wife*   412

118. A great castle made of sea: Why hasn't Susanna Clarke's *Jonathan Strange & Mr Norrell* been more influential?   416

119. Gulp or sip: How do you read?   419

120. Quincentennial: Arthur C. Clarke's *Imperial Earth*   422

121. Do you skim?   426

122. A merrier world: J. R. R. Tolkien's *The Hobbit*   429

123. Monuments from the future: Robert Charles Wilson's *The Chronoliths*   434

124. The Suck Fairy   437

125. Trains on the moon: John M. Ford's *Growing Up Weightless*   441

126. Overloading the senses: Samuel Delany's *Nova*   445

127. Aliens and Jesuits: James Blish's *A Case of Conscience*   449

128. Swiftly goes the swordplay: Poul Anderson's *The Broken Sword*   456

129. The work of disenchantment never ends: Kim Stanley Robinson's *Icehenge*   459

130. Literary criticism vs talking about books   463

1. Introduction

This book is made up of a series of blog posts I wrote on Tor.com between July 2008 and February 2011. They appear here in order, and with their original dates. These are about a fifth of the total posts I made during that time. You don't have to read them in order, but sometimes one will refer back to another and develop an argument. I wrote them as blog posts, and so they are inherently conversational and interactive—they were written in dialogue with each other and also with the people reading and commenting. I think they are still interesting when taken out of that context, but if reading them here makes you splutter "but, but" and reach for the follow-up key, the posts are still online, and I am still reading comments. Interaction remains a possibility. I'm still writing new posts too. (If, however, you are reading this in a far distant future in which this is no longer a possibility, hello! Nobody would have liked to talk to someone from your world more than I would, and any regrets are on both sides.)

The brief I was given when I started writing for Tor.com was to talk about what I was re-reading. Patrick Nielsen Hayden said that I was always saying "smart things about books nobody else had thought about for ages," and that's what I tried to do. You won't find any reviews here. Reviews are naturally concerned with new books, and are first reactions. Here I'm mostly

1

talking about older books, and these are my thoughts on reading them again. There are posts on books in many genres and published between 1871 and 2008, but the emphasis is on older science fiction and fantasy. There are also posts here about the act of reading and re-reading, and about the genres of science fiction and fantasy and the boundaries between them. When I talk about books that aren't science fiction and fantasy, I'm looking at them from a genre perspective, whether it's how George Eliot should have single-handedly invented science fiction or wishing wistfully that A. S. Byatt had read Delany.

My general approach to the books in these pieces is as a genre-reader, but not as a generic reader. There's no impersonality here, no attempt at objectivity. These are my thoughts and opinions, for what they're worth, my likes and dislikes, my quirks and prejudices and enthusiasms. I select the books I re-read based on what I feel like reading at the moment, so these are my tastes. I do from time to time write about books I don't enjoy, for one reason or another, but what you'll mostly find are attempts to consider the question I ask in the title of this collection—what makes this book so great?

2. Why I Re-read

There are two kinds of people in the world, those who re-read and those who don't. No, don't be silly, there are far more than two kinds of people in the world. There are even people who don't read at all. (What *do* they think about on buses?) But there are two kinds of readers in the world, though, those who re-read and those who don't. Sometimes people who don't re-read look at me oddly when I mention that I do. "There are so many books," they say, "and so little time. If I live to be a mere Methuselah of 800, and read a book a week for 800 years, I will only have the chance to read 40,000 books, and my readpile is already 90,000 and starting to topple! If I re-read, why, I'll never get through the new ones." This is in fact true, they never will. And my readpile is also, well, let's just say it's pretty large, and that's just the pile of unread books in my house, not the list of books I'd theoretically like to read someday, many of which have not even been written yet. That list probably is at 90,000, especially if I include books that will be written in the next 800 years by people as yet unborn and books written by aliens as yet unmet. Wow, it's probably well over 90,000! When will I ever read all those books?

Well, I read a lot more than one book a week. Even when I'm fantastically busy rushing about having a good time and visiting

3

my friends and family, like right now, I average a book every couple of days. If I'm at home and stuck in bed, which happens sometimes, then I'm doing nothing but reading. I can get through four or six books in a day. So I could say that there are never going to be sufficient books to fill the voracious maw that is me. Get writing! I need books! If I didn't re-read I'd run out of books eventually and that would be terrible!

But this argument is disingenuous, because in fact there is that towering pile of unread books in my bedroom at home, and even a little one in my bedroom here in my aunt's house. I don't re-read to make the new books last longer. That might be how it started. . . . The truth is that there are, at any given time, a whole lot more books I don't want to read than books I do.

Right now, I don't want to read *Storming the Heavens: Soldiers, Emperors, and Civilians in the Roman Empire* by Antonio Santosuosso, and/or *The Phoenicians and the West: Politics, Colonies and Trade* by Maria Eugenia Aubet and Mary Turton. I do want to read both of these books, in theory, enough theory that they came home with me from the library, but in practice they both have turgid academic prose that it's work to slog through. I am going to try to slog through the Phoenician one before I go home to Montreal and the book goes home to Cardiff library, but the other one is going back unread. (The Phoenicians, unlike the Romans, are insufficiently written about for me to turn down a solid book for bad prose.) But yesterday, when I was picking up books to take to read on the train to London, both of them glowered at me unwelcomingly. I was already in the middle of one (pretty good) book on Hannibal's army, I wanted fiction. And I didn't just want any old fiction, I wanted something good and absorbing and interesting enough to suck me in and hold my attention on the train so that I wouldn't notice the most boring scenery in the world—to me at least, who has taken the train between Cardiff and London quite often before. I didn't want to have to

4

look out of the window at Didcot Parkway. I had some new fiction out of the library, but what I wanted was something engrossing, something reliable, and for me, that means something I have read before.

When I re-read, I know what I'm getting. It's like revisiting an old friend. An unread book holds wonderful unknown promise, but also threatens disappointment. A re-read is a known quantity. A new book that's been sitting there for a little while waiting to be read, already not making the cut from being "book on shelf" to "book in hand" for some time, for some reason, often can't compete with going back to something I know is good, somewhere I want to revisit. Sometimes I totally kick myself over this, because when I finally get around to something unread that's been sitting there I don't know how I can have passed it over with that "cold rice pudding" stare while the universe cooled and I read C. J. Cherryh's *The Pride of Chanur* for the nineteenth time.

My ideal relationship with a book is that I will read it for the first time entirely unspoiled. I won't know anything whatsoever about it, it will be wonderful, it will be exciting and layered and complex and I will be excited by it, and I will re-read it every year or so for the rest of my life, discovering more about it every time, and every time remembering the circumstances in which I first read it. (I was re-reading Doris Lessing's *The Good Terrorist*. "The first time I read this was in a cafe in Lytham St. Annes in 1987," I mentioned. "How can you remember that?" my husband asked. "I don't know. It was raining, and I was eating a poached egg on toast." Other people remember where they were when they heard that Princess Diana was dead. I haven't a clue, but I pretty much always remember where I was when I first read things.)

This ideal relationship doesn't always work out. Even when I like the book in the first place, sometimes a re-read is a

5

disappointment. This usually happens when the thing that was good about the book was a temporary shininess that wears off quickly. There are books that pall when I know their plots, or become too familiar with their characters. And sometimes I read a book that I used to love and find it seems to have been replaced with a shallow book that's only somewhat similar. (This happens most often with children's books I haven't read since I was a child, but it has happened with adult books. This worries me, and makes me wonder if I'm going to grow out of everything and have nothing to read except Proust. Fortunately, when and if that day comes, in several hundred years, Proust will be there, and still pristine.)

A re-read is more leisurely than a first read. I know the plot, after all, I know what happens. I may still cry (embarrassingly, on the train) when re-reading, but I won't be surprised. Because I know what's coming, because I'm familiar with the characters and the world of the story, I have more time to pay attention to them. I can immerse myself in details and connections I rushed past the first time and delight in how they are put together. I can relax into the book. I can trust it completely. I really like that.

Very occasionally, with a wonderfully dense and complex book I'll re-read it right away as soon as I've finished it, not just because I don't want to leave the world of that book but also because I know I have gulped where I should have savoured, and now that I know I can rely on the journey that is the book, I want to relax and let it take me on it. The only thing missing is the shock of coming at something unexpected and perfect around a blind corner, which can be one of the most intense pleasures of reading, but that's a rare pleasure anyway. Re-reading too extensively can be a bad sign for me, a sign of being down. Mixing new possibilities with reliable old ones is good, leaning on the re-reads and not adventuring anything new at all isn't. Besides, if I do that, where will the re-reads of tomorrow come from? I can't re-read the same 365 books for the next 800 years. I've already read some dearly beloved books to the point where I know them by heart.

Long before I am 800 I will have memorized all the books I love now and be unable to re-read them, but fortunately by then people and aliens will have written plenty more new favourites, and I'll be re-reading them too.

3. A Deepness in the Sky, the Tragical History of Pham Nuwen

Vernor Vinge's *A Deepness in the Sky* (1999) wouldn't be a tragedy if it existed alone. It's a tragedy because it's a prequel to *A Fire Upon the Deep* (1992) and the reader knows things about the universe the characters do not know. All the other things I can think of that make this trick work are historical or mythological. *Deepness* does it entirely within SF and entirely within Vinge's invented universe. I think it's an incredible achievement.

In *A Fire Upon the Deep* we learn early on that our immediate cosmic neighborhood is divided into Zones, working outwards from the Galactic core. In each Zone, cognition and technology work better. So in the core it isn't possible to be intelligent at all, in the Slow Zone it's possible to be as intelligent as a human but no better and you can't go faster than light, in the Beyond you can have FTL and anti-gravity and enhanced intelligences, and in the Transcend you can have godlike intelligences and Clarke's Law tech. The novel takes place in the Beyond, with an excursion to the Slow Zone, and concerns a problem from the Low Transcend risking upsetting the whole thing. (Vinge apparently thought up this brilliant universe as a way around his idiotic

8

Singularity non-problem, which just goes to show that a) constraints can produce excellent art and b) every cloud has a silver lining.)

The whole of *Deepness* takes place in the Slow Zone, among characters, human and alien, who have absolutely no idea that their universe works that way. They don't know there are other Zones out there, they think they're part of a baroque and complex civilization that stretches for light-years, that's held together by a thin skein of trading spaceships.

The universe they believe they live in has a long history of Failed Dreams—AI, FTL, really good life-extension techniques—which have kept receding as they are chased. There's a profession of "Programmer/Archaeologist" where your job is to excavate the underlayers of the old programs your computers are running—and they're very old; in some cases, there are slower-than-light starships running on Linux.

The plot of *Deepness* is an exciting one, with aliens going through a technological revolution, with two groups of opposed humans trying to use them and each other, and with tiny incremental advances in technology meaning a huge amount. Whole civilizations are perishing in the background because they've got as far as it's possible to go—their planets are at the point where one little bit of overload will bring it all down around their ears. There's mindwipe, and the fascinating idea of Focus (enslaving people and fixing their brains in one direction so that they become obsessive about it), and a carefully timed revolt, and secrets among the aliens. There are great characters and a great character-driven plot, and I didn't even mention how terrifically alien and yet entirely comprehensible the aliens are, who have evolved on a planet around a star that goes out regularly and freezes even their air. There's a happy ending.

But in the end what brings me back to *Deepness* again and again isn't any of that but the terrible tragedy that surrounds that happy ending, that Pham Nuwen wants to find the secret at the heart of the galaxy and he sets off in the wrong direction to find it.

At the end of the movie *Far from Heaven* the hero, a black guy in a segregated 1950s US, leaves the white heroine and gets on a train in Hartford, Connecticut, towards the US South. "No!" I said in an anguished whisper. I wanted him to walk across the platform and get on the train going the other way. In Montreal even then he could have married the girl. He's heading in the wrong direction and he doesn't even know there's a possible way out.

It's a heck of an achievement for Vinge to make me feel the same way in an entirely SFnal universe, and without a word about it in the book.

4. The Singularity Problem and Non-Problem

I mentioned in my post on Vinge's *A Deepness in the Sky* that I don't believe the Singularity is a problem. Commenters Dripgrind and Coveysd asked about that, and I decided the answer was worth a post. Vinge came up with the Singularity in *Marooned in Realtime* (*Analog,* May–August 1986; Bluejay, 1986), which I read in 1987 when it came out in Britain. I thought then that the Singularity was a terrific SF idea—the idea was that technological progress would spiral so fast that something incomprehensible would happen. In the book, most of humanity has disappeared, and the plot concerns the people who missed it. (Incidental aside—the reason I re-read *Marooned in Realtime* is for the journal of one of the people who missed it. The plot, the ideas, the other characters have all worn fairly thin over time, but Marta's journal as she lives alone on a far-future Earth remains compelling.) I was astonished at reaching the end of the book to discover a little afterword in which Vinge claimed to believe in the coming Singularity. I thought it was a great idea for a story, maybe even two or three stories, but too obviously silly for anyone to really believe.

Since then, the Singularity has come to be an object of almost religious faith in some quarters. In *The Cassini Division*

(1998), Ken MacLeod has a character call it "the Rapture for nerds," and that's just how I see it.

I understand how Vinge, a brilliant writer who had worked in computing for years, could, in 1986, have seen how incredibly quickly computers had developed, and extrapolated that to other things. I mean it's like someone seeing in 1950 that a hundred years before, the fastest speed was twenty miles per hour and now it was supersonic and extrapolating that line straight forward to having FTL by 1983. Nevertheless, I regard this as a kooky belief. Yes, in 1950 we were supersonic, and gosh, we're in 2008 and . . . we're still traveling in jets only very slightly faster than in 1950, and cars, and subways, and buses. Even computers are only incrementally better than they were in 1987, and this isn't entirely because they're mostly handicapped with Windows. I'm not saying they haven't improved. I'm just saying that if we'd carried on the extrapolated curve between 1950 and 1987 we'd have something a lot better. Instead, we got the Internet, which is a lot better, which is a new thing. That's what people do. They come up with new things, the new things improve, they have a kind of plateau. It doesn't go on forever. A microwave is shiny and science-fictional but a toaster makes better toast, and most people have both, and few people have much in their kitchen that's much newer. And people are still people, traveling fast, using the Net, and though they may go through paradigm shifts, I don't think we'll ever get to the point where understanding the future would be like explaining Worldcon to a goldfish, and even if we did, it wouldn't be very interesting. If you want to argue about how much closer to the Singularity we are than we were in 1987, fine, but I'd suggest taking a look at *The Shock of the Old: Technology and Global History Since 1900* by David Edgerton first. But my view remains, nice SF idea, not going to happen.

I wouldn't care at all about people believing in the Singularity, any more than I care about them believing in the Great Pumpkin, if it wasn't doing harm to SF for everyone to be tiptoeing around it all the time.

What irritates the heck out of me is that so many other people have come to have faith in this, despite zero evidence, and that this is inhibiting SF. It's a lovely science fiction idea, and so are Gethenians, but I don't see people going around solemnly declaring that we must all believe there's a planet out there with people who only have gender once a month and therefore nobody should write SF about gendered species anymore because of the Gethenian Problem. Yet somehow the Singularity resonated to the point where Charlie Stross called it "the turd in the punchbowl" of writing about the future, and most SF being written now has to call itself "post-Singularity" and try to write about people who are by definition beyond our comprehension, or explain why there hasn't been a Singularity. This hasn't been a problem for Vinge himself, who has produced at least two masterpieces under this constraint. But a lot of other people now seem to be afraid to write the kind of SF that I like best, the kind with aliens and spaceships and planets and more tech than we have but not unimaginable incomprehensible tech. (Think Heinlein's *Citizen of the Galaxy* or pretty much anything by C. J. Cherryh.) I recently asked about this kind of SF in my LiveJournal and got only one recommendation for something I wasn't already reading. Maybe it's just a fashion, but I blame the Singularity—and that, to me, is the Singularity Problem.

5. *Random Acts of Senseless Violence: Why isn't it a classic of the field?*

Jack Womack's *Random Acts of Senseless Violence* is one of my favourite books, and indeed, one of the favourite books of everybody who lives in this apartment.

Outside of this apartment, I know only a handful of people who have even heard of it. It always strikes me as strange when there's something like that, a book that's brilliant and ought to have been seminal, a book that clearly should have set the world alight and yet sank with barely a ripple.

Random Acts is written in the form of the diary of Lola Hart, a twelve-year-old girl in a near-future New York City. As the book progresses she changes from being a sweet middle-class child to a robbing murdering street girl as society changes around her. Presidents are assassinated and money is devalued and martial law is declared as she worries about her sexuality and groans about being forced to read *Silas Marner* for school. At the start of the book she's writing in standard English with the occasional odd word choice, by the end she has progressed into a completely different dialect, and you have progressed step by step along with her and are reading it with ease. I can't think of a

14

comparable linguistic achievement, especially as he does it without any made-up words. (Random example: "Everything downcame today, the world's spinning out and I spec we finally all going to be riding raw.") I also can't think of many books that have a protagonist change so much and so smoothly and believably. What makes it such a marvellous book is the way Lola and her world and the prose all descend together, and even though it's bleak and downbeat it's never depressing.

So, why haven't you read it?

There are four reasons I can think of.

First, it might be because it didn't get much attention. It had some reviews, but it wasn't even nominated for any awards. It was published in 1993, in Britain first, by HarperCollins Publishers, and then in 1995 in the US by Grove Press. This probably messed up its award eligibility. I was just looking on the *Locus* index of awards, and I saw that Womack's previous (and only slightly less terrific) *Elvissey* (1992) won the Philip K. Dick Award and was on the short list for the Locus Award, but *Random Acts* doesn't seem to have been nominated for anything. It would have been eligible for the 1993 BSFA Award in Britain, which was won that year by Christopher Evans's *Aztec Century,* thus proving that there's no accounting for taste. Secondly, it might be because it has had singularly appalling covers. The original British hardcover was fairly bad, but sufficiently appealing that I got it out of the library on a cold day just before Christmas 1993, when I was feeling particularly desperate for something to read. The paperback covers—British and US—are just eye-gougingly awful. Despite having already read it and loved it I recoiled from the British cover. I've had friends who sounded intrigued by my description of the book change their minds when they actually see it.

Thirdly, it might be because the title is off-putting. You may have noticed I haven't been calling it *Random Acts of Senseless*

Violence every time I mention it, and there's a reason for that. It's not a bad title for the book, but it's off-putting for the kind of people who would enjoy it. It's also off-putting, according to some Amazon reviews, to the kind of people who would really love a book with that title and don't want the diary of a twelve-year-old as the world goes to hell around her.

It seems to me that the purpose of the title and the cover are to help the book find its friends. This hasn't worked here. I'm the only person I know who started the Dryco series—which also includes *Terraplane* (1988), *Heathern* (1990), and *Ambient* (1987)—with *Random Acts;* the rest of the handful of people I know who have read it read it because they already loved the others. Yet it's the first—chronologically—and the best place to start.

Now awful covers, a worrying title and no attention are damning enough for a book, but I think the thing that really relegated it to such undeserved obscurity is that it was a novel that didn't meet the zeitgeist. It didn't meet the expectations of what SF was supposed to be doing. It doesn't fall into an easy category and so it's hard to sell. The UK edition has a William Gibson quote on the back that says, "If you dropped the characters from *Neuromancer* into Womack's Manhattan, they'd fall down screaming and have nervous breakdowns." Gibson said that, and he meant it in a good way . . . but in the late eighties and early nineties Gibson was what people were looking at and cyberpunk was what they were expecting, with the New Space Opera just starting to come along to replace it. Gibson's affect is very cool, very noir, and that of his imitators even more so. What Womack was doing was hot and realistic and emotional, as well as edgy and weird. It didn't quite fit, so people didn't know how to take it—and very few of them did take it. I think it might do better today in today's more fragmented SF field, but in 1993 being totally astonishingly brilliant clearly wasn't enough.

6. From Herring to Marmalade: the perfect plot of Dirk Gently's Holistic Detective Agency

You know those polished wooden egg puzzles that people buy for you, the kind that are beautiful when they're an egg but that fall apart into shards that seem impossible for mortals to reassemble? Then maybe after a lot of trying suddenly all these impossible three-dimensional jigsaw pieces suddenly slot together and you have a lovely fragile egg again? Douglas Adams's *Dirk Gently's Holistic Detective Agency* (1987) always reminds me of one of those.

I didn't read it for ages. It wasn't that I didn't like *The Hitchhiker's Guide to the Galaxy,* it was just that I thought the plot had rather fallen apart in the later books. Indeed, the "throw in everything including the kitchen sink and St. Anselm's ontological proof of the existence of God" style of the Hitchhiker books had lent the series high initial energy but did not lead to continuous plot, or even necessarily making sense. They were inventive and amusing, but he seemed to be juggling too many balls and letting a lot of them drop. I wasn't in a hurry for more Douglas Adams in 1987. I didn't get around to picking Dirk Gently up until Emmet insisted on lending it to me in the mid-nineties. I read it for the first time on the train, the long six-hour (if nothing went wrong) train journey between Cambridge and Lancaster. I read it with a five-year-old Sasha reading Tintin and Asterix comic books beside me and asking (admirably rarely) if we were nearly at Crewe yet and (regrettably frequently) to explain a pun to him. (There's nothing like discovering how much sheer context and world knowledge a pun requires like explaining the puns in Asterix to a five-year-old.) Despite the inauspicious circumstances, Dirk Gently kept making me giggle, whereupon I resolutely refused to read the funny bits aloud. "You'll want to read this yourself one day," I said, and time proved me right. When he read it, aged about twelve, he loved it. I'm going to give you one example, the one that had me laughing so helplessly on the train that people were turning around to look and poor Sasha was embarrassed to be seen with me. Dirk Gently has a holistic detective agency of the kind that you'd expect to find in a Sheckley novel. Earlier, his secretary has torn out the middle of the dictionary to fit it into a drawer.

> "Luckily," he said, "you have come to exactly the right place with your interesting problem, for there is no such word as impossible in my dictionary. In fact," he added, brandishing the abused book, "everything between herring and marmalade appears to be missing."

It's the timing that's so beautiful, and the unlikeliness of the words. What brings me back to it isn't the funny bits, though some of them remain funny long after they've stopped being surprising. (Dirk's later offered a herring, and says there's no such word in his dictionary . . . and all of this is buildup and foreshadowing for something that is in our world but not in theirs, yet.) What's beautiful about it is the way the plot looks as if it's bumbling along tossing elements into the blender and making a big messy stew, just like *Hitchhiker,* and then suddenly it gives a glorp and assembles itself into a perfect precise layer cake. In retrospect, every element of the book makes perfect glorious sense and needs to be there. It all fits together, from the way the sofa won't go either up or down the stairs to the appalling dinner conversation about music on Radio Three. Things that look like jokes and asides are actually all setup. Every piece fits with every other piece like a perfect machine. It's almost impossible to summarise or synopsise because of this. If you wanted to tell someone about it you'd have to say, "Well, there's this time machine. And the person from Porlock. And ghosts. And Bach was written by aliens. And it's SF and very funny and it all totally makes sense eventually." I admire it to no end.

There are very few other examples of books I re-read to glory in the way they're put together. There's Barry Hughart's *Bridge of Birds,* and John James's *Not for All the Gold in Ireland* and perhaps— another time travel story—Tim Powers's *The Anubis Gates.*

7. "That's just scenery": What do we mean by "mainstream"?

In the "Handicapping the Hugos" thread, there's a discussion of what "mainstream" means.

In the simplest sense, "mainstream" is everything that is not genre. It's a marketing category like "mystery" or "SF" or "chicklit" or "literary fiction." It's everything that's mimetic. That's a fairly useless category, though, because it's too huge. We joke about simplistic equations like, "If you loved *Dragonflight* you'll adore *Mission of Gravity*" but categories exist to help people find books they'll like, and "If you loved *Middlemarch* you'll adore *The Hunt for Red October*" isn't going to do much for anyone. Anyway, marketing categories may be useful for finding books, but they're not interesting to think about as edges of genre.

"Mainstream" is a term from within SF culture. Mainstream writers don't know they're mainstream, and I believe Tor (which started off publishing mostly fantasy and SF) is the only publisher to label a portion of its list "mainstream." Mainstream is defined in opposition to SF. Damon Knight famously said that SF is what we point at when we say SF, and mainstream is the same, it's what we (SF readers) point at when we say mainstream.

20

What I find interesting is when there are books that are "obviously" SF but that some people think are mainstream.

I think what people mean when they say *The Yiddish Policemen's Union* (an alternate history about a Jewish state in Alaska) is "mainstream" is that it has mainstream sensibilities, mainstream expectation, and, most of all, mainstream pacing. They may also mean that it had mainstream publication and that Michael Chabon is a writer who made his name selling mimetic fiction—which is still true even though his last three books have been genre and he's spoken well of SF and even joined SFWA. I just made this kind of argument myself in that thread when I said that Ian McDonald was a long-standing SF writer who went to cons. The status of the author shouldn't make any difference . . . except that it kind of does. If some people are detecting mainstream sensibilities in *Brasyl* (a novel about quantum alternities in a historic, present and future Brazil) then I suppose they are. I don't know how, and I'd be interested to know how, because I just don't see it.

Samuel R. Delany has talked about the importance of reading protocols, and reading SF as SF. I tend to read everything as SF.

When mainstream writers come to write SF, it's normally the case that they don't understand the idioms of SF, the things we do when we (SF readers) read SF. This is very noticeable in things like Marge Piercy's *Body of Glass* (1991) (published as *He, She and It* in the US) where Piercy had clearly read Gibson but nothing much else, or Doris Lessing's *Shikasta* (1979) and sequels. The mainstream writers know how to do all the basic writing stuff, stories and characters and all of that, sometimes they know how to do that really well. They really want to write SF—in Lessing's case she clearly admires SF—but they don't know how SF works. They explain too much of the wrong things and not enough of the right things, they come up with embarrassing acronyms (SOWF, the "spirit of we feeling" from *Shikasta,* is burned onto my brain) and they don't understand how to put things over. They don't get the thing I call "incluing," where you pick up things about how the world works from scattered clues within the text. I don't feel that Chabon has this problem in the slightest, because he is an SF reader and knows how to inclue—indeed I very much admire the brilliance of his worldbuilding—but he's very unusual.

I had a great revelation about this some time ago when I was reading A. S. Byatt's *The Djinn in the Nightingale's Eye* (1994). This is a mainstream story in which a female academic buys a bottle containing a djinn and gets it to give her wishes. It's a mainstream story because she finds the bottle on something like page 150 of 175. In a genre story she'd have found the bottle on the first page. It has mainstream pacing and expectations of what's important. The story is really about how simple answers are not fulfulling. The djinn is a metaphor in exactly the way Kelly Link's zombies aren't a metaphor. People talk about SF as a literature of ideas, as if you can't find any ideas in *Middlemarch* or *The Hunt for Red October*! I don't think it's so much the literature of ideas as the literature of worldbuilding.

In a science fiction novel, the world is a character, and often the most important character.

In a mainstream novel, the world is implicitly our world, and the characters are the world.

In a mainstream novel trying to be SF, this gets peculiar and can make the reading experience uneven.

In the old Zork text adventures, if you tried to pick up something that was described but not an object, you'd get the message "that's just scenery." The difference between a mainstream novel and an SF one is that different things are just scenery.

8. Re-reading long series

I'm re-reading C. J. Cherryh's Atevi books. There are nine of them, and another three promised, which makes them one of the longer SF series around. I was thinking, as I made my way through book two, *Invader,* that there are some things about a long series, any long series, that are quite different from an individual novel, perhaps in the same way an individual novel is different from a short story.

A novel is one story. It has a beginning, a middle, and an end. In Diane Duane's *Door Into . . .* books, when people are going to tell a story they begin, where we'd start "Once upon a time," with the formula "This is the story of /whatever/ and this is the way I tell it." I find it quite useful myself to think of that as the unwritten first line of any novel, because knowing what story it is and how I tell it is a very useful thing. The *Iliad* starts off with "Sing Goddess, of the wrath of Achilles" and the story you get is the wrath of Achilles, not the whole saga of the Trojan War—it begins ten years into the war, with the reasons for Achilles' wrath, and ends when he stops being angry, with Troy still unfallen. Eric Frank Russell's *Next of Kin* is the story of how Leeming single-handedly won the war against the Lathians. *Citizen of the Galaxy* is the story of how Thorby learned to be a free man. *Random Acts of Senseless Violence* is the

23

story of how Lola and her world went to hell together . . . and so on.

But when you have a long series, it isn't like that. There are artifacts of publishing where one story gets spread over multiple volumes (Charlie Stross's *The Family Trade* and *The Hidden Family,* or *The Lord of the Rings* for that matter) but I'm not talking about that. There are also very long series, like Kate Elliott's *Crown of Stars* books, where you have one very long story in separate volumes that have individual narratives but aren't really separable. I'm not talking about that either, though that's interesting and I might talk about that some other time. And you get things like Ken MacLeod's Fall Revolution books or Kim Stanley Robinson's Three Californias where the different parts stand alone but comment on each other, which is also really nifty, but not what I want to talk about.

What I'm talking about is something like Cherryh's Alliance-Union Universe or Atevi books, or Brust's Vlad books, or Bujold's Vorkosigan books, or Patrick O'Brian's Aubrey/Maturin books, where you have individual books that each tell a story and can be read alone, but each book is part of a longer history, and the books illuminate each other and the longer story and the way that is told begin to emerge as the series progresses. It isn't Achilles' wrath but the whole Trojan War, but it isn't a rambling set of anecdotes either, it's a lot more like a whole mythology.

The length itself has something to do with it. I always feel that re-reading a series like that is like embarking on a voyage, because you have many volumes in front of you. When you set off, you know you're committing yourself to a long time in the world, you're launching yourself into something you know is good and absorbing and is really going to last. I love that feeling, when you step again into that universe, knowing what happens, knowing the long road you have to go along before you reach the end—or the present end. When a series is still ongoing, I usually re-read it when a new volume comes out. Then there's a lovely sense that the new volume is waiting there at the end for me, that I can sail happily through the known waters with unknown waters ahead. I re-read the whole Vlad series in preparation for *Dzur,* and may well again for *Jhegaala.* Ooh! What a treat!

When I do this, of course, one thing I really notice is any minor inconsistencies. I used to have a problem understanding this. If I could see them, why couldn't the author see them and reconcile them? If I could launch myself into the universe and re-read so happily, why couldn't the author? Since then, I have written series myself, and now I am far more sympathetic. Re-reading one's own work is unlikely to bring the same warm glow of trusting yourself to the words on the page and the world they create. And remembering one's own work, one remembers what one meant to do and the broad sweep of intent, not every detail of what one actually put down. Oh well.

I also notice the felicities of connection that I might have missed before. This minor character will become a major character several books later! This antagonist will become a friend, and this friend a traitor. (Cherryh is particularly good at this.) Also, you can really appreciate setup. Through nine Vlad books, Brust mentions Valabar's as a wonderful restaurant, but before *Dzur* we never see it.

It isn't just seeing details, though. I think there's a way that a quantitative difference becomes a qualitative difference. Really long series can do different things. Partly the difference is just a case of having longer to build your spear to drive home your spearpoints. If the reader has lived with the characters for a long time and knows them really well, a line like "Ivan you idiot, what are you doing here?" can bring tears to their eyes. (Bujold's *Memory* [1996]. Read the other seven books first.) The same goes for Dorothy Dunnett's *Pawn in Frankincense* (1969), where I've known several people who have read only that book not be knocked over by the events at the end, whereas people who have read from the beginning of the series (it's book four) reliably are.

Beyond all this, in a long series we have history. This can be the ability to give a historical perspective—Cherryh's Alliance-Union books are brilliant at that, because they're written from different angles on a long history. But even books that use the same points of view can do it—we see history change in Bujold's Miles books and in the Atevi books. We see people go from being a glint in someone's eye to viewpoint characters in a length of time that feels emotionally long enough for that to happen. In a really long series, there's time for characters to really grow and change in a way that doesn't feel rushed or forced. And in SF, as we've noted before, the world is a character. So there's time and space for the world to grow and change. The world growing and changing is what history is, and seeing it happening before our eyes is a wonderful thing that provides a new and fascinating kind of perspective.

9. The Dystopic Earths of Heinlein's Juveniles

Heinlein isn't usually noted for his dystopias. Indeed, his Juveniles are usually considered upbeat cheery fare, suitable for twelve-year-olds of all ages. But as I was gazing out over the cornfields of Iowa (does anyone really need that much corn?) I found myself thinking about U.S. rural poverty, which led me naturally to reflecting on U.S. rural poverty in *Starman Jones* (1953). In *Starman Jones,* Max is a dirt-poor farmer teen who leaves home in search of adventure and opportunity when his stepmother marries again. Max has an eidetic memory and is a lightning calculator, which is enough to get him promoted to starship captain practically as soon as he gets off the planet, but on Earth isn't enough for him to qualify as apprentice to a dustman. Earth has become dominated by Guilds, all of which demand fees and recommendations and kickbacks to allow people to join. Max cheats, lies and bribes his way off this horrible place to make good among the stars.

The other Earths of Heinlein's Juveniles aren't much better, as I remember. In *Citizen of the Galaxy* (1957), there's no slavery actually on Earth, but Earth is decadent, corrupt, controlled by corporations and full of people living on the profits of offworld slavery. Ugh.

In *Farmer in the Sky* (1950), a family emigrates to Ganymede to struggle with terraforming. Before they leave we see a little of Earth—food rationing, counting points, not wanting to waste the last scrape on a butter paper. This Earth is overpopulated and starving, even if it still has accordions and Boy Scouts.

Tunnel in the Sky (1955) is one of my favourites. Kids get to go on school trips through matter transmitters to other planets, and they can almost cure cancer, so far so good. But this Earth is overpopulated and repressive too. The Chinese are shipping out their population, and not very kindly. Food is being brought in from other planets, so nobody is starving, yet, but the smart characters are heading out for the stars as soon as they get the chance. How long will the colonies feed an Earth that loses schoolchildren for months in unexplored alien jungles?

In *Red Planet* (1949) and *Between Planets* (1951), Earth is a pretty fair stand-in for George III's England, repressive, aggressive and useless, with the plucky colonists of Mars and Venus as the fledgling US. In *The Rolling Stones* (1952), nobody even considers visiting Earth in their tour of the solar system.

Time for the Stars (1956) has one of the worst imaginable future Earths. It's so overcrowded that you have to have a license to have children, and if you have more than three you pay extra tax and get a big enough apartment allocated. Also, women wear hats all the time, even indoors and at the table. . . . Just horrible. It doesn't seem all that much nicer when the hero gets home three generations later in time to marry his great-great-niece, but at least it's more colourful.

It's funny how it's overpopulation and political unpleasantness that cause the problems, never ecological disaster. Maybe that wasn't on the horizon at all in the fifties and early sixties? I suppose every age has its own disaster story. It's nice how little they worry about nuclear war too, except in *Space Cadet* (1968), which is all nuclear threat, Venusians and pancakes. (They don't make them like that anymore. Come to think it's probably just as well.)

Have Space Suit, Will Travel (1958) has an Earth just like the US of the 1950s, with soap competitions and soda jerks. Yet it's almost bad enough for the benevolent aliens to condemn it, and us.

In *The Star Beast* (1954), children can divorce their parents and live in government hostels, bureaucrats rule the world, and everyone is kowtowing to aliens. It's not all that bad, but I wouldn't want to live there.

No individual one of these would be particularly noticeable, especially as they're just background, but sitting here adding them up doesn't make a pretty picture. What's with all these dystopias? How is it that we don't see them that way? Is it really that the message is all about "Earth sucks, better get into space fast"? And if so, is that really a sensible message to be giving young people? Did Heinlein really mean it? And did we really buy into it?

10. Happiness, Meaning and Significance: Karl Schroeder's Lady of Mazes

Karl Schroeder's *Lady of Mazes* is one of the best pure SF novels of recent years. I read it in 2005 when it came out and was surprised it got so little attention. It seemed to me to be one of those books everyone would be talking about. I've just read it for the second time, and it holds up as well as ever. What a good book!

Livia Kodaly lives in Teven, a coronal (ringworld) where tech locks limit nanotech and inscape (perceptible virtual reality) to various consensual manifolds of reality. You can be right next to someone who sees you as a tree and you don't see at all, you can duck out of a conversation and replace yourself with an anima who you can later reabsorb to review what you both said, you carry around with you a Society of chosen friends and relations who may or may not be connected to the real people they represent at any given moment. This is complicated and fascinating enough, but Schroeder sets it up only to destroy it and show us how Livia copes with that destruction and with the wider world outside Teven where she travels to understand what has attacked them and find help for her people.

Lady of Mazes is rigorous hard SF, but the questions it raises are philosophical rather than technical. The problem with writing about post-humanity and people whose experience is very far from ours is the difficuty of identification. This can sometimes be a problem for me with Egan and Stross. Schroeder avoids the potential pitfalls, in any case for readers who are prepared to pay close attention even at the beginning when everything is unfamiliar. *Lady of Mazes* has a very high new-cool-stuff-per-page density, but without ever losing sight of the perceptions of its point-of-view characters. It has worldbuilding and ideas casually mentioned that most writers would mine for a trilogy, and it has one of the best descriptions of suffering chagrin I have ever read.

Set in the same universe as Schroeder's earlier *Ventus, Lady of Mazes* also explores some of the same themes. Schroeder seems generally interested in what gives life purpose and agency in post-scarcity societies. Schroeder, like John Barnes, seems to think that many people would retreat into unreality. Schroeder appreciates that people tend to become very baroque when given the opportunity. In *Lady of Mazes* we see new art forms, new ways of living, angst over relationships and other hallmarks of humanity. The illusions they embrace are the illusions of meaning and significance. They are happy and fulfilled within their ultimately meaningless experience. Schroeder doesn't have any answers, but he's great on fascinating questions. Does it matter if what you do matters as long as you think it matters? What do you want to be, free or happy? How about if they really are mutually exclusive options? What is freedom anyway? How does humanity govern itself when each person can have anything they want? How does humanity govern itself when nothing is natural? And if a Chinese Room started to attack your home, how would you fight against it?

On this re-read I am more impressed than ever with Schroeder's breadth of vision and clever construction. I also had a great time hanging out again with Livia and her world. The shadow of the post-humans and half-understood technology may hang over them, they may live in very odd worlds, but these characters are recognisably people, and people one can care about.

11. *The Weirdest Book in the World*

For a long time I thought the weirdest book in the world was Robert Sheckley's *Mindswap,* in which a retiring college professor does a holiday mind swap with a colleague on Mars, only to find when he gets there that the colleague doesn't exist and his own body back on Earth has disappeared. Things get weirder from there on, and don't stop being weird by the end of the book. Then I discovered R. A. Lafferty and thought nobody could ever be weirder.

In 1995, Lafferty lost his title. Robert Reed wrote *An Exaltation of Larks,* which really did seem to be the weirdest book in the world, making Sheckley and Lafferty seem positively normal in comparison. Robert Reed is an absolutely brilliant writer. I think he may well be the greatest living writer of short SF, edging out Ted Chiang by a nose. Stories like "A Plague of Life" and "Veritas" are why I buy SF magazines. Gardner Dozois has said he could publish a *Best Robert Reed of the Year* collection every year. He's phenomenally wonderful, up to about 10,000 words. After that it's as if you can hear him thinking, "Oh. Better throw in something else now. Something new." Sometimes this works really well, as in *Sister Alice* and *Marrow,* where the recomplications just make the books better.

Other times, as in *Down the Bright Way,* you find yourself thinking at the recomplications, "You know, this might have been enough for any normal person?" Then there's *An Exaltation of Larks,* which is brilliantly written, fascinating, and essentially becomes a new genre every 10,000 words. It starts off on a college campus with weird things happening, and whenever you think you have some idea what's going on, you just don't. There's a section where the characters are alien turtles floating in space. It has been, for more than a decade, the indisputable weirdest book in the house.

But I may have just read something that beats it for sheer unadulterated oddity.

Kathleen Norris (1880–1966) was an American "women's writer" of the early twentieth century. Her novels are odd romances set in an era after divorce but before divorce was acceptable, after automobiles but before air-conditioning and penicillin. To someone used to Victorian novels and modern ones, they have a fascinating level of morality—in one of them, someone lusts in his heart and is falsely accused of murder and, eventually exculpated, he dies of TB caught in prison. Rich people have interesting trouble passing through eyes of needles. Adultery is a perpetual problem. Love is not enough, and neither is money.

I read half a dozen of Norris's books from the library, just for fun. (I do this sometimes.) The last one I randomly picked off the shelf was *Through a Glass Darkly,* which is science fiction and, you guessed it, my new contender for the weirdest book in the world.

There's a utopian world which is an alternate America that didn't fight the Spanish–American war and which has always made peace ever since. It's socialist to the point of having free food for everyone, and in a way that clearly grows out of Norris's experience of having lived through the Depression writing cheerful books about rich people's love troubles. This alternate world also happens to be Heaven, or one of the Heavens—there are at least seven, as everyone knows. People are born and die there, but people also arrive there from our world when they have died here in a particularly good way. Our hero, a young trainee doctor, turns up there after having died heroically in the battle of Midway. He is shown around in a typical mainstream-writer-writes-utopia visitor way, having how everything works explained to him.

He then sets out to practice as a doctor, his training being miraculously complete. (Don't ask.) He falls in love with a married woman and angsts about this at great length. Then he falls in love with and gets engaged to her daughter. The daughter finds out about the mother and allows herself to be swept away in a flood (where she's rescuing some kids) and drowns, and is reborn in our world. There she grows up in New York and becomes a nurse, is seduced and marries someone else to give her baby a name. In the end she realises she loves the someone else after all.

That's it. Two-thirds of the book takes place in the ideal otherworld, and one third in our world. There's no frame closure.

If you have contenders for books weirder than this, do let me know.

35

12. *The Poetry of Deep Time: Arthur C. Clarke's Against the Fall of Night*

I've been meaning to re-read some Clarke in a memorial kind of way ever since he died earlier this year. What I picked up immediately was the short story collection *Of Time and Stars,* the first thing of his I ever read, which holds up wonderfully. Looking along the shelf this afternoon I found myself wanting new vintage Clarke, and failing that, which I'm not going to get, one that wasn't utterly familiar. There comes a time with authors one really likes and re-reads a whole lot when the books that were the least favourites become the favourites, because they're the ones you can still actually read.

Against the Fall of Night (1953) was the first far-future SF I ever read. My memories of it were hazy—I remembered the far-future city Diaspar, the only city on the desert Earth, and the way it had stood for countless millions of years looking only inward. I couldn't have told you a thing about the plot and characters, and on re-reading it, yeah, they're there, I suppose, but they're not what's important.

There isn't much lyrical SF, and it's something more often associated with Zelazny than Clarke. In the story about SF, Clarke was the nuts-and-bolts engineer with a vision. Yet here we don't see any nuts and bolts, we're into Clarke's-law sufficiently advanced technology. What makes the book memorable and notable is the beauty of the words and the imagery that clothes the ideas.

Man has been beaten back from the universe and confined himself to Earth. Not everybody was writing in those terms even in 1953—this is where Heinlein looks like an enlightened feminist. But never mind. I didn't notice it when I was twelve. There is one female character, but it might as well be all "he" for all that it matters. For the purposes of this story the spirit of humanity, the only important character, is called Man, and he, and is to be considered male. The actual notable characters are two asexual teenage boys and a middle-aged asexual male librarian. Forget it. It's shooting fish in a barrel. It's probably part of the genetic engineering they've done so they don't want to leave the city. Gender barely exists, sex isn't an issue, passion isn't an issue. Cope. Billions of years have passed, the oceans have dried up, nobody leaves Diaspar and Alvin is the first child to be born in the city for seven thousand years.

It's an amazing span of time, between now and then, and Clarke really makes you feel it. You feel how old Diaspar is, with its forgotten connections to lost cities and its buried robotic levels. Nobody knows how the computers work, or the moving walkways. They're decadent, in a mild passionless way. Then you learn of the dried-up oceans, the fallen moon, the endless desert, the great span of history out among the stars before the city existed. This really does feel like the end of time, not only to the people who live there but to the reader as well.

> In utter silence, the ship drew away from the tower. It was strange, Rorden thought, that for the second time in his life he had said goodbye to Alvin. The little closed world of Diaspar knew only one farewell, and that was for eternity.

The ship was now only a dark stain against the sky, and of a sudden Rorden lost it altogether. He never saw it going, but presently there echoed down from the heavens the most awe-inspiring of all the sounds that Man had ever made—the long-drawn thunder of air falling, mile after mile, into a tunnel drilled suddenly across the sky.

Even when the last echoes had died away into the desert, Rorden never moved. He was thinking of the boy who had gone, wondering, as he had so often done, if he would ever understand that aloof and baffling mind. Alvin would never grow up, to him the whole universe was a plaything, a puzzle to be unravelled for his own amusement. In his play he had now found the ultimate, deadly toy which might wreck what was left of human civilization—but whatever the outcome, to him it would still be a game.

The sun was now low on the horizon, and a chill wind was blowing from the desert. But still Rorden waited, conquering his fears, and presently for the first time in his life he saw the stars.

The plot is quite simple. Diaspar is beautiful but entirely inward turned. Alvin looks out and discovers that there is more in the universe than his one city. He recovers the truth about human history, and rather than wrecking what is left of human civilization, revitalises it. By the end of the novel, Man, Diaspar, and Earth have begun to turn outward again. That's all well and good. What has always stayed with me is the in-turned Diaspar and the sense of deep time. That's what's memorable, and cool, and influential. Clarke recognized though that there isn't, and can't be, any story there, beyond that amazing image. It's a short book even so, 159 pages and not a wasted word.

They don't make them like that anymore.

13. Clarke reimagined in hot pink: Tanith Lee's Biting the Sun

After reading *Against the Fall of Night,* I felt like reading something else set at the end of time, but this time with some girls in it. Tanith Lee's *Biting the Sun* was the obvious and immediate selection. Re-reading it with that in mind, I wonder if this may have been Lee's intention in writing it.

> My friend Hergal had killed himself again. This was the fortieth time he had crashed his bird-plane on to the Zeefahr Monument and had to have a new body made. And when I went to visit him at Limbo, I was wandering around for ages before the robot found him for me. He was dark this time, about a foot taller with very long hair and a moustache all glittery gold fibres, and these silly wings growing out of his shoulders and ankles.

It's the far future. Humanity is confined to three very similar domed cities (the interestingly named Four Bee, Boo, and Baa) and the rest of the Earth is desert. Robots do everything. People are essentially immortal, and decadent. We have an adolescent protagonist. So far, so very similar to Clarke. After that point, everything is different. Lee's work is first person, up front, immersive, immediate, individual, and anything but distant. Her version of humanity has not been genetically engineered into contemplative asexuality and aeons of quiet dreaming—anything but. Lee gives us a slangy rebellious girl with a taste for sex and drugs and changing gender. This is the subversive feminist version of the desert city with robots at the end of time.

The normal life cycle in Lee's world is for the life-spark (or soul) to begin as a child, with at least one involved parent, or maker. The child goes to hypno-school and is educated. After this, the child becomes "Jang," adolescent, and is expected to stay at this stage for a century or two. Beyond that they become "Older People" and live a different lifestyle for some centuries until they're sufficiently bored with life to wipe their memory and return to childhood, this time with a robot parent.

Robots do everything. There's nothing significant for people to do. At one point we're shown people "working" where they have to press buttons—and if they don't press them, they pop up anyway in half a minute. This really is makework and futility. Even art is entirely computer-mediated—and when the protagonist tries to make a sculpture without that mediation, it falls to bits. There's no work, there's no art, robots have it all. This is an early take on the problem of post-scarcity leisure, and as such it also makes an interesting comparison with John Barnes's *A Million Open Doors* or Karl Schroeder's *Ventus*. If you can do anything you want and have anything you want, but none of it matters, what do you want to do or have? There's nothing in this world for humans to do except eat, shop, take drugs, dream designer dreams, follow fashion, and have sex, for which they get married for periods varying between one afternoon and forty days. Jang are supposed to sabotage things from time to time, and even that isn't any fun, and doesn't really achieve anything. Life's a cycle of romance, drugs and sex, no wonder people are killing themselves in droves. There's no scarcity of anything, and you pay for things with groveling thanks. If you think of some work you could do, you have to apply for permission, and you'll find the robots have already got it covered.

Clarke's robots are wise, ageless, inscrutable and have the good of humanity at heart. Lee's are petulant, have personalities, and are not beyond cheating on their programming. They're sure they know best, after all. Clarke's are wise servants, Lee's are stifling over-controlling parents. This may not be as good for the characters, but it does make for more conflict.

Life for humans is, on the surface, glittering and fascinating. There are about six words of new slang, giving a brave illusion of a new dialect. Almost everyone lives in a palace. Fashion is constantly changing. You can have a completely new body designed, and wake up in it right away. You should do this no more than every thirty days, but you can short-circuit the process by committing suicide if you're impatient. Killing yourself creatively and designing interesting bodies are almost the only real art forms. You can change gender as easily as you can change height, weight, hair and skin colour. Most people have a gender preference, but it tends to be fairly mild. One character describes himself as "eighty percent male" and appears as female only once in the novel; others switch gender as often as clothing. This is done brilliantly, because it's accepted so casually. It bears comparison with the best of Varley's Eight Worlds stories.

The book has an interesting title history. It was originally published in the US as *Don't Bite the Sun* (1976) and *Drinking Sapphire Wine* (1977). I own a 1979 UK (Hamlyn) edition of both volumes bound in one cover as *Drinking Sapphire Wine*. More recent editions include both books but use the name *Biting the Sun*. I think of it as *Drinking Sapphire Wine,* as that's what it's said on my copy every time I've read it for almost thirty years, but they're both great titles. *Biting the Sun* refers to a shard found in an archaeological site our protagonist spends time at in her

41

quest for relevance. The shard bears the message, "Do not bite the sun! It will burn your mouth," which she interprets as not fighting the system—which she nevertheless continues to fight throughout the book. The sapphire wine is the water of Lethe which will let you forget who you are and begin again at childhood.

Unlike *Against the Fall of Night,* I've re-read this at reasonably frequent intervals. I think it's fair to say that I like it a lot more— but then I am a sucker for characters and events in a book, and Clarke's is pretty much pure atmosphere. I adore Lee's first-person unnamed protagonist. I re-read it to visit with her and her world for a while. She's predominantly female and has been Jang for about twenty-five years and is sick of it. She has a circle of friends and a life that doesn't contain anything real. At the beginning of the book she steals a pet, a desert animal. The first volume is about her search for meaning in her life, and the difference her pet makes; the second volume is largely about her living alone and making the desert bloom. You can see that as growing up, in a very limited way, I suppose.

I don't know quite what it says about gender expectations that while Clarke's protagonist looks outside the city and causes a renaissance, Lee's settles for a garden.

14. Something rich and strange: Candas Jane Dorsey's Black Wine

This was only my second read of Candas Jane Dorsey's *Black Wine,* and I don't have all that much coherent to say about it except "Wow," and "You want to read it!"

> The child imagined the wind slipping and sliding down the dunes at Avanue. She imagined the dunes as some kind of geometrical slope, at thirty-five degrees, like this one, but the mother kept talking and the mind picture changed with each sentence, like the shape of the wind.
>
> "It's an amazing landscape there. It's all billowy and soft, like a puffy quilt. Or maybe like the body of some great voluptuous fat person turning over in bed, the covers falling off, the mounds of flesh shifting gently and sensually. You know, you can memorize the patterns and then a big wind-storm comes and when you go out the next day everything is different. The skyline is different. The shoreline is different. The sand has turned over in its sleep. While you slept."

Let's try that again: Wow! You want to read it!

("Do you find it easy to get drunk on words?" Harriet Vane asks Lord Peter Wimsey in Sayers's *Gaudy Night*. I have to reply with him: "So easily that, to tell the truth, I am seldom perfectly sober.")

Soberly, however, *Black Wine* was published in 1997. It won the Crawford Award for best first fantasy novel, the Tiptree Award for best book that makes you think about gender, the Aurora Award for best book in English by a Canadian, and was third in the Locus Poll for best first novel. From which you'd gather that it's a first fantasy novel, it's good, and it makes you think about gender, all of which is correct so far as it goes, but doesn't get you much further.

This is another book like *Random Acts of Senseless Violence* that I'd expect to be a classic that everyone has read, and yet which seems to have been read only by a small group of passionate enthusiasts. I don't even own a copy myself, and have read it (twice!) because of the kindness of my next-door neighbour Rene Walling.

It's fantasy, but it might just as well be science fiction. There are some small insignificant magic gifts. There are some prophetic cards that seem to work. It's another planet, anyway, a whole planet with as many cultures and climate zones as you'd expect, and a moon that rotates. There's some technology, airships, medical imaging, but it's unevenly distributed. There doesn't seem to have been an industrial revolution, most of what you see is handmade. They know about genes, but children are as often conceived between two same-sex partners as two opposite-sex ones. Against this world we have a story of travel towards and away from, of mothers and daughters, quest and escape, horizons and enclosures.

This is a difficult book to focus on, unexpectedly hard-edged where fantasy is often fuzzy, disconcertingly fuzzy in places where you expect it to be solid.

There's an immense richness of world and character, and of story arising out of the intersection of the two. We see four very different cultures close up, the culture of the Remarkable Mountains, of the Dark Islands, of Avanue and of the Trader Town. They're all at different stages technologically and socially, the way things are in the real world. They do things differently. They have different languages and different patterns of behaviour. Nobody could confuse them. Names especially are edgy things, and central. Every culture has their own naming custom, from the names the slaves give each other in their silent language of touch and gesture to the people of Avanue who are all called Minh.

The novel is built from the intertwined stories of a mother and daughter who come from different places. It's not told sequentially. You have to fit it together as you read. There were things I didn't understand the first time I read it, and the odds are there are still things I don't understand. I can see re-reading it fifty times and still be finding new things in it. It's a book that happens almost as much in your head as on the page, which is rare and wonderful. This is a story where trying my trick of figuring out what would happen in the second half and where the beats would fall would have got me nowhere. I couldn't even have guessed the plot.

It's beautifully written at all levels. The language is precise yet lapidary—literally. The words are like stones, sometimes sharp and sometimes jewel-bright, and all of them essentially placed in the structure of the novel. The words are sometimes frank and shocking, but that's right, so is what they're saying:

Near them two students in green tunics were struggling with a fallen bicycle, trying to straighten the handlebars. Essa saw that they needed it because one student was wounded in the leg and could not walk. She averted her

45

eyes as if from an intimate act. Essa pulled the hand of the trader, whose palm was slimy with hot sweat. If the smell of death, something she thought was a cliche which is not, had not been filling the square his and her fear would have been palpable. Essa could only feel grateful for the camouflage as they started to run.

She heard a ragged officious shout behind them. They turned, still running but ready to dodge, thinking they were the target. The two young soldiers were beating the two students. The boy who had given Essa directions raised the club he had unhooked from his belt and brought it down on the skull of the wounded student. Her long hair seemed to shatter into a spray of black and glittering red.

It's demotic language, but not demotic in the way Monette's Melusine books are; indeed it's not really like anything else at all. If I had to compare it to anything it would be to Silverberg's *Lord Valentine's Castle,* but with much more depth.

It's a great pity it isn't in print. I'd love to be able to share it with people.

15. To Trace Impunity: Greg Egan's Permutation City

There are readings of a book you can't have on first reading. One of them is the reading in the light of later work. Another is being impressed how much it hasn't dated.

I loved *Permutation City* when I first read it in 1994. It blew me away. It does everything science fiction ought to do—it has a story and characters and it's so full of ideas, you almost can't stand up straight.

I still love it. I noticed all sorts of things about it on that first reading, but I didn't then see it as part of Egan's passionately engaged one-sided argument against God. In 1994 Egan hadn't yet written *Teranesia* (1999), or *Oceanic* (1999) or "Oracle" (2000). The cumulative effect of these, with *Permutation City*'s concluding denial of the possibility of deity, is not so much an assertion of "I don't believe in this, and you can't either" as of the intellectual equivalent of watching the world champion heavyweight blind-fold shadow-boxer.

Permutation City takes a brilliant (but apparently impossible) SF-nal idea and works through it pretty much perfectly. This is the Dust Hypothesis, the idea that consciousness finds itself out of the dust of the universe and constructs its own universe where its existence makes sense. We first see this with an AI whose brain states are being calculated out of order, and eventually with entire infinite universes, human and alien.

The book begins in a 2050 that still plausibly feels like a possible 2050 we could reach from here—which is a major feat for a book written in 1994 and focused on computers. It palms the card of strong AI by putting us right into the point of view of a Copy, a simulated human. Because we're reading, and we're used to reading and empathising with a point of view, we don't ever stop to consider whether or not Copies are conscious. We just accept it and right go on into the Dust Hypothesis. Along the way we see the 2050 world, the far-future virtual world of Elysium, and the meticulously modeled autoverse.

The book has three central characters: Paul Durham, an obsessive who launches the virtual city out of the dust of the universe; Maria Deluca, programmer and autoverse junkie; and Peer, a Copy who persistently rewrites who he is. All of these, and the fourth point-of-view character, Thomas the guilty banker who sends his cloned self to hell, are among the best characters Egan has ever created. I don't think I've ever put down an Egan book without saying "Wow, look at those sparkly ideas," but this is the one I re-read to hang out with the characters.

Reflecting the Dust Hypothesis, the chapter titles, which recur and mark threads within the novel, are all whole or partial anagrams of the words *Permutation City*. So is the title of this piece, which comes from the poem that begins the book in which each line is such an anagram.

The last time I read this book, a couple of years ago, on what was probably my tenth or eleventh read, I got so caught up in the end that I missed my stop on the metro. About a year ago, my son Sasha read it and was enthralled. His top quality category of SF is what he calls "Books like *Spin* (2005) and *Permutation City*!" By that he means very well written SF with characters you can care about and plots that keep you on the edge of your seat, with ideas that expand the possibility of what you can think about. He wishes there were more books like that, and so do I.

16. Black and white and read a million times: Jerry Pournelle's Janissaries

Sometimes, not every month, but every few months, I come over all Victorian and have pains in my stomach and want to spend a day lying on the couch reading Jerry Pournelle. When I feel like that there really are very few books that satisfy me—I want black-and-white military fiction with good and bad clearly delineated, guns, obstacles, military training, things blowing up, glory, death, and the good guys definitely winning. Also, it has to be written to a certain standard. I don't want rubbish just because I'm in that particular mood.

It isn't only Jerry Pournelle that scratches this itch. He's the best, especially when he's writing on his own. He can bring tears to my eyes with lines like "The sergeant survived? Then the Legion lives!" There's also Piper, Weber, John Barnes's Timeline Wars books, and more recently I've discovered W. E. B. Griffin, whose books are not SF but straight military historical fiction. ("Wow," I thought when I read *Semper Fi,* "a whole book about Bobby Shaftoe!") I can also thank this reading mood for my discovery of Lois McMaster Bujold, who I adore even on days when I don't want to bite something.

But when I've got those cramps and that urge, the canonical most perfect book in the world for me is suddenly *Janissaries* (1975).

Janissaries would push a lot of my buttons at any time. There's a planet, Tran, where groups of people from Earth have been taken by aliens at 600-year intervals to grow drugs. So they have brilliant weird cultures, because they came from different parts of the planet and at different tech levels. There are Romans who have copies of Roman books we don't have. They also have interestingly weird tech, because it has merged oddly. So when our heroes give them gunpowder, things get interesting. You get new military formations, for instance. And beyond all of that and the good guys and bad guys and the things blowing up, there are fascinating hints of a wider universe and Other Things Going On. Oh, and it's got a girl. I mean, of course it's got a girl, even W. E. B. Griffin has girls, but it has a girl who isn't just there as a prize and a sexual partner—well, it has one of those too, but it also has a major female character who does significant things.

They don't make military adventure fiction better than this, and you get bonus extra history of tech stuff thrown in for free.

There are some sequels, by Pournelle and other people, or by other people on their own, which I have read once and never felt the urge to pick up again. My original copy of *Janissaries* has been read so much, it's in danger of disintegration.

As I was putting it back on the shelf, I admired the serendipity of alphabetical order, that allows Marge Piercy, H. Beam Piper, Plato, Karl Popper, Jerry Pournelle, and Tim Powers to sit so peacefully on the shelf together.

17. College as Magic Garden: Why Pamela Dean's Tam Lin is a book you'll either love or hate

This is one of my very favourite books, and one that grows on me with every re-read. But I know from other online discussions that it isn't a book for everyone.

Tam Lin (1991) is based on an old Scottish ballad. It's the story of a group of friends at a liberal arts college in Minnesota in the 1970s, talking, reading, discussing, seeing plays, falling in love, meeting the Queen of Elfland, coping with ghosts, worrying about contraception and being sacrificed to Hell.

That makes it sound much more direct than it is. The story, the ballad story, the way the head of the Classics Department is the Queen of Elfland, is buried in indirection. Many readers wake up to the fact that one of the main characters is about to be sacrificed to Hell as an unpleasant shock sometime in the last couple of chapters. It isn't just a book you like better when you re-read it, it's a book that you haven't had the complete experience of reading unless you've read it twice. Some readers have even argued that Dean wanted to write a college story and pasted on the magic to make it sellable—sellable outside the mainstream ghetto, no doubt. If you hate indirection and re-reading, you're probably not going to like it.

In fact the magic, the ghosts, the ballad story and the Queen of Elfland are integral to the whole thing. The central thing the book is doing is college as magic garden. The whole experience of going to university is magical, in a sense, is a time away from other time, a time that influences people's whole lives but is and isn't part of the real world. College is where you are, as the protagonist, Janet puts it, paid to read for four years. It's also many people's first experience of being away from home and of finding congenial friends. But it isn't, and can't be, your real life. It's finite and bounded. It falls between childhood and adulthood. And it's full of such fascinating and erudite people who can quote Shakespeare. Where did they come from? They certainly can't have come from high school, and "Under the hill" is *Tam Lin*'s very interesting answer.

The other thing some readers object to is the pacing. The first year takes up far more of the book than the subsequent years, and the climax is over with almost before you've had time to savour it. I didn't understand this properly myself until I wrote a play version of the ballad—the pacing of the novel is the pacing of the ballad. It's very impressive, and I kicked myself for not spotting it until I tried to do it myself.

Furthermore, you won't like *Tam Lin* unless you like reading, because a lot of it is about the meta-experience of reading and thinking and putting things together. (There are plenty of books you can enjoy even if you don't like reading. This just isn't one of them.)

You may not like it if you didn't feel the need to go to, or hated, university—you may find yourself passionately envious though. I mean, I was a Classics major myself, but not only did I never meet any magic people (so unfair!) but I was at a British university where I did nothing but Classics for three years, never mind all those fascinating "breadth" requirements. (Incidentally, I've known a couple of parents who have given this book to their teenage kids who are bored with high school and can't see the point of more education. This works.)

One of the main reasons I re-read certain books over and over is to hang out with the characters. The characters in *Tam Lin* are so cool to hang out with that I sometimes wish they were with me when I go to see plays. If you don't get on with them, then it isn't going to work for you. Myself, I think they're wonderfully real and three dimensional and fascinating.

Oh, and the last reason you might hate it? If you hate books that mention other books so that you wind up with a reading list of things the characters read at the end. Now I adore this, and not just with books. I found Rodin because Jubal Harshaw liked him, and Bach because Cassandra Mortmain liked him, and the Beatles because George Orr and some aliens liked them. Similarly, *Tam Lin* encouraged me to read Christopher Fry and *Rosencrantz and Guildenstern Are Dead* and Dr. Johnson. I hate it when books rely on knowledge of something external, when they lean on it as if everybody through all time knows who Cordelia is* and it's enough to namedrop a reference to get automatic free atmosphere. In a book replete with references, Dean never does this. Even with Shakespeare she quotes enough and fills in enough that it doesn't matter to understanding the story whether or not you knew it beforehand, without boring those who did know before.

It's a fairly long book, but I'm always sorry when I get to the end and have to stop reading it.

Full disclosure: Pamela Dean is a friend of mine, I've beta read her latest book, and I've had her *Tam Lin*–conducted tour of Carleton College. But if you think that makes any difference to what I think about the book, you should see all the friends I have whose books I keep meaning to get to sometime.

---

* Cordelia could mean Lear's daughter, Miles Vorkosigan's mother, or somebody in *Buffy*.

18. Making the future work: Maureen McHugh's China Mountain Zhang

China Mountain Zhang (1992) is a fascinating example of a near future science fiction mosaic novel. There are a number of notable mosaic novels—my favourite other examples are *Hyperion* (1989), *Tales of Nevèrÿon* (1975) and *The Jewel in the Crown* (1966). A mosaic novel seems at first more like a short story collection all set in the same world, like *Four Ways to Forgiveness* (1995) or *Capitol* (1979), but it soon becomes apparent that it is more than that. A normal novel tells a story by going straightforwardly at it, maybe with different points of view, maybe braided, but clearly going down one road of story. A mosaic novel builds up a picture of a world and a story obliquely, so that the whole is more than the sum of the parts. *China Mountain Zhang* is one of the best mosaic novels ever written, and this was reflected in the attention it got on publication. It won the Tiptree and Lambda and was nominated for the Hugo and Nebula. I read it because of the Hugo nomination (after all, how many first novels get Hugo nominations?) and I've read it again probably every couple of years since, because reading it is a very enjoyable experience.

It's a very unusual book. It's not just the mosaic thing. It's also a small-scale book about ordinary people winning small-scale victories without changing or saving the world. Yet it's immensely readable and very hard to put down. It raises the stakes for what the stakes can be. Also, it has terrific characters.

China Mountain Zhang centers on Zhang Zhong Shan. His story spirals through the novel, and all the other stories and characters touch his. Zhang is fascinating. He's a gay man from New York with spliced genes who's passing—not only passing as straight, but also passing as Chinese. His voice is immediate and compelling—indeed, one of McHugh's strengths is in the splendid solidity of the voices of her characters. But the real central character of *China Mountain Zhang* is the world.

This is a world dominated by China. At some time in the past, the US has had a proletarian revolution, and at some time only about fifteen years ago had the Cleansing Winds Campaign, an overwhelming event like the Cultural Revolution in China. Global warming has made much of the interior of the US uninhabitable. Mars is being settled. Everything is socialist, but there are cracks. Stories often take place in the cracks, and this one is no exception.

This is a book about ordinary people getting by and coping with their everyday problems in a world that's both weirdly different and weirdly similar to our own. It's a very political book in the sense people normally mean. It's showing us a world after a proletarian revolution in the US, for goodness' sake. And yet it certainly isn't a fantasy of political agency. None of the characters in the novel have any political agency at all. They're all helpless against the system, and getting by as best they can in the cracks.

Zhang is an ordinary working-class working guy getting by without thinking about things too much. He's an engineering tech who, during the course of the book, becomes an engineer. He uses futuristic cyberpunk equipment to do his job, but he takes it all for granted. He jacks in to his tools with a sigh. There is no glamour, even when he's using computer systems to design houses organically. He's also gay, in a much more unromantic and realistic way than I'm used to seeing with gay characters written by women. He has casual sex. He has a terrible time when he's forced to live on Baffin Island where there's no possibility of meeting anyone. He's forced into an embarrassing situation taking the daughter of his boss on a date.

We also have the points of view of Martine, a twenty-year veteran who's now lonely among her goats on Mars; Angel, who races a kite (a huge powered hang glider) through the skies of New York City; Alexi, another Martian settler, who wants to get better at engineering; and San Xiang, an ugly girl who gets a new face and finds out it isn't really what she wanted.

It's surprising how unusual it is to have a book where the characters really work. Maybe I've just read too many quest novels and too many stories about interstellar traders. But it seems that in most fiction while characters may have a job, the story takes them away from it. We don't see much in the way of actual work being done. Zhang's work is futuristic and half-cyberpunk, but he has to do it, and keep doing it. The economic relationship between work and living is more realistic in this novel than in any other SF future I can think of. In the end, you're left with a mosaic picture of a man in his world. Zhang's world has clearly descended from our world. It's better in some ways and worse in some ways. If not a plausible future, it's not a future that has dated itself out of existence in the fifteen years since the book was written. If not a hopeful vision, it's not a disastrous one either. It has texture and ambiguity. I value that, and I'd like to see more of it.

19. Anathem: What does it gain from not being our world?

Tom Shippey, who isn't an idiot, called Neal Stephenson's *Anathem* (2008) "high fantasy" in *The Times*. So in my second reading of *Anathem* in the two months since it came out, I was trying to figure out what he meant when he used that term about a book that includes spaceships and the scientific method.

Shippey defines high fantasy as "a story set entirely in a secondary world, the creation of which is a major part of the author's appeal and intention." Certainly, the world of *Anathem* is deeply appealing. It's not just that geeks live in giant clock-monasteries, cool as that is. It's not the way different parts of those monasteries are enclosed for different amounts of time. It's the angle on time that encourages. Our narrator, Erasmas, is only nineteen, yet it's second nature to him to say: "When there's an economy extramuros, we can sell the honey outside the Day Gate and use the money to buy things it's difficult to make in the concent. When conditions are post-apocalyptic, we can eat it." Or "For three thousand years it had been the concent's policy to accept any or all folding chairs and collapsible tables made available to it, and never throw any away. . . . We had folding chairs made of aluminum, bamboo, aerospace composites, injection-molded poly, salvaged rebar, handcarved wood, bent twigs, advanced newmatter, tree stumps, lashed sticks, brazed scrap metal and plaited grass." This is a large part of why I love it, and why I missed it after I finished it and wanted to read it again soon. However, this isn't a fantasy thing. SF has worlds with funny words and customs and interestingly anthropological ways of looking at things.

Shippey also says that Stephenson intended the book to proselytise for the ideas, for potential fraas and suurs, which, if it were the case, would hardly have led him to end it the way he does.

I started thinking about why Stephenson had chosen to set the story in a different world, rather than set it four thousand years or so in our own future. There's a good plot reason, of course, which is having people from our world show up later. But he could just as well have set it four thousand years in the future and had aliens, rather than people from our world and other cosmoses. Since the first time I read *Anathem* I've been assured by people I trust who know about science (Marissa Lingen and Chad Orzel) that essentially the many-worlds alternate physics stuff is all wrong. While the French is cute and all that, it could have been aliens and been fine. The bit I like least about *Anathem* is the bit in space, the probabilistic Millenarian ex Machina stuff. So he could have lost that and not annoyed Mris and other physics people and still kept everything I adore about the book. My general feeling is that SF is better if it's connected to our world. I have an emotional preference for futures we could get to from here.

Nevertheless, I think it's better for *Anathem* to be in its own world. There's a way of writing fantasy where you use history but put it into a subcreated world so that you can talk about the essence of the history and not the details. Guy Gavriel Kay does this a lot, and I have done it myself.

Anathem is doing that same thing only with the history of science and natural philosophy.

That rocks.

20. A happy ending depends on when you stop: Heavy Time, Hellburner and C. J. Cherryh's Alliance-Union universe

Cherryh has been writing the Union–Alliance books since *Downbelow Station* in 1981. They're a series of standalone novels within a shared universe. The major characters from one book may be seen briefly in another book, but you don't generally need to have read any specific book to understand any other book in the series. Cherryh delights in turning the reader's brain inside out anyway, so there are books from all kinds of points of view, and one book may make you sympathise with characters and positions that other books made you detest. I regard this as a major achievement and part of what makes Cherryh a great writer.

In internal chronological order, the series begins with the duo *Heavy Time* (1991) and *Hellburner* (1993) (published in one volume as *Devil to the Belt*, 2000), and that's where I'm beginning my re-read. I'm not sure I'd recommend this as a place to start, not because you need series knowledge to follow them (you definitely don't) but because *Heavy Time* is so relentlessly grim. Cherryh is seldom a barrel of laughs, but *Heavy Time* is grim even for her. Most of her books are a lot more fun than this. Yet if you did read them first, they might not seem so grim, because a lot of what makes them grim is the inevitability of what's coming, which you know only from the other books. After all, there's a definition of tragedy as a story where you know the end.

Unlike most Union-Alliance books, these are a pair, concerning the same characters, and should be read in order. Also unlike the others, they are set in the solar system. We don't see much of Earth, but this is as close to it as we ever get in these books.

The asteroid belt crawls with miners all hoping for a big strike that's going to make them rich, but the Company grinds them down worse each year. In *Heavy Time* a couple of prospectors pick up a ship that's sending a distress signal and complications ensue. Ben and Bird just want to get a bit ahead and Dekker just wants to fly, the Company just want to screw everyone over, and the Fleet just want recruits with the kind of reflexes you can get from being an asteroid miner. In *Hellburner* our protagonists (those who survived *Heavy Time*) are in the Fleet and hoping to get along, until they get involved with trials of a prototype rider-ship.

If Cherryh were a weaker writer, if she didn't make the characters and the places of her novels so real, it wouldn't matter that these books are intensely claustrophobic, and that Dekker is on the edge of crazy for most of the time you spend in his head.

These are great feminist novels. There are women in them who succeed on their own merits and yet are questioned because they are women. They're not in a magically non-sexist future. They're accused of making it by "whoring around on Helldeck," to which one of them replies, "You a virgin, Mitch? Didn't think so."

It's also a terrific future. All the details hang together. Asteroid miners being screwed by the Company is somehow more realistic than the scenarios of asteroid miners SF usually offers. And in the background negotiations going on in *Hellburner* you can see the beginnings, if you know what's coming, of the long betrayals that are up ahead. Cherryh's future history really has the texture and grain of history, and the books feel to me very much like historical novels. Yet on a series re-read when you know what's coming, they also have history's inevitability.

Both of these books have ends that approximate happy endings, and if you were to read them without knowing any more about the universe, they could be read as happy endings. At the end of *Heavy Time,* being drafted comes as a relief, an escape from problems in the Belt. At the end of *Hellburner,* the immediate problems have been solved and it looks as if everything is going to be all right.

These are happy endings to compare with the Albert Finney film version of Churchill's *The Gathering Storm,* in which the happy ending is that World War II starts. I think you're assumed to know about the implicit happy ending of WWII. But it's still a long way off from September of 1939. It's even worse here, where the end of the War is a quarter of a century away, and even then it isn't good for the Fleet. Still, Cherryh artfully stops the books at points where we can feel reasonably positive, if we lack foreknowledge, and that's really very clever of her.

21. Knights Who Say "Fuck": Swearing in Genre Fiction

A little while ago the Mighty God King posted a marvellous collection of doctored book covers, with the titles he felt the books he'd loved as a teenager should have had. The genius of this was the way he used the exact right fonts every time, so that Mercedes Lackey's *My Little Pony Goes to War* had just the font you were expecting to see on that cover. One of them that made me laugh out loud was his cover for George R. R. Martin's *A Game of Thrones.* (I love those books.) His new title was *Knights Who Say "Fuck,"* which amused me not only because of the clever Python reference but also because it's true, they do, and that's one of the things that makes it different from traditional high fantasy. He's not the only person whose knights are saying "fuck" these days—Sarah Monette's charmingly foul-mouthed Mildmay leaps to mind—but it is something you never used to see. It didn't fit the register of fantasy. The register has broadened. Interesting.

I'm reading Cherryh's *Downbelow Station,* which was published in 1981. I started it immediately after finishing *Hellburner,* which is set earlier but was published in 1992. I noticed immediately that in *Downbelow Station* the troopers "breathe an obscenity into com," "swore quietly," "swore at length," "adding an obscenity." In *Hellburner* in equivalent situations they're saying "Shit, shit, shit!" and "Fuck!"

Now I read both of these books pretty much when they came out, and I didn't notice anything odd about the level of permitted swearing in them. Yet something definitely changed between 1981 and 1992, and it wasn't C. J. Cherryh. The number of times someone breathes an oath, an obscenity, or swears viciously in *Downbelow Station,* you can tell she knows the words the troopers are saying. In fact it reminds me of the coy dashes you get in Trollope, where the fact that a husband called a wife a "___" in *He Knew He Was Right* is plot-rocking, and no, you never find out what the word is. (The footnotes think "harlot." As I'm not even faintly shocked by "harlot" I've decided to fill in that blank, and all Trollope's blanks, with the worst words I know.)

So, was Cherryh being effectively censored by what you were allowed to say?

The thing that surprises me about that is the date. I thought it was the sixties when people in books were allowed to use actual oaths, rather than just mighty ones. Did genre fiction lag behind? Certainly it was the New Wave that started talking about sex, but how careful were the words? I noticed when reading W. E. B. Griffin that you can say "shit" all you like in his books as long as you're not talking about "human excrement" and similarly "fuck" is fine unless you're talking about "sexual intercourse." Obscenities are different from description, and use of the words can vary in either direction. These words are charged, and they have very specific registers, they're significant markers.

You used to see fake "futuristic" swearing. (Who can forget Larry Niven's "tanj"?) When did that stop? *Drinking Sapphire Wine* has it, and that's 1976.

So, things clearly changed in the eighties. Why? Was there a specific change, a specific book or date that it changed, within genre fiction? Or was it a general cultural change of what was acceptable slowly bleeding through into genre? Did it get to SF first and seep into fantasy later? *A Game of Thrones* is 1996.

And when did it stop being daring for people to swear "like a trooper" and become normal? My memory is that in South Wales when I was a child adults swore in Welsh, and what they said, translated, meant "God" or "the Devil," and "bloody" was pretty strong swearing in English. But my memory of being a young adult in Britain in the early and mid-eighties didn't include other young women casually saying "fuck" the way they do now. I think there has been an actual change, and it isn't just that literature was coy about recording what people said, as that what people say has changed. I'm sure this is also a difference between Britain and North America, and maybe between different areas too.

And in the future? Well, there are fashions in these things. Perhaps our texts with their liberal scatterings of "fuck" will eventually look as quaint as Trollope's dashes.

22. "Earth is one world": C. J. Cherryh's Downbelow Station

Downbelow Station was published in 1981 and won the Hugo in 1982. It is in many ways the central book of the Union-Alliance series. It's about the Company Wars. Most of the books in the series are dealing with the aftermath of those wars, flotsam and jetsam left in their wake. *Downbelow Station* is central, it has many points of view (many of them important people), and it's about the end of the war and the formation of the Alliance. It has a marvellous perspective on humanity in the wider universe. I have to admit, though, it's a hard book to like.

There's a story that after Cherryh had written this book, someone told her every scene had to do three things (any three things), so she went through and removed all the scenes that only did one or two, without replacing them with anything. I don't suppose for a moment that this really happened, but it's one of those legends that's truer than the facts. *Downbelow Station* is a dense, complex book written in a terse, futuristic style, from multiple points of view, some of them alien and many of them unpleasant. It feels disorienting and slightly disconnected and as if something somewhere has been left out. It's definitely immersive, and the history is real enough to bite, but even on a re-read it isn't a book I can sink into. I bounced off it the first time I tried to read it, and even now it's my least favourite and the one I read only when I'm doing a full re-read of the whole series. Again, I don't think this is a good place to start.

All of Cherryh's characters are ambiguous, but nowhere more than here, where there are so many of them. The plot is a complex maneuvering of factions and realignment of interests. There are space battles, and there are economics of space stations. There's a compelling beginning where a warship turns up with freighters full of desperate refugees that have to be accommodated at the space station without warning. And there are all these factions and points of view.

The Mazianni are a Company fleet that have been fighting too long. They're exhausted, hard as nails, and can't stop. Signy Mallory, one of their captains, is ruthless, competent, deadly . . . and really not very nice.

The Konstantins are nice. They run Pell, a space station circling an alien planet and clinging to its independence at a time when Earth is giving up space to Union, seen here as unmitigatedly terrifying and appalling. They're definitely nice, all of them—we get three Konstantin points of view, Angelo, Emelio and Damon—but their very niceness is their fatal flaw, the hamartia that causes their tragic downfall—except not quite, because the novel is a eucatastrophe, not a tragedy.

Elene Quen is a merchanter who is married to Damon Konstantin and staying on Pell for a while when she learns that her own ship, and family, have all been killed.

Josh Talley is a Union spy who after his brainwipe becomes something very interesting but also very ambivalent.

Satin is a hisa, an alien from Downbelow. The alien point of view is convincingly alien, but the hisa are, regrettably, furry noble savages. Cherryh has done much better aliens absolutely everywhere else she has aliens. I find the hisa embarrassing with their pidgin English and their names "Sky sees her" and "Bigfellow" and "Sun her friend."

Ayres is a Company man, come from Earth to sell out the Mazianni and all of space. He starts off seeming deeply unsympathetic, but by the time Union have been horrible to him for most of the book, I feel terribly sorry for him.

Jon Lukas is a resident of Pell who tries to play both sides against the middle. He's hardheaded, self-interested and very unpleasant, but that doesn't mean he's always wrong.

Vassily Kressich is a resident of Q, the Quarantine Zone where the refugees lead lives of riot and gangs, and who is so desperate, he's the pawn of anyone who uses him.

I used the word "desperate" several times, and I could have used it several more if I were talking about what happens to these people as the book goes on. It's a novel about desperate people, desperate space stations, desperate aliens, a desperate space fleet that's out of choices. It's desperately claustrophobic too, with people hiding in tunnels filled with unbreathable air, not to mention that the whole of Pell is an inescapable trap. It's marvellous that Cherryh manages to pull a happy ending out of all that.

That said, *Downbelow Station* is a book I re-read only because I'm in love with the universe, kind of the way one puts up with one's spouse's irritating relations.

23. "Space is wide and good friends are too few": Cherryh's Merchanter novels

Merchanter's Luck (1982), *Rimrunners* (1989), *Tripoint* (1994) and *Finity's End* (1997) are all stories of individual spacers in the time immediately post–*Downbelow Station*. They're all excellent books, and they are where I suggest people start with this universe, so that when they get to *Downbelow Station* they are already invested in the universe. The title of this post comes from "Sam Jones," a song that Cherryh wrote and Leslie Fish sings, and which I think of as another story in this set.

Imagine the universe of *Traveller* or *Elite*. Then imagine it made sense in depth and had up-close personal human stories happening in it. These books take place in merchant ships and space stations. The very occasional living world glows like a jewel in the dark. The ships started off slower than light coming out from Earth building stations as they went, and built up a culture like that, but then pretty much at the same time they discovered other living planets, faster-than-light and rejuv—a drug that keeps people at about the biological age when they start taking it until they're well over a hundred. Then came the War, between Earth and Union, with the merchanters caught in the middle, until the Treaty of Pell that ended the war and formed the Merchanter's Alliance.

In these books we see ships and people of all kinds. There's an independent whose family were killed in the War barely making it as a trading ship, and a thriving family ship where rejuv keeps so many generations alive that young people can't hope to have useful work before they are themselves old. There are Union ships and Alliance ships that have been militarised. There's a Mazianni supply ship and a beached Mazianni trooper who finds herself aboard an Alliance military ship with very mixed feelings. Most of all these are the stories of spacers, with their sleepovers on stations, their thin margins of profit, their shared experience of the deep dark and going FTL through Jump.

They are also all about the very human need to belong, to have someone to love and somewhere to call home.

More than anybody else, Cherryh has thought about what it would mean to live in space. I don't know whether it's scientifically plausible, but it feels entirely real in its nested implications. They don't have day and night, ships and stations work all the time, in shifts, they have mainday and alterday which overlap when morning for one is evening for the other. The ships are communities, families, villages, matrilineal with children concieved with partners off the ship but growing up aboard. They dock at the stations and because they don't have the rotation they use in motion to create gravity, they have to sleep off the ship. This leads to romance in *Merchanter's Luck* and to rape and revenge in *Tripoint*. The way Jump stretches age means there's a crew member in *Rimrunners* who started off on sublight ships, and is very significant for the protagonist of *Finity's End,* who got left at a station while the ship went on.

These books all stand alone, with very little overlap of characters with any of the others, though there's considerable overlap of locations and history. They can be read in any order. And every single one of them has a happy ending, or stops at a point that could in any case plausibly be taken for a happy ending.

24. "A need to deal wounds": Rape of men in Cherryh's Union-Alliance novels

From Signy Mallory to Ariane Emory, Cherryh has a tendency to write female characters who are not just powerful but actually abusive and male characters who are not just helpless but actually raped. What's with that?

Rape of men by women is remarkably rare in literature generally and yet remarkably prevalent in these books.

This is Signy and Talley, early in *Downbelow Station*:

"You're getting off here," she told him, staring at him who lay beside her. The name did not matter. It confused itself in her memory with others, and sometimes she called him by the wrong one, late, when she was half asleep. He showed no emotion at that statement, only blinked indication that he had absorbed the fact. The face intrigued her: innocence, perhaps. Contrasts intrigued her. Beauty did. "You're lucky," she said. He reacted to that the same way as he reacted to most things. He simply stared, vacant and beautiful. They had played with his mind on Russell's. There was a sordidness in her sometimes, a need to deal wounds . . . limited murder to blot out the greater ones. To deal little terrors to blot out the horror outside. She had sometimes nights with Graff, with Di, with whoever took her fancy. She never showed this face to those she valued, to friends, to crew.

Now what that says is that she knows he has been damaged and she has been systematically abusing him all voyage, "dealing little terrors." Ick.

In *Cyteen* Ariane Emory even more directly rapes Justin, with the help of drugs, and rapes his mind, too, in complete violation. The text does see this as a terrible thing to do, and we sympathise with Justin and hate Ari for it. It's also entirely plot necessary, and far and away the worst thing in the book. Ari also confesses to having hurt Florian. And there's also the whole issue of azi. Any relationship with an azi is non-consensual, no matter how enthusiastic the azi in question has been programmed to be. They're not capable of giving free consent. They get tape to make them like it, the same as for anything. This is fundamental to what azi are. This is all entirely necessary to the story.

In *Rimrunners* Bet Yaeger kills two potential (male) rapists in the first few chapters. But when she thinks about what happens to newbies on the decks in Africa and what she has herself done, it's also rape. This is what Bet's like, and it isn't graphic or even onstage, but it also isn't particularly necessary.

In *Tripoint,* Marie Hawkins, who is very unstable, has been raped, and she has fantasies of raping her rapist in return, specifically of violating him without consent. Also her son Tom, the product of the rape, has sex forced on him during Jump when he isn't in a condition to give consent. It's rape even if he enjoys it—he doesn't understand what's going on or who is with him.

Again, I wouldn't say this was necessary to the plot or the themes of the novel.

So what is going on? Clearly, Cherryh's seeing rape here as part of a power balance thing. Historically, it has usually been men who have had more power. In a non-sexist future, some women will also have power. Men with power in this universe are fairly hard to find, but when you do find them they quite often tend to be rapists, too: the male Mazianni captains, Austin Bowe, Geoffrey Carnath vs non-rapists Angelo and Damon Konstantin, the captains of *Finity's End* and *Dublin Again,* Denys and Giraud Nye. So it does seem as if she's working on an axiom that some human beings will rape other human beings if they can get away with it, which has been historically true of men, and it would be sexist to think it would not be just as true of some women if women also had power.

I do find this more than a little disturbing, but it's completely logical unless women are inherently nicer than men, which I do not believe. It's a pretty unpleasant thought though, when you drag it out and examine it.

25. How to talk to writers

Writers are people, and they were people before they were writers. They change lightbulbs and buy groceries just like everyone else. Really. Because they're people, they vary. Some of them are jerks, but many of them are very interesting people to talk to.

Writers will usually talk about their writing if you want to talk to them about it. But they can also talk about other things!

Writers mostly aren't celebrities. They have a little bit of demi-fame within the community, and that's it. For the few who are celebrities it's different, but most writers are only too glad to have their name recognised.

However well you feel you know a writer because you have read their books or their blog, until you've met them you don't know them, and they don't know you. They'll probably be happy to talk to you at a signing or a convention, but they're not your instant best friend.

If you happen to be introduced to a writer you haven't read, do not say, "I'm sorry, but I haven't read any of your books." This just causes embarrassment. The normal state of affairs for an ordinary writer is that most people they meet haven't read any of their books. This may be different for Terry Pratchett and J. K. Rowling. But ordinary writers that you might happen to meet won't expect you to have read their work. This totally isn't a problem unless you mention that you haven't. What are they supposed to say in response? "Oh, that's all right"? "Go away, you illiterate ass"? There just isn't a good answer and it leaves the writer spluttering. (Anyone who wants is welcome to my answer: "Oh, that's OK, you can give me the five dollars now.") I understand the urge to say you haven't read them. It comes from guilt. But don't say it. If you feel guilty just quietly go and buy one of their books later. And there's no reason to feel guilty. Nobody expects you to have read every book in the world, least of all the writers. Writers see their sales figures. They know that statistically it's unlikely that you've read their books.

Do not say "Where can I buy your books?" The answer is "The bookstore!" (Or "The dealers' room!" or "Your usual online bookstore!") Asking this question makes the writer feel as if you think they're self-published and sell their books out of the back of their car. (My husband's boss asks me this every time she sees me.) Ellen Kushner is irate about it in her journal. I think people ask this because they want to demonstrate good intentions, but again, don't ask. If you want one just go and buy one quietly where you normally buy books.

If you have read their books and you adore them, do say so if you'd like to. You can't go wrong with "I really like your books!" or "I really like *Specific Title*." The worst thing that can possibly happen is that the writer will say "Thank you," and you'll stand there tongue-tied by being in their presence. This still happens to me occasionally when I meet writers I really admire. The last time I met Samuel Delany I managed an actual sentence with words in it, rather than just awestruck gurgling. Most writers can cope even with the gurgling if they have to.

If you have read their books and you hate them, don't say, "I have to say, I really hate your work." You don't have to say it at all. Again, it leaves the writer with no possible honest and polite reply. If you're having an actual conversation with the writer

76

about something and it's actually relevant to say that you hate all alternate history including theirs, or their treatment of dragons, then it can be OK. But marching up to them and saying you have to say it—and it's something people always feel they have to preface that way—is just a waste of time.

Pick your time to approach. If a writer is eating or busily engaged with other people, don't interrupt them just to gurgle at them. There'll probably be another moment.

Oh, and finally, if you meet a writer and they turn out to be four feet tall, or immensely fat, or terribly ugly, or old, don't say, "I thought you'd be taller/thinner/prettier/younger." As I was saying, writers are people and can have their feelings hurt by this kind of thing just like anyone else.

26. "Give me back the Berlin Wall": Ken MacLeod's *The Sky Road*

Ken MacLeod's Fall Revolution books consist of *The Star Fraction* (1995), *The Stone Canal* (1996), *The Cassini Division* (1997) and *The Sky Road* (1999). That's the order they were published in originally in the UK, in the US they were published in the order *The Cassini Division, The Stone Canal, The Star Fraction* and *The Sky Road*. Tor have republished *The Star Fraction* and *The Stone Canal* in one trade paperback called *Fractions,* and I bet (without any inside information, just because it makes sense) that they're fairly shortly going to do the other two in one volume called *Divisions.*[*]

I really like these books. They're a fully imagined future where the capitalist criticism of communism is entirely true, and so is the communist criticism of capitalism. They're kind of libertarian (several of them won the Prometheus Award) and they're grown up about politics in a way that most SF doesn't even try. These aren't fantasies of political agency, not at all. But they contain revolutions, political, technological and social, and they

---

[*] 2011. I was absolutely right about this!

have an awareness of history that makes them stand out. MacLeod has written more accomplished books since, but not more passionate ones. Anyway, because of the publication order differences, it's always possible, when two or three Ken MacLeod fans are gathered together, to get up an argument about reading order. The books are chronologically sequential in the original publication order. But it doesn't really matter. You can make a pretty good argument for any order—except that everyone always agrees that you should read *The Sky Road* last. So, out of sheer perversity, I decided to re-read it alone, and to consider whether it works as a standalone novel.

Surprise: it does. You can start with *The Sky Road*. And it's even a good idea.

The Sky Road and *The Cassini Division* are alternate futures to the stories in *Fractions*. And if you read *The Sky Road* in sequence, that's a lot of what you're going to be thinking about. Most of the conversations I've had about the book have been about that. But it's a cracking good story in its own right. It has two storylines, alternating chapters throughout the book. One is the first-person point of view of Clovis colha Gree, a student of history in a distant future, and the other is the third-person point of view of Myra, a disillusioned and life-extended communist about a century from now. They are connected by revelation, and because Clovis is trying to write a biography of Myra—The Deliverer. You want to know how things got from A to B, and slowly, over the course of the book, you find out.

The thing I never really appreciated, reading it as the culmination of the series, is the way in which Clovis's story is shaped like fantasy. The woman comes to him through the fair, she is beautiful and perilous, she is something more than she seems, and they fall in love and she takes him into a world of enchantment. Myra's story is all end-game cynicism, while Clovis's is, in complete contrast, almost idyllic. There's also time, history, technology, boilerplate spaceships, computers that are half organic and half babbage engine, the background terraforming of Mars, and all the tortured compromises Myra has made along the way from the ideals she held in 1970s Glasgow. For this book, I really don't think it matters who appeared in the earlier books. The story more than stands alone. The background of the earlier books just gives it more depth, more history. If you have that context, it hooks on for you, if not, I really don't think it would matter. The alternate-ness certainly doesn't matter, except in the way that missed opportunities are always cause for wistfulness. And I'm not sure I don't like Clovis's world better than Ellen May's anyway.

MacLeod always plays fair with his ideologies. The text doesn't take a position. He doesn't extrapolate to meet his own prejudices—well, not more than people do just by being human. In the Clovis parts of *The Sky Road,* the greens and barbarians have won, but it doesn't seem like such a bad thing. Clovis follows the religion of Reason:

> In the beginning, God made the Big Bang, and there was light. After the first four minutes, there was matter. After billions of years there were stars and planets and the Earth was formed. The water brought forth all manner of creeping things. Over millions of years they were shaped by God's invisible hand, Natural Selection, into great monsters of land and sea.

The conclusion of someone who has lived from Myra's time until Clovis's is that the people of his day are more able to withstand the problems and temptations that destroyed the world once.

I think *The Sky Road* is my favourite of the quartet because I find both characters sympathetic.

I'm tempted now to re-read them all in reverse order and see how it goes, but I think I'll restrain myself. And if you haven't read them, you should by all means be sensible and start with *Fractions,* which is even in print.

27. What a pity she couldn't have single-handedly invented science fiction! George Eliot's Middlemarch

It's too much to ask, of course. Nobody could, a quarter century before *The War of the Worlds,* and when Verne was only just beginning to be translated into English. But it's such a pity, because she would have been so very good at it.

I started to read George Eliot only a few years ago. She suffered in my mind from a geographical, or rather alphabetical, contagion with Dickens and Hardy. (I have no idea how it is that my grandmother didn't own any Mrs. Gaskell, when Mrs. Gaskell would have been so very much to her taste. It makes me a little sad every time I read *Cranford,* to know she never did.) In any case, whatever you may think, George Eliot isn't tedious or depressing or shallow. What I loathe about Dickens is the shallowness of his caricatures, the way he pushes them around his ludicrous plots not even like puppets (because I could admire a well-done puppet show) but like children's toys that might topple over at any moment and get a grinning "Aw shucks" from the mawkish and badly played omniscient narrator. Hardy, on the other hand, was a good writer. I loathe him for the morbidity of his imagination and the sheer misery of his stories. Even his "lighter" works are blighted, and his best and most serious ones are barely endurable. But would I have liked *Middlemarch* any better when I was ten? Maybe it is a book you shouldn't read until you're forty.

But she should have been a science fiction writer! And she could have been because she saw the world in an essentially science-fictional way. She saw how technology changes society—she understood that thoroughly. In a way, she was someone who had lived through a singularity—she had seen the railroad coming and had seen how it entirely transformed the world she grew up in, with second-order effects nobody could have predicted. Her books constantly come back to technology and the changes it brings. Her whole angle of looking at the world is much closer to Wells than to Dickens. She didn't often speculate, but when she did, you have lines like: "Posterity may be shot, like a bullet from a tube, from Winchester to Newcastle: that is a fine result to have among our hopes." (From *Felix Holt, the Radical*.)

And she understood the progress of science, the way it isn't all huge and immediate:

> He meant to be a unit who would make a certain amount of difference towards that spreading change which would one day tell appreciably upon the averages, and in the meantime have the pleasure of making an advantageous difference to the viscera of his own patients. But he did not simply aim at a more general kind of practice than was common. He was ambitious of a wider effect: he was fired with the possibility that he might work out the proof of an anatomical conception and make a link in the chain of discovery. (*Middlemarch*)

The trouble with mimetic fiction isn't that you can tell what's going to happen (I defy anyone to guess what's going to happen in *Middlemarch,* even from halfway through) but that you can tell what's not going to happen. There isn't going to be an evil wizard. The world isn't going to be destroyed in Cultural Fugue and leave the protagonist as the only survivor. There aren't going to be any people who happen to have one mind shared between five bodies. There are unlikely to be shape-changers. In science fiction you can have any kind of story—a romance or a mystery or a reflection of human nature, or anything at all. But as well as that, you have infinite possibility. You can tell different stories about human nature when you can compare it to android nature, or alien nature. You can examine it in different ways when you can write about people living for two hundred years, or being relativistically separated, or under a curse. You have more colours for your palette, more lights to illuminate your scene.

Now, the problem with genre fiction is often that writers take those extra lights and colours and splash them around as if the fact that the result is shiny is sufficient, which it unfortunately isn't. So the most common failing of genre fiction is that you get shallow stories with feeble characters redeemed only by the machinations of evil wizards or the fascinating spaceship economy or whatever. What I want is stories as well written and characterised as *Middlemarch,* but with more options for what can happen. That's what I always hope for, and that's what I get from the best of SF.

If Eliot could have taken her SFnal sensibility and used it to write SF, she could have swung the whole course of literature into a different channel. She could have changed the world. All the great writers who followed her would have had all the options of SF, instead of the circumscribed limitations of the mimetic world. We wouldn't see books, like Piercy's *He, She and It,* that are well written in character terms but incredibly clunky in SF ones because they don't have the first idea how to embed SF tropes in a narrative.

Meanwhile, *Middlemarch* remains an extremely good book, and I enjoyed it as much on a second reading as I did on the first. You'd think from the bare bones that it would be as depressing as Hardy: it's the story of two people who passionately want to succeed but who fail. Dorothea wants to help a great man in a great endeavour, and finds herself utterly miserable in marriage to a man jealous of her, and engaged on writing footnotes on footnotes. Lydgate wishes to make medical discoveries, and finds himself miserably married to a social climbing woman who weighs him down in debt, everyday cares and the shallows of life. Eliot shows us exactly why they make the decisions that seem like a good idea at the time and how they lead inexorably to disaster. It isn't a miserable book though, not at all. It doesn't grind you down. It's very funny in parts, it has a huge cast of minor characters, some of them seen in great detail (she knows how to use omni deftly) and Dorothea's story at least ends happily, if unconventionally. That is, unconventionally for a Victorian novel. She doesn't get to be the ambassador to Jupiter, more's the pity. She always wants to rush off and do good. "Let us find out the truth, and clear him!" she declares, when she hears base rumours about Lydgate. I'd like her to be in a universe where everyone's response to that wasn't to tell her to be sensible and calm down.

Middlemarch is a panorama, and a terrific novel of life in provincial England just before the Reform Act. It's the kind of book where you want to gossip to your friends about the characters and what can become of them. I love it, and I heartily recommend it. But I wish she'd invented science fiction instead, because she could have, and it would have been so amazing if she had.

28. The beauty of lists: Angelica Gorodischer's *Kalpa Imperial*

There's one way around the problem of clunky translation and that's having a world-class English language stylist do the translating for you. It doesn't happen often, but we're lucky it ever happens. Ursula Le Guin's translation of Angelica Gorodischer's *Kalpa Imperial* is wonderful.

Kalpa Imperial was originally published in Spanish. Gorodischer is one of Argentina's leading writers. I'd never heard of her until Le Guin began publishing this translation—I read part of it in the anthology *Starlight 2,* which is how I knew I wanted it and why I picked it up as soon as it came out.

It isn't like anything else. Well, a little like Borges perhaps, but much more approachable. And it's a little like Le Guin's own *Changing Planes,* but much better. I occasionally come across something where I read a page and then immediately read it again, more slowly, or even aloud, just out of sheer pleasure at the way the words go together. (The first chapter of Doctorow's *Someone Comes to Town, Someone Leaves Town* (2005), the beginning of McKinley's *Spindle's End* (2000) . . .) and this book is like that all the way through. This is how it starts:

The storyteller said: Now that the good winds are blowing, now that we're done with days of anxiety and nights
of terror, now that there are no more denunciations,
persecutions, secret executions and whim and madness
have departed from the heart of the Empire and we and
our children aren't playthings of blind power; now that a
just man sits on the Golden Throne and people look
peacefully out of their doors to see if the weather's fine
and plan their vacations and kids go to school and actors
put their hearts into their lines and girls fall in love and
old men die in their beds and poets sing and jewelers
weigh gold behind their little windows and gardeners
rake the parks and young people argue and innkeepers
water the wine and teachers teach what they know and
we storytellers tell old stories and archivists archive and
fishermen fish and all of us can decide according to our
talents and lack of talents what to do with our life—now
anyone can enter the emperor's palace out of need or
curiosity; anybody can visit that great house which was
for so many years forbidden, prohibited, defended by
armed guards, locked and as dark as the souls of the
Warrior Emperors of the dynasty of the Ellydrovides.

Isn't that lovely? If your answer to that is "No!" then don't go
any further, because what that sentence has is what the book has,
in miniature.

Kalpa Imperial isn't exactly a novel. It's more like a collection
of related short stories, or a very fanciful history book. And it
isn't exactly fantasy—there isn't any real magic. It's the history of
an empire that never was. A lot of time passes. Dynasties rise and
fall. Even the empire falls and is reborn. We have all tech levels
from nomadic hunters to planes and cars, not necessarily in a
sequence you'd expect. A number of the individual stories have

the story nature, but some of them are interesting in the non-fiction way. They don't relate a history so much as a series of vignettes, so that they echo, in a macro-structure way, this amazing style that evokes by listing and naming.

I really enjoyed the book the first time I read it, and I really enjoyed it again now. The first time I took the whole thing entirely on a fantastical level—why shouldn't an Argentinian write about an imaginary empire, or why should it have any significance? But this time I was wondering about that, about what it means that someone from a new country with a quite short history should write about an incredibly ancient country with a convoluted history? This wasn't written as a fantasy novel, though it's entirely readable as one, and I don't have the context this book was written in. It doesn't open any windows on Argentinian culture for me, or illuminate anything but itself. I may be—am, I'm sure—missing a lot of levels. But nevertheless, what there is to be gleaned on the surface is well worth having. It's gorgeous, and a lot of fun, and the stories are lovely.

29. Like pop rocks for the brain: Samuel R. Delany's *Stars in My Pocket Like Grains of Sand*

Samuel Delany is intimidatingly brilliant, and *Stars in My Pocket Like Grains of Sand* (1984) is (arguably) his best book. Even though he's been one of my favourite writers since I was a teenager, and I've read all his books multiple times, I try not to re-read him when I'm writing, because he sets such a high standard, I feel that I might as well give up now.

You know how life and real history are always more complex and fractal than fiction can manage? Delany manages it. He does the thing where his science-fictional innovations have second- and third-order consequences, where they interlock and give you worldviews. Other people do it, but he does it all the way down. He's astonishing. This book has the density of very sparkly neutronium.

I first read *Stars in My Pocket* in 1985 on the night before an exam. (Don't worry, I aced it, and though my essay style may have been a little Delanyan, nobody noticed.) I was at Lancaster University, and living off-campus in a converted barn out in the countryside, with friends. We were in town buying food and walking along what had been a boring street when I discovered that Lancaster had suddenly sprouted a science fiction bookshop, Interstellar Master Traders. I insisted we go in, and I rushed around buying U.S. imports (this was 1985! There was no Internet. U.S. books were treasure!) while my friends stood there, bored and twitching. I went home with a huge pile of books and sat down to read the Delany first.

Reading Delany is like pop rocks for the brain. He scintillates. Things sparkle and explode all over, and it's not entirely comfortable but it is quite wonderful.

Stars in My Pocket begins with a prologue, in third person, set on the planet Rhyonon (though it is not named in the prologue) and dealing with Rat Korga, though he isn't named in it either. What it's really about is how reading can blow the top of your head off and open it up to the universe, so it's recursive in the very best way. There's a passage in Byatt's *Possession* where the narrator says that books have their bravura descriptions of sex and food but they don't describe the joy of reading, and then goes on to do it. When I read that, years later, I stopped dead and tried to figure out a way of getting Byatt to read Delany. (I'm still working on it.)

The problem with talking about *Stars in My Pocket* is that it's too big and too great. I could write a whole post of the length I usually write explaining what's so amazing about the prologue, which takes up the first eighty-four pages in the Grafton edition I own. There's so much in it, so much history and culture and scientific speculation and plot that it's hard to cover any of it at all and not just sit here burbling "brilliant, brilliant." I can't be detached about it.

First, I want to say that the surface level story and characters are very engaging. It's so easy when you start talking about clever details to lose sight of that. This is a book where I care deeply about the characters and where, the first time I read it, I stayed up half the night (with an exam the next morning) to find out what happened.

In Rhyonon, where Rat Korga comes from, sex between males is permitted for people over twenty-seven, but sex between tall people and short people of any gender is entirely and completely forbidden. The universe is a very big place, and the first-person narrator of the rest of the book, Marq Dyeth, is an Industrial Diplomat whose job[1] is delivering weird goods from planet to planet. (There isn't much interstellar trade, and what there is is mostly weird. The economics? Convincingly complex.) Marq comes from Velm, from the south of Velm, from a little city called Morgre, and there consensual sex between any species and any gender is freely available and a matter of preference. There are "runs," safe spaces you can walk through where people who like the kind of sex you like hang out and might be interested in sex with you. (I gather from things Delany has said external to the novel that this may be based on gay male culture in 1970s New York. I took this as entirely exotic and science-fictional, because it's like nothing whatsoever in my experience, then or now.) Marq and Rat are each other's perfect erotic object . . . and when Rat's world is entirely destroyed and he is the only survivor, the Web (which is a space-based organization a whole lot like Google only more powerful) sends Rat to visit Marq for what turns out to be only a few days.

Gender is constructed very differently. "She" is the standard pronoun for any sentient being, and "woman" is the standard term for a person. "He" is the pronoun for someone you desire. "Man" is an obsolete poetic word. "Mother" is a role anyone can choose if they are parenting. This use of pronouns is a little odd. It helps that Marq and Rat are attracted to men, but there are important human characters in this book where you literally do not know the gender because Marq doesn't find them attractive and doesn't mention whether they have breasts or not. The

91

names give no clue—and why do you need to know? Thinking about why you want to know is interesting. Reading all these people as female (because they're "she," after all) and then rethinking them as male can be interesting. Japril, in particular, reads very differently to me male, which is unquestionably revealing of my subconscious biases and expectations. This is one of the best feminist re-use of pronouns I've ever come across. It isn't clunky, it isn't awkward, and it doesn't get in the way of the story.

I mentioned Marq had a "job[1]." That's like a profession or a vocation. Your job[2] tends to determine where you live and tends to be more how you make your living. It is what a lot of people in our world call their "day job." (Delany, for instance is a writer[1] and a professor[2].) There's also homework[3] which is the kind of work that's never done. This is an interesting conceit, though not really explored very much because of the time period the story covers. Also on jobs, on Velm, at least in the south (in the north there's ethnic conflict between humans and the native lizardlike intelligences, the evelmi), tracers, who are rubbish collectors, have very high social status. This on its own would be enough background for some novels.

Humans have found alien intelligences on a lot of different worlds, but only one other starfaring civilization, the mysterious Xlv. Human/alien relationships are varied and complex. On Velm, in the south the humans and evelmi live close together and can be lovers or family members. In the north they're fighting each other. On other planets, other problems. The Xlv seem to have some interest in, concern with, or even involvement with Cultural Fugue, the real threat to civilization. Cultural Fugue is when a whole planet destroys itself, as Rhyonon does at the beginning of the book, and as other planets have from time to time. It's what everyone worries about when something goes wrong. It isn't defined, though what happened to Rhyonon is described in detail. There are two main paths of civilization, which stand opposed to each other. The Family (which has a cult centred in their belief in humanity's origins on a planet called Earth, since lost in the confusion), which is generally reactionary and rigid, and the Sygn, which believes in multiculturalism and relativism.

One of the most awesome things about this book is the way in which detail is layered on detail to make you believe in the complexity of the cultures, or the histories and the customs. Food in particular, which tends to be rather badly dealt with in SF, is positively fractal here. There's a description of an informal breakfast and a formal dinner that are nothing like anything from Earth, but that are wonderfully solid. And sex? I mentioned sex, but there's a throwaway mention that people from recently settled planets tend to use a lot of erotic technology. And as for technology, Rat has artificial eyes that go clear in bright light, look normal in normal light and reflect in dim light like a cat.

One of the themes of the novel is that a world is a very big place but the universe is a very small one. While most of the planets humanity has settled are dry and sandy, there aren't any "desert planets" here. And culturally—there's somebody Marq meets at a conference who uses weird honorifics that confuse him a little, and it turns out they're from a different city on Velm, and she'd learned them to make him think she was from home. . . .

There's a thing called General Information, which is like having Google in your head only more reliable. The one thing Delany got wrong there was that the Web isn't the Net of a thousand lies, information is reliable, when available. (But the book was published in 1984.) Apart from that, and that it is only an encyclopaedia that can give you brain-downloadable skills, the way they use it is exactly like the way I use Google now, and nothing like anything in the world in 1984, when as I understand it email had just been invented for people in the U.S. military. The future in *Stars in My Pocket* has not been made obsolete by computers, the way a lot of older SF has. Delany was aware that what you need is not information but a sorting system, and if you control that sorting system you're very powerful.

Stars in My Pocket was supposed to be the first half of a diptych, and the sequel, *The Splendor and Misery of Bodies, of Cities,* has never been written and probably never will be. It's worth knowing that *Stars in My Pocket* isn't a whole story, but as it is so good, unless you are absolutely addicted to knowing what happens, you can probably cope. Personally I've given up longing for it. If he can't write it, he can't. I do wish he'd write some more SF though.

30. Between Two Worlds:
S. P. Somtow's Jasmine Nights

S. P. Somtow's *Jasmine Nights* (1994) is one of my favourite books. It's funny and sweet and clever and awesome. It's about growing up, and sex, and racism, and magic, and life and death, reincarnation, and identity. No, it's more complicated than that, and better too. It's about all these huge wonderful things, but really, it's about this little boy.

Justin, or Little Frog, or Sornsunthorn, is twelve. He's an upper class Thai boy who has been left by his parents to live with his very odd Thai extended family. For the last three years he's been refusing to speak Thai and insisting on eating bacon and eggs for breakfast. He's been living two lives: in one of them he has servants and aunts and is a child, and in the other he has made a fantasy game for himself in a ruined house based on his reading of Homer and science fiction. ("Homer is a god, but he only wrote two books.") It is also twisted through with Thai mythology of spirits. In the ruined house one day he meets his great-grandmother:

> There is an enormous leather armchair in the room. It rocks. It faces away from me. Poking up from behind the chair's high back is a tuft of silvery hair.

There is someone there. The lightbulb sways. My shadow sways. The cobwebs sway in the wind from the electric fan.

I have seen *Psycho* fifteen times. I have visited the fruitcellar of the Bates house in my dreams. I know what is to be found in leather armchairs in abandoned houses. I feel my heart stop beating.

Will the armchair suddenly whip round to reveal the corpse of Norman Bates's mother? I step back. My Homeric drapery slides to the floor. "Who is there?" The chair has not moved. The voice is as ancient and as gravelly as the stones of Troy. It speaks in Thai. "Come on, who is it?"

Before I can stop myself I say "It's me, Norman."

His great-grandmother is dying, and he is on the verge of growing up. They become friends. She tells him he has a year to find out who and what he is, and the book is the story of that year, the discoveries he makes inside and outside himself, the friends he makes, and the adventures he has.

It's the books I love best that are the hardest to write about. I don't want to take one angle on them, I want to dive into them and quote huge chunks and tell you everything about them, and it just isn't possible.

Jasmine Nights is written in the first person of a child who lives mostly in his own head but who is just beginning to step outside it. The magic that is interwoven through this story he entirely takes for granted. Justin (it's his preferred name for himself, though he's made it up himself) doesn't quite know what's real and what isn't, and neither does the reader. His pet chameleon, Homer, dies, and his great-grandmother tells him that he has to take the spirit of Homer into himself and become like a chameleon. Homer appears in his dreams as Yama, god of death, and later he visits a magician who becomes Homer and continues the conversation from the dream. The magician's love potions work. All the magic we see unquestionably works—and yet this is one of those books where you're not entirely sure whether it's fantasy until the very end. It walks a very subtle line, very cleverly.

Also, it's laugh-out-loud funny. And it manages to be funny about very serious subjects, like race and sex. It's very interesting about race, too. S. P. Somtow is himself from Thailand. The book is dedicated to his four grandparents, one of whom was Queen of Siam. Justin is Thai, but his first language is English, his passions are Homer, Asimov, Shakespeare and Hollywood movies. He sees himself as an unmarked inheritor of Western civilization . . . and he has definitely inherited it. He has to find his Thai identity, like his ability to speak the Thai language. He's between two cultures, one of them not quite real.

The first two friends he makes are a servant boy, Piak, and an African-American neighbour, Virgil. In Virgil's treehouse, Virgil announces, they are in America and Piak isn't a servant. It's an idealised America, because this is 1963 and in the real America Martin Luther King has only just announced his dream. The race issue that first impinges on Justin isn't to do with the question of his own race (when he experiences racism against himself it pretty much goes straight over his head because he doesn't have the context for it) but the question of racism towards Virgil when they interact with white Americans and with a South African. To begin with, Justin and his Thai family have no context for black people. When Virgil says Thais are too superstitious, Justin counters:

> "What about you people with your cannibals and your voodoo? You sit around worshipping King Kong for God's sake! You strangle your wives, too," I added, learnedly.

He's perfectly prepared to go on from that naivety to being friends, and fortunately Virgil's response is to roar with laughter. But when, during a rehearsal for Justin's play about the fall of Troy the South African and the European-American try to lynch Virgil, Justin comes to a consciousness of race, and of race in the context of Western culture which is all the more clearly seen against the background of Thailand. His solution is to write a play about Orpheus that will reconcile everyone. But it takes Kennedy's death to make Justin's dream of having all the boys in the treehouse come true. And Somtow sees that this is a limited dream, that the girls (white, black and Thai) are left out, and the climax of the book concerns them.

Jasmine Nights seems pretty thoroughly out of print, but fairly easily available used. I'd love to see it in print again, but in the meantime do seek it out. Somtow has written lots of books, some horror, some SF, some fantastical. My favourite of his other books is *The Shattered Horse* (1986), a sequel to Homer. If you're new to his work, the collection *Dragon's Fin Soup* (1998) seems to be available. The short story "Dragon's Fin Soup" is just brilliant. I keep hoping one of his books will be a big bestseller and all his older books will come back into print so I can recommend them in good conscience. Meanwhile, he's the director of the Bangkok Opera, which seems entirely appropriate.

31. Lots of reasons to love these: Daniel Abraham's Long Price books

Last August I asked for suggestions for different cool fantasy that I ought to be reading, and I'd like to thank everyone who rec-ommended Daniel Abraham to me. Wow, these are good books. And they're a perfect example of what I wanted—they look like generic fantasy books, but they just happen to be brilliant. They are *A Shadow in Summer* (2006), *A Betrayal in Winter* (2007), *An Autumn War* (2008) and the forthcoming *The Price of Spring* (2009).

For those of you who haven't yet picked them up, I thought I'd point out some things about them that make them different and exciting, with absolutely no spoilers at all.

First, there are four books, and they're all written. The fourth one won't be out until July, but I have an ARC right here. It's written, done, ready to go to press. No interminable waiting.

Also on the "no waiting" front, each of these volumes has unu-sual amounts of climax and closure. They're all part of one thing, but each volume has its own story, which is complete in that volume. There's fifteen years between each book. They're one evolving story of a people and a world and their problems, and after reading one I definitely wanted the others ASAP, but they don't end on cliffhangers and they didn't leave me unsatisfied.

It's a great world. It borrows things from a lot of different history from around the world, but it doesn't slavishly imitate any one culture. Also, the magic is totally integrated into the history. It's more like science fiction in many ways. It's a consideration of the consequences of having the world work that way. There are poets who can capture "andat," which are the perfect expression of an abstract idea. For instance there's one called "Stone-made-soft" who can make stone soft and has made some famous mines. The andat are people, are solid, are characters in the books, but they're also held in the world by the poet's constant struggle. They have enormous and very specific powers, and they have an agenda, and they keep their cities safe because the threat of them is enough to stop anyone thinking of attacking them. There was an empire once that had andat and it was destroyed, and what's left now is a set of cities ruled by Khai. The Khai are allowed to have only three sons (subsequent sons go to train to be poets, few of them make it) and those three sons struggle to kill each other to become Khai. The rest of the world, lacking andat, look on jealously.

There's no struggle between good and evil. There are good points on both sides. Good people do terrible things for what seem like sensible reasons, and live with the consequences. Good people become awful people. Awful people do good things. People compromise. People change. The issues are really murky and some people are really twisty. Oh, and while we're talking about people—there are terrific female characters in a world where women have to make more effort to achieve things. There are also very different female characters, and very different male characters too. The characterisation generally is such a strength, I almost didn't mention it. Great characters.

The world keeps expanding as the books go on and actions have consequences, but there's no retconning. Things that are throwaway mentions in *A Shadow in Summer* are seen to have great significance later. The plot and worldbuilding and history are rock solid. I hate it when I can't trust that kind of thing, it's like leaning on a wall and the house falls over. Here I feel I really can. The technology and the magic and all the details of how the world works make sense and integrate.

This may seem like a strange thing to say, but these are post-9/11 fantasy. I've read post-9/11 SF already, but this is the first fantasy that had that feel for me. I don't mean they have allegory, or even applicability. They're their own thing, not a shadow-play of our world. But they have that sensibility, in the same way that Tolkien was writing about Dark Lords in the shadow of Hitler and Stalin and Marion Zimmer Bradley was writing about Free Amazons during the seventies upswell of feminism. This may eventually make them seem dated, or very much of this time. But right now is this time, and I found this aspect of them interesting to observe.

They're rattling good stories of the kind that are easy to sink into and pull over your head. I dreamed about that world every night while I was reading them. If fantasy is Tolkien's "history, true or feigned," here's some really solid feigned history of just the sort I like best. I wanted to know what happened. I wanted to keep reading them through meals. I'm sorry to have come to the end of them and I know I'll be re-reading them before too long. I'll let you know more about them when that happens, and my considered reflections on them. For the time being, if you like fantasy at all you almost certainly want to read these.

Thank you again for recommending them to me.

32. Maori Fantasy:
Keri Hulme's The Bone People

Keri Hulme has, according to the little piece about the author, "Maori, Scottish and English ancestry" and has always lived in New Zealand. *The Bone People* (1985) is a book rooted in the physical locations of rural littoral New Zealand and in the mythological and folk traditions of the Maori people. The very specificity of the places and details make the magic, when you get to it, feel real and rooted and entirely believable. This is above everything a story about a colonised people getting their spirit back, and getting it back in a way that is itself uniquely theirs but does not exclude. In Hulme's vision of cultural renewal, the New Zealanders of European ("Pakeha") origin are included as also belonging now to the land. The book takes you slowly into the heart of it and it takes you spiralling out again. This is a story about three people, and in their three points of view, the part-Maori woman Kerewin who is an artist who is blocked, the Maori man Joseph who has wanted so much and failed at everything, and the mute child Simon, who is all European and who washed up on the shore from a wreck. Terrible things happen to them, and wonderful things, and things that are very hard to read about.

The Bone People is a wonderful book, and one it's definitely a lot more fun to re-read than it was to read for the first time. There's a lot in the book that's very disturbing, and there's one passage that in many re-reads I've never seen without tears coming between me and the words. It's a story where halfway through the first time I almost felt I couldn't go on, except that I had to, and yet knowing the well-earned ending it has, over time, become a comfort read for me. The present edition says it was the most successful book in New Zealand's publishing history. It won the prestigious Booker Prize sometime in the mid-eighties, and the award did its job by attracting a lot of attention to the book, including mine. I first read a library copy (on a train to Skegness) and then I bought a new paperback, and then I read my paperback to death and I've recently replaced it with another paperback. I love it. I love the fish and the food and the magic, I love the people, I've read it so often that I can read the Maori phrases without looking at the translations at the back, and yet the only way I can get through the book is knowing that in the end there is redemption. I think Hulme knew that, because she put the end at the beginning, just as a little incomprehensible prologue, to let you know they come through.

I think this is a book most people would really enjoy. There's the unusual perspective, the interesting culture, the deep-rooted magic, the wonderful end, but I have to say it isn't an easy book. Joseph Gillayley drinks and beats his foster son, Simon. And yet he loves him, and Simon loves Joe, and Kerewin thinks at one point, "What kind of love is it that has violence as a silent partner?" and that's what the book goes into, in more detail than you might be able to take. It does not romanticise the situation or shy away from it. Terrible things happen to Simon, but the worst of them for him is that he loses his home. The hardest thing to read is not Simon being hurt but Joe hurting him. Getting into the point of view of a man beating a child, understanding where that comes from is a major writing achievement, and deeply upsetting.

At the beginning of the book, all three of the main characters are screwed up. The story is the process of them being healed, and in the process renewing their culture, but they are healed by going through annealing fire. Simon is mute and about eight years old, he doesn't know where he comes from and thinks that he is bad, and that when people find that out about him they will hurt him. This has been the pattern of his life. Kerewin is artistically blocked and cut off from her family, from human connection and from love. Joe has lost two vocations and a family and he has a child who does misbehave, who does do wild things, who deliberately invites violence because he sees it as redemptive. Simon wants everything to be all right again and he wants that to happen after punishment, because that's what he understands. He thinks he is the scapegoat. He doesn't want to be hit but he wants to be loved, and being hit is part of that, and he will deliberately provoke it. Simon's healing involves being very badly hurt, being taken away from his father, and then eventually coming to see value in himself and a way of going on that is not the way of violence. And Joe, who was beaten himself as a child and comes out of a pattern of this, goes through prison and then physical distress and then being trusted with something real and magical before he can start seeing the world differently. Kerewin tears down her tower (she has the best tower, but it's the wrong thing) and almost dies before she can come to renewal, to be able to create again.

The magic works like stone soup. It gives them the confidence to begin again, to do what needs to be done, to rebuild, and then everyone comes to help and add their little bit. The book wouldn't work without it. It's there and real and alive, like everything else in the story. I'm afraid I've made it sound cold, but it isn't at all, it's a very warm and welcoming book. It's also very readable, with beautiful use of language and point of view. The place and the people feel real and close enough to touch, which is why you can come to care about them so much.

33. Better to have loved and lost? Series that go downhill

In my post on *A Million Open Doors* I mentioned the advice given to someone on rec.art.sf.written when they asked about the reading order for the *Dune* series. "Read the first one. Then stop." In the comments, R. Fife said:

> I feel your pain. I have not read Barnes in particular, but I have read the first three *Dune* books. After the third one, I was left with a kind of disillusioned aftertaste that has led me to not finish the other three. Same with *Sword of Truth,* where I forced my way to *Naked Empire* then gave up (and had to start forcing after *Faith of the Fallen*). Heck, *The Dark Tower* by Stephen King did it to me after *Wolves of the Calla* (read two pages of *Song of Susannah* and threw the book).
>
> So, is it better to have loved and lost than never loved before? Is it better to pretend the series could still be good and never read the disappointing sequels, but still know they are out there, somewhere, and possibly even why they were disappointing, than to experience it firsthand?

I think that's a very interesting question. And there's a related question. Is it worth reading the early good books, if the series isn't going to live up to its promise?

There has been no case in the whole of my history where somebody has told me not to read the sequels and I have listened to them. I have always gone on to read the disappointing sequels, and been disappointed. Occasionally, I've read the sequels and liked them despite the consensus. But mostly the consensus is right, and I just haven't listened. Once I stop, I stop, I don't keep on and on if I'm no longer enjoying something. But I'm hopeless at not seeking out sequels as long as I have enjoyed the series up to that point.

So, better to have loved and lost?

I think a lot of it depends on the way in which the sequels are bad. If there's an initial brilliant volume and then the sequels fade off with less and less originality until they're just going through the motions, then I haven't really lost anything. I'm thinking of the Pern books. I haven't read all of those (goodness me, there's one called *Dolphins of Pern*!) but I've read enough of them to be able to tell you that none of them is *Dragonflight* (1968), but they're all perfectly reasonable extra helpings of books with dragons and weyrs. None of them are going to spoil the experience of *Dragonflight*, except perhaps by diluting it a little. And you can't really get back the experience that was *Dragonflight*, because let's face it, you have to be twelve. If I was camping in the rain and there was nothing to read but *Dolphins of Pern*, I'm sure I could pass a happy enough afternoon with it. The same with the sequels to David Feintuch's *Midshipman's Hope* (1994). I've read all of them. I'd urge you to stop with the first book, but the sequels haven't done me any harm.

Where there's a real problem is when the sequels spoil the original book.

The books about which I feel most strongly negative are all

sequels to earlier books that I really like, and which spoil those earlier books. I'm immediately thinking of Card's *Xenocide* (1991) and Mary Gentle's *Ancient Light* (1987). In those cases, I can't re-read the earlier books without the memory of the later books coming between me and the page. I know the Ender series has gone on far past *Xenocide,* and though, or perhaps because, I loved *Ender's Game* (1995) and *Speaker for the Dead* (1986) so much, I haven't been able to bring myself to read them, and I can't really re-read the first two either. With *Ancient Light* it's not so bad, I have after many years been able to forget it sufficiently that I can re-read *Golden Witchbreed* (1983). But I'm afraid *Xenocide* has poisoned the universe forever for me.

I think my problem here was that part of the fundamental pleasure of reading SF for me is putting the hints and clues together and extrapolating where they're going, and in re-reading seeing how they go together when I know where they're going. I can't do that if I have to turn my eyes away from where they're going. I honestly wish I hadn't read those books. When we were talking about *Eternal Sunshine of the Spotless Mind,* I said that if Lacuna was real, the thing I'd have wiped would be my memory of *Xenocide.* "But then you'd read it again!" Sasha said. And he's right! (In fact, the only way I know this hasn't happened already is that I read *Xenocide* about three days after it was published.)

So, why is it worse when this happens in a sequel?

When a writer takes a book in a new direction, it can feel jarring, and if it's a direction I don't like and that doesn't fit with what has gone before, I won't like it. But it's happening while I'm reading, and though I may be invested in the plot and the characters and the world, it won't disappoint me as much as when this happens in a sequel, where I may well have read the first book(s) several times before the new one comes out. There are a number of books that I think go downhill in the last third, but I don't start foaming at the mouth when I think of them. But when it's a series and when I already love all of the earlier books and have read it and read it and read it, sometimes when I hear there's going to be a sequel I'm as afraid as I am delighted. This happened recently with *Regenesis* (2009).

I think whether it's worth starting a series that goes downhill depends very much on how self-contained the good books are. In the case of *A Million Open Doors* and *Dune* that isn't a problem. The books stand alone. With something like a fantasy series (I haven't read either of R. Fife's examples of King and Goodkind) it's a lot less clear-cut, because a series like that is very much a voyage where you want to feel sure of your destination. A lot of this is a problem with trusting the author. If I trust the author, I'll put up with a lot, but once I start feeling distrusting, I start picking fault with everything.

And a lot of it is individual taste. Mostly when this has happened to me, I've started the series before all the books are out. I know there are people out there who won't read series unless they're complete. But it's very difficult if someone says, "Read this one, and then stop."

34. More questions than answers: Robert A. Heinlein's The Stone Pillow

When you read a book that's been so tremendously influential on the whole genre of SF and inspired a whole subgenre of its own, it's hard to see it clearly. It's hard to see what it was that seemed so wonderful when it was new that fans rushed to give it the Hugo and pros the Nebula. Even when I first read it in the early eighties it knocked me over, but I have to recapture my inner twelve-year-old to really appreciate *The Stone Pillow* now.

If *The Stone Pillow* were a new book today, I'd call it derivative. But the reason for that is the tremendous influence it has had. Is there a word for a book that was genre-changing and is historically important but that has been left behind by changing times? I don't know.

Before *The Stone Pillow,* nobody had written about a world where the stars go out. Oh it's a familiar conceit now, it's been done by Robert Charles Wilson (*Spin*), Robert Reed (*Beyond the Veil of Stars*), Greg Egan (*Quarantine*), Joanna Russ (*Edge and the Border*), Margaret Atwood (*Exceed His Grasp*) and even Arthur C. Clarke ("The Nine Billion Names of God"). That isn't the only way the book has been influential—it introduced Heinlein's theme of older aliens and younger women, so prevalent in the genre today. It was the first introduction of aliens with an agenda and affected SF from Ken MacLeod to *Battlestar Galactica*. It prefigured the first-person kick-ass female protagonist in *Friday*. It was also, astonishingly so late, the first story in which all the women went away.

Did the genre really need the introduction of robotic sex kittens?

As always with Heinlein, when I'm actually reading it, I get caught up in the story and I don't care about the flaws. OK, Desdi likes to be wolf-whistled at, I guess some women do. OK, her nipples go "spung," maybe mine are defective, they've never made any noise at all. The future world without stars is well drawn—and in so few words, too! Heinlein's really astonishing skill at sketching detailed backgrounds with a few brief strokes was never better. I like the aliens, well, I mostly like the aliens. If I have issues with the Crazy Greys it's in their motivation sneaking around that way. My problem is with Desdi. When I was twelve this went right past me. But now I have to ask, why does she go with them at the end? And why do all the other women and femmbots? What's so wrong with Earth? Why is the epilogue from the point of view of the men left behind (with no stars!) and not with Desdi and the others aboard the spaceship? And why did the ship change from a saucer to a teapot? I remain perplexed.

And I appreciate that it's influential, but why are all those books the same story? I mean at the end of *Spin* men as well as women leave the planet, and at the end of *Beyond the Veil of Stars* they leave the planet as mind vampires and I suppose you can call *Exceed His Grasp* and *Edge and the Border* feminist reimaginings and *Quarantine* a geek reimagining, but in my opinion only Clarke had the courage to do something really different with this story.

I mean, it's undeniably influential. And I guess it's a good book. It's certainly still a thought-provoking read. But I'm not sure it's quite as good as everyone thought it was back in 1940.

April Fool! If you are perplexed, you should know that this was a jape published on April 1. *The Stone Pillow* was a title of an announced Heinlein book that he never actually wrote. Robert Charles Wilson mentioned it in his short story "Divided by Infinity." The conceit here is taking an imaginary book and making it the ancestor of a mixed set of books, some real and some made up. The Wilson, the Reed and the Egan are all real, and all really about worlds without stars. Clarke's "Nine Billion Names of God" is also a real short story on this subject.

35. Weeping for her enemies: Lois McMaster Bujold's Shards of Honor

Kate Nepveu mentioned Bujold's Vorkosigan saga as a series where the quality increased as they went on, and the more I thought about that the more I felt like reading them, and as today is a "mostly horizontal" day, I spent the morning with *Shards of Honor* (1986). As *Shards of Honor* is now published as the first half of a book called *Cordelia's Honor,* with *Barrayar* (1991) as the second half, and as plotwise *Barrayar* is the second half of the story, even if it was written a lot later when Bujold had become much more accomplished, I had intended to spend this afternoon reading that and then do one post on the whole story. But as I put *Shards of Honor* down and realised I had to get out of bed anyway, I thought it might be interesting to consider it alone, and as a very unusual beginning for the series. And then it occurred to me that it might be interesting to re-read the books in publication order, which I don't think I have ever done.

Shards of Honor was Bujold's first published novel. It introduces the universe in which all the books in the series take place. Otherwise, it couldn't be less like a standard first novel in a series. The main character (of the series) isn't even born and this is about how his parents met. Major events happen that do cast their shadow a long way, but here they are mostly interesting in the context of Aral and Cordelia, who are minor characters in most of the subsequent books. This totally isn't a case of writing something and following it with more of the same.

What's really good about *Shards of Honor*, what totally grabbed me about it on first reading and on every subsequent read, is the character of Cordelia. The book is written in a very tight third person in Cordelia's point of view, and Cordelia is a wonderful character. She's empathic and practical and she's from no-nonsense egalitarian Beta colony. She is the commander of the exploration starship *Rene Magritte*, when on a newly discovered planet she encounters the aggressive forces of Barrayar. The universe is just sketched in compared to the way it is developed later, but it's already interesting. The plot provides enough events to get from one end of the book to the other. The writing is nothing like as good as Bujold has since become, but it's very absorbing. The other thing that's notable is the emotional depth she manages to get into this space opera plot. It's not so much the romance (though the romance is actually very sweet) as the genuine ethical dilemmas. Again, this is something where Bujold improved by orders of magnitude, but even here in this first novel she had enough to hook me completely.

I said that the background of the universe is only sketched in, and that's true. Everything she says later is reasonably implicit in what's mentioned here, but an awful lot isn't mentioned. The phrase "the Wormhole Nexus" isn't used. Jackson's Whole is mentioned as a name, and the Cetagandan war, but no other planets except Escobar, Beta, Barrayar and Earth. There's nothing—and there should be nothing—about how the ships are powered, but the pilot we see does have implants.

Shards of Honor is about the specific contrast between Beta and Barrayar, and Beta and Barrayar a generation before we mostly know them. For Beta we have Cordelia, female, a theist, competent and practical, an explorer, whose weapon is a stunner. For Barrayar we have Aral, male, an atheist, a militarist, a romantic, who has seen someone killed because he only has a stunner. ("How did they kill him with a stunner?" "They didn't. They kicked him to death after they'd taken it away from him.") Aral is practical too, but with a completely different kind of practicality. Of course they fall in love—and Bujold does it rather well by not dwelling on it. Beta here is democratic—except that nobody admits to having voted for the president. Malefactors are treated with therapy, which seems very enlightened until Cordelia is threatened with therapy that will peel her brain like an onion looking for the seeds. Barrayar is feudal and militaristic and has been having a problem with political officers and a Ministry of Political Education. Ezar, the dying emperor, gets rid of that but at a terrible cost.

The immediate contrast between Barrayar and Beta is one of the things that does prefigure the rest of the series. But it's surprising how little of what I know about Barrayar is mentioned here—there's no mention of the Time of Isolation, no mention of the poisonous native vegetation, or the radioactivity of Vorkosigan Vashnoi. Also, we barely see Piotr. All of those things are clearly there, to an eye who knows to expect them, but they're not explicit. Bujold has always said she reserves the right to have a better idea, but there's remarkably little retconning or contradiction—just more information, as things become fractally more complicated as you get closer to them. When Cordelia mentions interrogation drugs, I'm pretty sure Bujold had not yet thought up fast penta, but when she has her allergic reaction to Dr. Mehta's drug it prefigures Miles's idiosyncratic reactions to fast penta even so. Similarly, Jackson's Whole may just have been a name when she wrote it, but what I know about it from the later books fits in without a twitch.

I mentioned the emotional depth. The depravity of Vorrutyer and Prince Serg, and the explicit minimizing of that evil compared to Ezar's plan, is very impressive. But most interesting of all is Bothari, who is a monster, but an entirely three-dimensional one even here.

There are a number of things that are quite intentionally set up for later books. What they are setting up is not *Barrayar* but *The Warrior's Apprentice* (1986), which takes place eighteen years later but is what she wrote immediately next. Arde Mayhew is the pilot who takes Cordelia to Escobar, Vordarian is mentioned, Aral's Regency, and Aral and Cordelia's hope for children. *Shards of Honor* has a happy ending, I suppose. Aral and Cordelia are married, Aral is Regent, nothing bad has happened yet. Very few people would turn from that to poor Miles breaking his legs again as he fails to get over the obstacle course. But that's why Bujold is such a terrific writer, and was, even at the beginning of her career.

36. Forward Momentum: Lois McMaster Bujold's The Warrior's Apprentice

The Warrior's Apprentice (1986) is where I normally tell people to start the Vorkosigan books, and it is the other logical beginning to the series. It was written immediately after *Shards of Honor* but set a generation later—a literal generation. Cordelia and Aral's son Miles, blighted before birth by a teratogenic chemical attack on his parents, is a manic-depressive dwarf with brittle bones but is still determined to serve in the military. On the first page of the book he fails the physical test to enter the military academy. After that he goes to visit his grandmother on Beta Colony and events spiral in the manner of "The Sorcerer's Apprentice" until he finds himself the admiral of a fleet of space mercenaries. If you like MilSF you'll love it, and if you don't like MilSF you might just love it anyway, because really that's the least of it.

What makes this so good is that it has about 90 percent more depth than you'd expect it to have. The plot may be "seventeen-year-old with physical disabilities becomes admiral of space mercenaries" but the themes are much deeper and more interesting. This is a story about loyalty, duty, the weight of family expectations, and what it means to serve.

Miles's grandfather was a general, his father was an admiral and regent, his mother keeps telling him great tests are great gifts. He's spent a lot of his childhood crippled physically and under a weight of expectation. The other person who brought him up was Sergeant Bothari. Bothari has been Miles's bodyguard and batman since Miles was born and he is a deeply screwed-up guy. He has a daughter, Elena, and the mystery of Elena's parentage (no mystery if you have read *Shards*) is one of the unusual plot strands of *Warrior's*. Bothari raped Elena's mother and made a fantasy that she was his wife. Elena, born out of a uterine replicator, is supposed to be his atonement—but one human being cannot be that for another. Miles loves Elena but once she gets away from Barrayar she never wants to go back. You'd expect from the first chapter of the book that Miles and Elena would be engaged at the end, but far from it, she rejects him to marry a deserter and remain a mercenary.

The book largely takes place in Tau Verde space, with Miles taking over the Oseran mercenaries with hardly a blow being struck. ("Now I understand how judo is supposed to work!") But the emotional heart of it is on Barrayar. In *Shards,* Cordelia says that Barrayar eats its children, and here we have that in detail. After Miles has assembled the fleet and is hailed as Admiral, he goes home to stand trial for treason. The climax of the story is not the surrender of the Oserans but Aral begging for Miles's life. (Incidentally, she must have had most of what happens in *Barrayar* in mind if not on paper before she wrote this.) The whole plot happened because Miles wants to serve . . . something.

Also unusual—how often do you see a bleeding ulcer instead of a bloody boarding battle? I think it was absolutely the right choice, but what a nerve! And Miles's depression balances his mania—he manages astonishing feats, but he also has his black moods, his days of sitting doing nothing while everything goes

118

to hell around him. Yet unlike some depressive characters in fiction, it's always entertaining to be around Miles. And the conflict of *Shards* between Cordelia representing Beta and Aral representing Barrayar is internalised in Miles, who holds both planets, both accents, both value sets, and tries to reconcile them in his own person. Psychologically and plotwise it all makes perfect sense, it's just, again, not the kind of choice you'd expect to see in a book like this. And again, you can spin this as a book about Miles winning, but it's really just as much if not more about how much he lost, Bothari, Elena, his grandfather. . . . On this re-read, I was impressed with how much we see Miles play-acting outside of the part of Admiral Naismith. He gets out of bed to mime the mutant villain, he pretends to be rehearsing Shakespeare with Elena, he plays the Baba in Elena and Baz's betrothal scene. Clearly acting parts has been part of his life for a long time, and that explains (partly) how he can take on roles so easily.

Again, though, this isn't a great first book that sets a pattern for the series. It's a lot closer to most of the books—it's Miles-centred, it features the Dendarii Mercenaries, it introduces some key recurring characters, Ivan, Alys (barely glimpsed), Emperor Gregor, Elena, Bel Thorne, Elli Quinn. I suppose some of the others are even on this pattern. *The Vor Game* (1990) and *Brothers in Arms* (1989) are both "adventures with the Dendarii where the heart of the thing is Barrayar." But none of the others have that shape. And on the writing level, this is perhaps a little smoother than *Shards,* but only a little. If you look at this as the beginning, it's a good book and I'm deeply fond of it, but the series does get a lot deeper and more complex as it goes on from here.

37. Quest for Ovaries: Lois McMaster Bujold's *Ethan of Athos*

Ethan of Athos (1986) is Lois McMaster Bujold's third published novel and the third book in the Vorkosigan saga. It's absolutely nothing like the other two. Athos is a planet where, like Mount Athos in Greece, women are not allowed. Ethan is an obstetrician there, before he gets sent on a mission to the wider galaxy to bring back new ovarian cultures. There he meets the mercenary Elli Quinn, who upsets all his ideas about women, and becomes involved in a complicated plot involving two sets of interstellar thugs (from Cetaganda and Jackson's Whole), a telepath, and the whole future of his planet.

The thing that makes this good is Ethan's unruffled innocence; the charming utopian Athos, where you have to earn social duty credits to be entitled to a son; the quiet acceptance of homosexuality as the norm on Athos (there is no actual onstage sex in the book); the ecologically obsessed Kline Station; and the fast-paced plot that doesn't give you time to think.

My favourite moment is when Terrence Cee reveals himself as a telepath to Ethan:

"If you truly possess such a talent it would seem a shame not to use it. I mean, one can see the applications right away."

"Can't one, though," muttered Cee bitterly.

"Look at pediatric medicine—what a diagnostic aid for pre-verbal patients! Babies who can't answer Where does it hurt? What does it feel like? Or for stroke victims, or those paralysed in accidents who have lost all ability to communicate, trapped in their bodies. God the Father!" Ethan's enthusiasm mounted. "You could be an absolute savior!"

Terrence Cee sat down rather heavily. His eyes widened in wonder, narrowed in suspicion. "I'm more often viewed as a menace. No one I've met who knew my secret ever suggested any use for me but espionage."

"Well—were they espionage agents themselves?"

"Now that you mention it, yes for the most part."

"So there you are. They see you as what they would be, given your gift."

It's interesting that Athos is a Planet of Men, because it's the only one I know of, and I can think of quite a few examples of Planets of Women (Russ's Whileaway, Griffith's *Ammonite* [1992]) and others of Women and Men Live Apart (Sargent's *Shore of Women* [1986], Tepper's *The Gate to Women's Country* [1989], Brin's *Glory Season* [1992]). I couldn't have imagined what a feminist notion a planet of men is, and how tied up with nurturing children Athos is, accounting for the costs in a way that doesn't dismiss it as "women's work." In the end Ethan comes to realise that Athos has mothers too, or at least ovarian donors.

Elli Quinn, who was a very minor character in *The Warrior's Apprentice* but who will be important in the series later, is the only repeating character in this book. Other things that will later become important are the Cetagandans and (especially!) House Bharaputra of Jackson's Whole. Barrayar is barely mentioned. The name Vorkosigan is not mentioned. And in the rest of the series, the things that are so important here are barely mentioned. Kline Station is never revisited; neither is Athos, and they're barely mentioned again. Terran-C is mentioned once briefly in one of the stories in *Borders of Infinity* (1989). It's possible that Bujold is planning to revisit the planet of peaceful gay guys in a few generations when they're all telepaths, but so far she has done no more with it. So it's perfectly possible to see this book as a detachable appendix to the series, like *Falling Free*. But it was written immediately after the first two books, and published immediately after them. It was as if Bujold had three tries at starting the series. She began it with Cordelia, again with Miles, and then a third time with Ethan and Elli before settling down to write a lot more about Miles. Was she waiting to see what people wanted? Or was it just that she had a lot of different interesting ideas and working them out within the context of one universe gave her a solid base of history and geography to go on from?

38. Why he must not fail: Lois McMaster Bujold's Borders of Infinity

Borders of Infinity (1989) is a collection of short stories about Miles. One of them, "The Mountains of Mourning," is about Miles Vorkosigan on Barrayar, and the other two are about Admiral Naismith, galactic mercenary (daring rescues a specialty).

Brothers in Arms and the collection *Borders of Infinity* were both published in 1989. When I re-read the way I normally do, chronologically, I'm never sure which order to read them in, as the stories take place at such different times. The frame story is clearly after *Brothers in Arms* and yet *Brothers in Arms* opens with Miles surveying the damage from "The Borders of Infinity." (It's probably a good thing the collection doesn't exist in that form anymore except for hardback collectors so people who want everything chronological can have it in the new versions.)

But I'm reading in publication order, and they were both published in 1989. With the computer off, I couldn't tell which had actually been published first. So I grabbed *Borders of Infinity* on the grounds that at least some of the stories are earlier. Looking around, it seems I was wrong, sorry.

The frame story is set immediately after *Brothers in Arms* and does not develop the main internal chronological plot of the series at all. Miles is having the bones of his arms replaced with plastic bones, and ImpSec is being audited. It's a very shallow frame, barely an outline to hang the three novellas from. It's a fairly clunky device. Having said that, I kind of like it. It gives us a bit more Miles, a bit more Simon, and it actually does some setup for *Memory,* though it probably could have done that better if it had known what it was doing. In losing the collection in favour of inserting the stories at the right chronological points, the frame is lost entirely, and I think I'd miss it.

"The Mountains of Mourning" is set immediately before *The Vor Game,* which of course she hadn't written yet. It's the best written thing in the series so far. Miles, fresh out of the Imperial Academy, goes up to the backwoods of the Dendarii mountains and discovers what he's fighting for. It's the most significant part of the whole sequence as far as understanding Miles goes, because Miles doesn't work without his heart in Barrayar. Miles is interesting most especially because he's pulled in many directions, and this one is what matters most. This is Miles's emotional core. The story is quiet and understated and people mentioned in the *Warrior's Apprentice* post that it's online.

"Labyrinth" gives us a close-up look at Jackson's Whole and thus sets up *Mirror Dance.* It also introduces Taura, and has a quaddie, connecting back to *Falling Free* and forward to *Diplomatic Immunity.* It's an interesting model of daring rescue, actually. Miles is sent in to kill a monster, when what's necessary is to rescue a princess. He thinks this himself, and Taura's transformation from monster to princess (or at least mercenary) is what the story is about. It all goes very smoothly.

"The Borders of Infinity" is clearly a thought experiment of Miles carrying on naked. I noticed that in *Shards of Honor* Cordelia thinks Aral could do it, and here Miles does it. It's another daring rescue, he rescues thousands of prisoners of war from a prison camp after getting them organized using nothing more than willpower. This gets the Cetagandans really mad at him, which becomes important in *Brothers in Arms*. He also traumatises himself by losing a woman out of the shuttle, as if he needed to be any more traumatised.

Through all of these Miles continues convincingly manic-depressive and to make his physical problems seem trivial. He sometimes manages to carry on through unconvincing amounts of pain, or at least sufficiently more pain than I could carry on through, and I'm fairly used to it myself. Having said that, she never really pushes it into total unbelievability—and here the frame story helps, by showing us Miles completely helpless.

In the context of the series, she wrote these three stories that are oh-so-definitely about Miles, and contextualising the whole universe around Miles, while at the same time writing the next Miles novel, so she must have definitely made some decisions about direction. It's a good place to start the series, or at least a lot of people seem to have happily started it here and gone on to love it. It's taking the series forward by focusing on Miles. I mentioned that the most interesting thing about Miles is his dual nature, the way his heart is on Barrayar and yet he can only really relax, and only really succeed, and only really serve when he's being Admiral Naismith. The novels all play on that. These stories divide him up, one on Barrayar, two in space. The frame roots them to Barrayar.

39. What have you done with your baby brother? Lois McMaster Bujold's Brothers in Arms

Brothers in Arms (1989) is the first Bujold book I read. I didn't like it much. I can therefore confidently say that it isn't a good place to start the series. The reason why I didn't like it relates to my spearpoint theory. Briefly, a spearpoint is a tiny sharp point that needs a whole long spear behind to make it go in. Similarly the weight of significance of things in fiction some-times need long buildups to make them get proper impact. This is a book that needs the weight of earlier books to have the impact it needs. A lot of what's good about it depends on knowing things already, out of the context of this book. So it's weird really that it's only the second novel about Miles, in pub-lication order.

Six months after I read this, when I picked up *Shards of Honor,* all I remembered about it was the cat blanket, mercenaries and lots of running around after a clone. So much of what's good about it went right over my head without context. I can't believe Galeni made no impression on me, but he didn't. (Galeni is one of my favourite characters in the whole series, perhaps my very favourite after Mark and Miles.)

In the thread about *The Warrior's Apprentice,* JoeNotCharles talks about how much better Bujold has got at setting up implausible situations and making them believable. For me as a reader I've never had any problem with the implausibility of her situations except in *Brothers in Arms,* where the clone of Miles being controlled by Galeni's father didn't convince me. If I'd already known Miles as Naismith and as Vorkosigan, if I'd had the grounding in Barrayar you get by reading the other books, I'd probably have had no problem with this either. But it's not just that. I'd have cared already. With spear-building a lot of it is ensuring that the reader cares about the right things. I came to this book without already caring, and it didn't make me care. I liked it enough to finish it, and to pick up another book by the same author when I came across one, but it took *Shards* to hook me.

Having said that, when you do already care about Miles, Ivan, Barrayar and the Dendarii Free Mercenaries, there's a lot more here. Galeni is introduced, and with him the complexities of another generation on Komarr. It's very nifty to see how Komarr is introduced as a title for Aral, pretty much, "The Butcher of Komarr" in *Shards,* and of course everything we hear about it there is in the context of Aral's career and Barrayaran politics. Then we hear about the battle from Tung in *Apprentice,* and here we see how things have played out. We get more Komarr again later, especially in *Memory,* and more Galeni too. I love the way politics and technology move and change and interact and things go on outside of the stories. This is one of Bujold's real strengths.

Mark is especially interesting, and so is Miles's attitude to Mark. Miles thinks of Mark almost at once as a brother, and as something he wants, and as someone to rescue, not as an enemy. Mark is a shadow of the way we see him in *Mirror Dance* (1994), but having a clone of Miles is a very interesting thing to do, and in only the second novel she'd written about Miles. Miles is already doubled and torn, Naismith and Vorkosigan, now he's literally doubled too.

If this were a normal series, and she'd decided to write about Miles, you'd expect another book like *The Warrior's Apprentice,* a caper with mercenaries, and with Miles's loyalties being stretched. You wouldn't expect this book about a clone, you wouldn't expect an eight-year gap, you wouldn't expect Elli Quinn, who was a fairly minor character the last time we saw her, to be such a significant love interest. You would expect Ivan to make an appearance, which he does, but you wouldn't expect him to be so intelligent. Ivan's eight years older too, and he doesn't do anything idiotic in this volume at all. (I'm fond of Ivan too.) Aral and Cordelia do not appear. Indeed, there isn't much Barrayar at all. Barrayar is represented by the embassy, and we don't see much of that except for Galeni, and for Galeni to work you need the Barrayar/Komarr contrast.

The other thing this book really needs is "The Borders of Infinity," the novella. Now, that was published in 1987, two years before the book, but it takes place immediately before, and an awful lot of the action of *Brothers in Arms* is a direct consequence of the events of the novella. I'm very glad it's now bound in with it, and I think it always should have been.

One last thing—this is the only time we see Earth in the series, and I remain unimpressed by it. The other planets are much more interesting.

40. Hard on his superiors:
Lois McMaster Bujold's
The Vor Game

The Vor Game (1990) was Bujold's first Hugo-winning novel, and it's here that the series really hits its stride, and also where it (briefly) starts to look like a normal series. Chronologically, *The Vor Game* follows on from *The Warrior's Apprentice,* with the novella "The Mountains of Mourning" (which also won a Hugo) coming between them. And *Young Miles* gives you just that, and I think that every single time I've read this series (certainly every time I've re-read it) I've read them in just that order. I had never actually consciously realised that Bujold had written *Brothers in Arms* first and come back to fill in this piece of the continuity.

I think *The Vor Game* would probably be a perfectly reasonable place to pick up the series, and as this is the first published novel where the writing quality is really high, it might even be a good place. It has an entirely self-contained and very exciting plot. And it's largely about what it means to be Vor, and Miles's subordination problems.

At the end of *The Warrior's Apprentice,* Miles's reward is entry into the Imperial Academy. In *The Vor Game* he has just graduated from it and been given an assignment—weatherman on an infantry base on Kyril Island. He's told if he can keep his nose clean he'll get ship assignment in six months, and of course he doesn't keep his nose clean. He is sent on a secret mission to the Hegen Hub for ImpSec. He's along to deal with the Dendarii, his superiors are supposed to find out what's going on. He finds out what's going on, and goes on to rescue the emperor and defeat the Cetagandans.

As a plot summary this does read just like more of *The Warrior's Apprentice* and kind of what you'd expect in another volume—"Barrayar and duty" vs "the mercenaries and fun." And there's a lot about this story that is pure bouncing fun. He does retake the mercenaries wearing slippers. (He's so like his mother!) At one point Miles has his three supposed superiors, Oser, Metzov, and Ungari, all locked up in a row, and Elena remarks that he's hard on his superiors. In *The Warrior's Apprentice,* it's MilSF fun with unexpected depths. Here the depths are fully integrated and entirely what the book's about. Practically all the characters are as well-rounded as the best of them are in the earlier books. We see a little bit of Ivan, a lot of Gregor, a little of Aral, of Elena, Bel, and there are the villains, Cavilo and Metzov, complicated people, and interesting distorting mirrors of Miles.

And Miles here is the most interesting of all. For the first time we see Miles longing to be Naismith almost as an addiction—Naismith is his escape valve. In *Brothers in Arms* there's the metaphor of Miles as an onion, Admiral Naismith being encompassed by Ensign Vorkosigan who is encompassed by Lord Vorkosigan who is encompassed by Miles. Here we see that working. It isn't just his subordination problem, the way he sees his superiors as future subordinates. (All my family are teachers, and I had the exact same problem in school of failing to be awed by the people assigned to teach me.) The most interesting thing about Miles is the tension between Betan and Barrayaran, between his personalities. He says to Simon at the

130

end that he couldn't keep on playing ensign when the man who was needed was Lord Vorkosigan, and thinks, or Admiral Naismith. He genuinely feels that he knows best in all situations and he can finesse it all—and so far, the text is entirely on his side. Miles does know best, is always right, or at worst what he does is "a" right thing to do, as Aral says about the freezing incident.

The book is called *The Vor Game* because one of the themes is about what it means to be Vor and bound by duty. I disagree with people who think "Weatherman" should be in *Borders of Infinity* and not here. Even if it wasn't absolutely necessary because it introduces Metzov and dictates what comes after, it would be necessary to introduce that Vor theme—Miles can make threatening to freeze stick not because he's an officer but because he's Vor, and because he's Vor he has to do it.

Feudalism is an interesting system, and one not much understood by people these days. Bujold, despite being American and thus from a country that never had a feudal period, seems to understand it deeply and all through. Vor are a privileged caste on Barrayar, a warrior caste, but this gives them duties as well as privileges. Miles standing freezing with the techs who refuse to endanger their lives, unnecessarily cleaning up the fetaine spill, is a man under obligation. Similarly, Gregor, who has tried to walk away from it all, accepts his obligations at the end. Gregor, with supreme power, is the most bound of all. (And he wishes that Cavilo had been real.) He isn't a volunteer, and yet by the end of the book he has volunteered. It's a game, an illusion, and yet it's deadly serious. In *The Warrior's Apprentice,* Miles uses it to swear liegemen left and right, here we see how it binds him. And that of course feeds back to "The Mountains of Mourning," which shows us why it is actually important, at the level it actually is.

The Vor Game looks like a sensible safe serieslike sequel to

The Warrior's Apprentice: it's another military adventure, it's another conflicted Barrayaran plot, and Miles saves the day again. It's the first book in the series that does look like that—and pretty much the last one too. What Bujold is setting up here is *Mirror Dance*. To make that book work, she had to have not only Mark from *Brothers in Arms,* she also had to have all this grounding for Miles and Gregor and the Vor system.

I started this post by mentioning that it was Bujold's first Hugo-winning novel. People who don't like Bujold talk about her fans as if they're mindless hordes of zombies who vote her Hugos unthinkingly and because she's Bujold. This is total bosh. When she writes something good, it gets nominated and often wins. The weaker books, even the weaker Miles books, don't even get nominated. I think she's won so many Hugos because she's really good and because she's doing things that not many people are doing, and doing them well, and thinking about what she's doing—and because what she's doing is something people like a lot. I think the system is working pretty well here.

41. One birth, one death, and all the acts of pain and will between: Lois McMaster Bujold's Barrayar

Barrayar (1991) is where the Vorkosigan books stopped being really good and lots of fun and became brilliant.

I started this thinking about series that improved. What has improved by this point is everything: the writing, the plotting, the depth of background, the significance of the issues, the characterisation—and remember that *Shards of Honor* was already well ahead of expectations on most of these things.

Barrayar is a direct sequel to *Shards of Honor*. It should be a story with no tension, because we already know what happens, if we have read anything about Miles at all. "I was a casualty in Vordarian's Pretendership before I was born!" he thinks in *The Vor Game*. This is that story. But despite knowing what's going to happen—Vordarian will start a civil war, Cordelia's unborn baby will be harmed by a gas attack, the baby will survive with teratogenic damage—it's an incredibly tense book, especially near the end.

It's very interesting to read a fast-paced science fiction novel about motherhood. There are fewer of them than you might think. Indeed, considering how much death there is in SF, there's not as much birth as you might expect. When there is birth it's usually high-tech and detached, and even then it's usually written by women. Here we have pregnancy and birth up close and surprisingly exciting. It is important—giving birth, giving life, does matter. If *Ethan of Athos* is making the point that reproduction isn't just for girls, *Barrayar* is really making future birth central and significant.

Someone mentioned that Bujold overshot the end of *Shards,* and that makes sense. It would be interesting to know how far that went. However it was, she must have rewritten that overshot. *Shards* has a lot of unexpected political and emotional honesty, but it's a first novel and it's written relatively clunkily. Delany talks in *The Motion of Light in Water* about the expected rhythm of prose and how you can go with that and use cliches and go along with the expected flow of language, or how you can push back and vary it and do things against the expected beat to make it syncopate or harmonize. On a prose level, *Shards* slides along with the expected thing every time. The language is in charge. By *Barrayar,* Bujold was entirely on top of language and pushing it for all it would do stylistically. There's a scene early on where Cordelia's at a party and she thinks that on Beta there would have been cameras and everything would have been done for the camera angles, but on Barrayar:

> The only recordings were made by ImpSec, for their own purposes, which did not include choreography. The people in this room danced only for each other, all their glittering show tossed blithely away in time, which carried it off forever; the event would exist tomorrow only in their memories.

The insight's the important thing and she could have had the insight in *Shards,* but here the mature Bujold is dancing with the language as well as the ideas.

From a series point of view, she was going back and filling in some more. She wrote *Brothers in Arms* and left the Mark plot dangling there for years while she did the necessary setup for *Mirror Dance.* This is the opposite of the standard series thing where the first book has all the ideas and the other books try to repeat or extend them. Far from writing something just like the last thing, or something more about mercenary adventures, she went right back to the beginning and wrote this slow-starting firecracker book about motherhood. And it won a very well-deserved Hugo. Oh, and it contains the awesome "Shopping" scene, which isn't in context funny at all, to me, because Cordelia is right on the edge there, she isn't putting up with any more from Barrayar at that point, she's almost as mad as Bothari. It's a great scene though.

This is the book where Piotr gets the character development he deserves. Miles and Ivan are both born. (Ivan's birth is one of the most nail-biting moments in the book.) We see Gregor as a small child. Alys Vorpatril, who has been mentioned but barely developed, gets a lot of development, setting her up for the position she holds in the rest of the series. One of the very clever things Bujold manages is making people seem as if they've been there all along. Alys has been mentioned briefly as Ivan's mother, when we find out about the rest of her job it just seems as if it wasn't mentioned because it wasn't important, never as if it's being shoehorned in. The same goes for the Koudelka daughters, who drift into the series in *Mirror Dance,* as a direct consequence, I'm sure, of Drou and Kou's romance here which probably had no existence before *Barrayar.* But they don't feel tacked on. Bujold has a genius for making things flow, for expanding her sketches into bas-relief and then three-dimensionality without any visible jerks. (I have to go back and change things to get this to work. I could never make it work over multiple volumes in cold print.)

Barrayar is about Betan Cordelia being swallowed by Barrayar. It's also about Barrayar adapting to her, by giving her spaces it doesn't believe are important, like the education of the emperor up to the age of twelve, like the marriage of a grocer's son and a corporal's son in the Imperial Residence, like the importation of uterine replicators and technology to choose the gender of your children.

My son, Sasha, has a joke about the three standard plots being "Man versus Man," "Man versus Plan," and "Man versus Canal." Most of the Miles books could perfectly sensibly be categorised as Man versus Plan. Barrayar has a certain amount of that, but it's also Man versus Canal—the way technology changes things. There's more technological change and sociological change and the effect technology has on society, and economics, and the effect economics has over time, in these books than in anything else I can think of—and it passes almost invisibly, perhaps because so much of it is classifiable as "girl stuff."

I gave *Barrayar* to a friend who had read *The Handmaid's Tale* and wanted to know more about this SF stuff, and she loved it, after initially having terrible problems with the cover. This isn't a "guilty pleasure" type read, this is as good as it gets, speculation and consequences and action and significant human issues. Whatever it looks like, we can put this with Le Guin and Delany and Vinge, this is a book that should make us proud of our genre.

42. All true wealth is biological: Lois McMaster Bujold's Mirror Dance

Mirror Dance (1994) is my favourite of the Vorkosigan series. It's the third Hugo winner of the series, and Bujold's third Hugo Award–winning novel in a row.

It's a very long book. It doesn't look any longer than the others, but it's 560 pages, in contrast to *Barrayar*'s 386 and *The Vor Game*'s 342. It needs to be longer, because a lot happens in it.

Mirror Dance is a direct sequel to *Brothers in Arms* (1989), though it could be read alone. (All of these books except *Memory* (1996) could be read alone.) It's Mark's book, though Miles is in it, it's the story of how a nameless clone became Lord Mark Pierre Vorkosigan. It's about identity and survival and better living through multiple personality disorder. It's surprising and brilliant, it does things you wouldn't think any series book could get away with, and the pacing is astonishing.

The best thing about the book is Mark, becoming a person. The most astonishing thing is that Miles spends half the book dead. In *Brothers in Arms,* Mark was another doubling of Miles. Here he is trying hard not to be. Also, Miles is hyperactive, brittle-boned, and charismatic. Mark is none of those things. Mark is short but solid, and he has been trained as an assassin.

In the beginning, Mark again poses as Miles and this time successfully takes a Dendarii ship, Bel Thorne's *Ariel,* and a battle group, Sergeant Taura's Green Squad. His plan is to rescue fifty clones from Jackson's Whole. The clones are being grown for life-extension purposes—not their lives, the lives of their originals, who will have their brains transplanted into the clone bodies, while the clone brains, personalities and all, are classed as "medical waste." This is a really horrible process, analagous to nothing in the real world, but entirely plausible as just the sort of thing unethical rich people would do. In this book we see Jackson's Whole in revolting close-up detail—again, Bujold makes me feel the details would have been there all along if only I'd been focusing on them.

Miles comes back to the Dendarii happy and confident; his only problem is that Quinn won't marry him. He collects some cryo-revival cases, cleverly setting us up with more detailed information on cryo-revival than we'd had before, though it has been mentioned right back to *The Warrior's Apprentice* (1986). He goes to the fleet, only to find the *Ariel* gone. He rushes off in pursuit. Meanwhile, Bel has figured out that Mark is Mark, but goes on with the mission for its own reasons. The mission goes horribly wrong, Miles arrives, rushes down to rescue Mark, and is killed.

The first time I read this, I was totally shocked when I got to Miles's death. Nothing had prepared me for it, not Murka in "The Borders of Infinity," not the body he hides under in *The Vor Game,* not any of the other deaths Miles has been close to. Death is there in military science fiction, death is right there but your protagonist always has a hairsbreadth escape. It's very hard to emotionally believe that one could really die oneself, that the world could keep going on but you wouldn't be in it, and point-of-view characters in fiction get this same special protection, especially after you've been reading about them for books and books. By the time *Mirror Dance* came out, I'd caught up to the rest of the series, this is in fact where I started buying them as they came out. And I was online, yes, it was 1994, that's when I went online. I remember seeing (and not reading) "*Mirror Dance* (spoilers)" threads on rec.arts.sf.written and not being able to wait for the UK edition. Anyway, Miles's death is another example of those things you just don't expect.

Miles stays dead for a long time. When you're reading about Aral and Cordelia trying to deal with Mark as the potential next Count Vorkosigan, the first time you have to ask yourself whether you are going to have to deal with him as the potential protagonist. I like Mark. But I was terribly worried about Miles.

When Sasha was ten, he read (in internal chronological order) all the Miles books up to *Brothers in Arms* in about a fortnight. He then wanted to read *Mirror Dance,* and I wasn't at all sure about it. There's some very disturbing stuff in it, and I wasn't sure if ten was old enough. I am all in favour of there being books appropriate for adults and not children, and I think it's the parent's responsibility to make sure kids don't get upset by things that are likely to really upset them. "Maybe you should wait on this one until you're older," I said. He hadn't just read half a ton of Miles for nothing. "How about if I read the ones about Cordelia, then?" "Great!" I said. "Because after I've read them, I'll *be* older. . . ." I gave in, but when I gave him *Mirror Dance* I said that if there was anything that upset him I was there to talk about it. He came downstairs at seven o'clock the next morning. "Jo! Miles is dead!" "I told you there were upsetting things in that book." "He does come alive again, doesn't he?" ". . . Yes." "I'm not going to school today." "Why not?" "How can I go to school while Miles is dead?"

Miles does indeed come alive again, though not without cost. But there's a great big chunk of the book when he's dead, and it's actually the most interesting bit. Mark goes to Barrayar and meets his parents and Gregor and Illyan and Kareen Koudelka. He stops trying to be Miles and starts to discover who he is himself. He joins in the search for Miles, having learned Miles from a different perspective and grown ready to value him. "All true wealth is biological" is what Aral says when he thinks he's dying. Mark doesn't understand it for a long time—he means you cannot buy love, or friendship, or family, and he is at that point thinking Miles is permanently dead, inviting Mark to be family.

All the books up to this point have contrasted the feudal masculinity of Barrayar with the egalitarian femininity of Beta Colony. *Mirror Dance* puts the integrity of Barrayar against the conniving of Jackson's Whole. Bujold has always been good at giving characters the virtues of their flaws, and for that matter, the flaws of their virtues. It's easy to hate Barrayar in *Barrayar,* but here we see what is most attractive about it, and we see it begin to heal Mark, or find a way for Mark to heal himself, to become Mark.

When Mark decides to return to Jackson's Whole to rescue Miles, the story goes back to Miles, but Miles newly awakened and amnesiac. Miles is endearing trying to figure out where he is, what's going on, and how to get on top of the situation. But it's all very tense. We remain in Miles's point of view for long enough to get used to it, then alternate between Mark and Miles as Mark is tortured by Ryoval and Miles is kept prisoner by Bharaputra. Mark waits for ImpSec to come, or the Dendarii, they'd have come for Miles . . . and horrible things are done to him. But he heeds Aral's advice and does not sell himself to his enemy in advance, and he manages to kill Ryoval and escape. (The torture sequences, and the psychological effects of that, brilliantly done as they are, are what I actually thought unsuitable for a ten-year-old—in fact he had no problem with them, I think the most distressing aspects probably went over his head.)

A note on the pacing here—Bujold never uses suspense for its own sake, but the sequence of information of what we know when about Miles, and about Mark and Ryoval, is very cleverly done, not just in what it leaves out but in when it gets us information.

At the end of the novel Mark has beaten Ryoval, has beaten Jackson's Whole, and Miles is alive but fragile. The two of them are a lot more equal than they have been, and they have become brothers.

There are two moments in *Mirror Dance* that brought tears to my eyes the first time I read it, and they're one for each of them. The first is when Miles gets his memory back and he thinks immediately of Bothari: "Oh sergeant, your boy really messed up." I don't know why I should find that so heart-stirring, but I do. The other is when part of Mark, in dissociation, talking to himself, shyly thinks that Aral is a killer too. I just find that incredibly touching.

Barrayar is about being a parent. So is this. Miles is in one sense Mark's parent, and so are Aral and Cordelia, trying to find a way to cope with a new grown-up and screwed-up son. Mark has to learn to have parents, and a home. "For the first time in his life, he was going home," he thinks as he returns to Barrayar at the end. *Mirror Dance* is about finding identity—not only for Mark, but for poor amnesiac Miles as well.

On re-reading, the first part, up to Miles's death, has the inevitability of Greek tragedy. The shadow of "remember you must die" falls across all what we see of Miles being happy and relaxed. Mark isn't given a name, in his own thoughts, because he doesn't yet have one in his own mind.

I find it a very difficult book to analyse. It's so good, and so immediate that it sucks me right in, it's hard to stand back from it at all.

43. Luck is something you make for yourself: Lois McMaster Bujold's Cetaganda

I don't like *Cetaganda* (1995). I've never liked it. I often skip it on re-reads, to such an extent that re-reading it now was almost like reading a new book. (There's a disadvantage of re-reading as much as I do in that there are series where the books I don't like become, in time, the ones I like the best because they're the ones that retain freshness after I have the ones I like memorised. I can see *Cetaganda* getting on that list along with *Five Red Herrings* and *Our Man in Camelot*.)

Cetaganda is a very slight book, to have been written between *Mirror Dance* (1994) and *Memory* (1996). It's set two years after *The Vor Game* (1990). It features Miles and Ivan going off to Cetaganda to a diplomatic function, where they get into trouble and out of it again. It's notable in being the first of the series apart from *Ethan of Athos* (1986) that's definitely a mystery and not a military adventure, and I suppose that's the logic in binding it with *Ethan of Athos* and *Labyrinth* as *Miles, Mystery and*

Mayhem. Or maybe not. Most of the reprint compilations make perfect sense to me, but this not one.

Cetaganda is about Cetaganda, the mysterious empire that has, thus far in the series, been seen only as a mysteriously aggressive enemy. It's first mentioned in *Shards of Honor* (1986) when Cordelia thinks her camp might have been trashed by Barrayarans, Cetagandans or Nuevo Brasilians—maybe we'll see some of those one day. We then hear that there have been three wars between Cetaganda and Barrayar, and later encounter Cetagandans, always as bad guys. They are the invaders in *The Vor Game,* and the prison guards in "The Borders of Infinity." They're pursuing Admiral Naismith across London in *Brothers in Arms* (1989), and we know they have painted faces, ghem-captains, and itchy trigger fingers. In *Cetaganda* we find out a lot more about them . . . and unfortunately, I don't find them that interesting.

One of the things I've noticed on this re-read is that the amount I like the books tends to be directly proportional to how much Barrayar there is in them. It seems that the thing I really like about this series is the Barrayaran roots. So that's my new complaint, not enough Barrayar. The book starts with arriving on Cetaganda and ends with leaving it. That also means we don't see any of the familiar Barrayaran characters except for Miles and Ivan, though Illyan is referenced.

However, my original complaint about *Cetaganda* when I first read it was that it doesn't have any Admiral Naismith or Dendarii Free Mercenaries—Miles is Lieutenant Vorkosigan all through. So not only do we not have any of the familiar Dendarii characters, but there's no Miles duality to make it interesting either. And compared to the Miles I just left in *Mirror Dance,* Miles at twenty-two seems strangely shallow, without everything he has learned since—and the same goes for Ivan. I don't think this is a complaint because I wanted a MilSF adventure and got a mystery.

It's more that I wanted a novel and got a romp. This is particularly noticeable in publication order.

The stakes are also fairly low in this book. We know Miles and Ivan escape pretty much unscathed. What happens to them is amusing enough, but that's all. There's no real possibility of a Cetagandan explosion, because we know it didn't happen. We know they did attack Marilac, and seeing the complacent Marilacans beforehand is one of the nice touches.

What else do I like, apart from the Marilican Embassy? Ivan and the anti-aphrodisiac and the consequences of him getting away with it. Yenaro, the descendant of the General who failed to defeat Barrayar, who is a perfumer. The garden with the luminescent frogs who sing in chords. Miles getting the medal and saying he won't wear it unless he needs to be really obnoxious—which looks forward to the scene in *Memory* where he wears all his medals. Ghem-Colonel Millisor calling in from *Ethan of Athos,* which I had totally forgotten about until reminded here.

I don't find the Cetagandan political setup very plausible, and worse, I don't find it very interesting. The same goes for the actual mystery and solution, which I'd half-forgotten. I don't like Miles's desire to keep information to himself and be a hero charming, in the context of what's going to happen when he, as Elli puts it at the beginning of *Mirror Dance,* runs out of hairs to split with these people. I don't much care for the supernatural beauty of the haut ladies floating around in their bubbles. ("Mutants on purpose are still mutants.")

The duality here is between sincere (if rough around the edges) masculine Barrayar and highly civilised (if not all the way over into decadent—that kitten tree!) feminine Cetaganda. It's interesting that there's more to Cetaganda than a tendency to shoot first and ask questions later, but did they have to be quite this effete? This depth of Cetaganda is setup for *Diplomatic Immunity* (2002), but I don't like the Cetagandan bit of that either. Maybe it's just me and everybody else loves Cetagandans, the haut and the ghem?

It may be worth noting here that despite coming after three consecutive Hugo-winning novels this was not even nominated for a Hugo, as discerning Hugo-nominating Bujold fans, far from being mindlessly adoring of everything she writes, noticed that this was a minor work.

44. This is my old identity, actually: Lois McMaster Bujold's Memory

Memory (1998) is in my opinion the worst place to start the Vorkosigan saga, because it is a sequel to all the books that have gone before it. I know that by saying this I'll be prompting several people who started with it to say that no, it absolutely hooked them, but even so, I think you will get more out of *Memory* if you come to it with knowledge of the earlier books, and the most if you come to it with all of the earlier books fresh in your mind. It contains some very sharp spear points on some very long spears. *Memory* was nominated for a Hugo but did not win, and I suspect that might have been partly because it is so very much a sequel. (It was a very strong year, though. There are three of my all-time top favourite books on that ballot.)

The themes of *Memory* are temptation and elephants.

This is the book where everything Miles has been getting away with from the beginning catches up with him. The text—the universe—has always been on Miles's side. He has always been right, against all odds, he has always won, he has always got away with things. It hasn't been without cost, but he has always got away with everything. He's been incredibly lucky and he's even survived death. It's been the kind of life that real people don't have, only protagonists of series with the author on their side. In *Memory,* it appears at first that Bujold has stopped being on Miles's side. The first part of the book is really grim, and really hard to read. Then the plot begins, and it gets really distressing. I'm not safe to read *Memory* in public because it always dissolves me into a pool of tears. Then Miles wrestles temptation two falls out of three and wins, and wins through. The whole book is about Miles's identity, Miles's split identity as Naismith and Vorkosigan, Miles's discovery of his own identity, his own integrity.

Sasha, reading the first part of *Memory,* still ten years old, asked me if Miles ever got off the planet. I deduced from that that he wanted Miles to run off to the Dendarii, and when he'd finished reading it I asked if he was sorry Miles hadn't made that choice. "Jo!" he said, furious with me, "The one thing you can't give for your heart's desire is your heart!" After that, I let him read whatever he wanted, because once you know that, you can't go far wrong.

The elephants are an underlying motif, they keep cropping up. I thought about tracking all of them this read-through and decided not to bother. Somebody has probably done it. There are a lot of them. The temptations—well, there's the central one of Miles's temptation to run off back to the Dendarii. The first time I read it I, like Cordelia, would have bet he would go. But the centrality of his Barrayaran identity, of what he's fighting for, goes back to "The Mountains of Mourning" (1989), and the central turning point of *Memory* is his visit to Silvy Vale, where nothing has been standing still. He's tempted again afterwards, he's tempted, not to say bribed, by Haroche. Miles resists the temptations, he comes to his central (and much quoted) realisation that "the one thing you can't give for your heart's desire is your heart." The author is still on his side, he finds integration and integrity, and he gets to be an Imperial Auditor—which might work slightly better if we'd ever heard of them before, but never mind.

Haroche though, Haroche was tempted and gives in. The Haroche plot totally fooled me the first time through—of all the books in this series with mystery plots, this one is the best. All the clues are hidden in plain sight, it all makes perfect sense when you're re-reading remembering exactly what they are, and so does the reason you didn't see them the first time. The whole plot is brilliant. And the way it's interleaved with the themes and the incidentals is incredible. I would be in awe reading it, if I wasn't always in tears. The plot is against Illyan, who we have seen constantly in the background since *Shards of Honor* (1986) and who now comes into the foreground. I don't think for a moment that when Bujold wrote about his memory chip in 1986 she thought "and in 1998 I can write about it breaking down." This isn't that kind of series. I like Illyan. The description of his disintegration remains very distressing. The first time I read it I actually broke down and sobbed on the line, "Ivan, you idiot, what are you doing here?" Yesterday, on a bus, and expecting it, I just had tears in my eyes. The whole section is almost unbearably brilliant.

There's a lot of romance in this book. There's Gregor's marriage plans, Galeni's marriage plans, Ivan proposing to Delia and Martya Koudelka on the same day, Alys and Illyan, Miles and Taura at the beginning, Miles and Elli Quinn giving each other up at the end. That looks forward to the other books in the series, where romance becomes increasingly a theme.

Cetaganda (1995) is the last of the books to be written out of order. The series preceding *Memory* was written all over the place, chronologically. From *Memory* on it marches straight forward, one book succeeding the next, chronological and publication order are the same.

I've talked about the different ways the series begins, and I've talked about the way all the books stand alone and recapitulate important information so you don't necessarily have to have read the other books. I started this re-read thinking about how this is a series that got better as it went on, instead of starting with a brilliant book and declining. I think a lot of what made it get better was starting with adventures and a deeper level of realism than adventures normally get and then going on taking those adventures seriously and making the realism more and more realistic. There's this thing where a reader accepts the level of reality of fiction as part of the mode, part of the "givens" of the text, the controlling axioms. So we don't really think that a seventeen-year-old could create the Dendarii out of bluff and illusion, but we go along with that because we get enough details, and because the emotional level of plausibility is there, and the cost is there—Bothari, and Elena, and Naismith not being Miles's name. And by *Memory,* the mode is different, and what we have is a psychologically realistic novel about the psychological cost of having got away with all of those things for so long.

Endings are a problem with an unplanned series, because the series isn't working towards an end point, just going on and on. Bujold is particularly good at endings on individual volumes, there isn't a single book that doesn't have a satisfactory climax. But the series as a whole doesn't have an end, doesn't go anywhere. *Memory* is one possible place for the story to end. It's a capstone for all that's gone before. It's not as if there isn't more that can happen to Miles—and indeed, we have three more (and a fourth being written) books about Miles. But what happens from *Memory* on is a set of different things, going on from there, not really reaching back to the earlier books. You can see it as two series—three. One about Cordelia, one about Miles growing up and being Admiral Naismith, stretching from *The*

Warrior's Apprentice to *Memory* and the third post-*Memory,* a series about Miles's love life and his career as Imperial Auditor. *Memory* is a climax for the whole series so far, and I think if it had ended there there would have been a feeling of rightness, a satisfaction, about that. I do not urge people to stop reading at *Memory,* but when you're looking at the series as a series and how it works, it's worth considering it as a possible end.

It is also my opinion that *Memory* is the point where the series stopped getting better. The other three books, while they're a new direction for the series, while they're never repetitive or just more of the same, are no better than *Memory.* (The new one when it comes may well prove me wrong, as Bujold has certainly gone on getting better as a writer in her post-Miles career.)

45. But I'm Vor: Lois McMaster Bujold's Komarr

Komarr (1998) has two alternating points of view: Imperial Auditor Miles Vorkosigan, on a mission to investigate an accident to the artificial sun of Barrayar's conquered subject planet Komarr, and Ekaterin Vorsoisson, the wife of a minor administrator in Komarr's terraforming project.

The plot of *Komarr* is one of the best and tightest in the series. Like *Memory* it's a perfect mystery, with all the clues in plain sight for a re-read but cleverly misdirected. It also has plausible villains who think of themselves as heroes.

The strength of the book stands or falls on Ekaterin. If you like her, you'll like the book, because it is largely a character study. What we have here is someone repressed to the point of inhibition, in an abusive relationship, and struggling to have any little piece of ground for herself. It's very well done.

This is the first of the books where Miles is having an adventure as Lord Auditor Vorkosigan, where Naismith and the Dendarii are entirely behind him. It's a mystery, and it's a new direction for the series—the direction was indicated in *Memory,* but this is where it settles into it.

We don't see any of the familiar recurring characters except

Miles. I think this is the only book in the series with only one familiar character since *Ethan of Athos*. Lots of them are mentioned, but none of them appear.

I love the way we see Komarr here as a real place. I really like the way Komarr has developed throughout the series, from Aral's bad reputation in *Shards of Honor* to a source of terrorist plots throughout, with the Galen/Galeni stuff and then Laisa. Here though we actually get down onto the planet and see some ordinary Komarrans. The plot to close the wormhole is very clever—and I like the way the physics all fits with everything we have had back to *The Warrior's Apprentice* about how the wormholes and Necklin rods work—but what I really like is what a sensible idea it is, from a Komarran point of view, how a bloodless engineering coup fits with their culture, how they're not raving loons like Ser Galen. It's Dr. Riva who really makes it work for me, Dr. Riva who figures it out and doesn't want to tell ImpSec, because she is a Komarran and it's such a beguiling idea. If your planet was conquered a generation ago and despite their paternal assimilationist policies you weren't quite equal to the conquerors and weren't quite trusted, well, doing something that would get rid of them forever would seem attractive. We get a lot of angles on Barrayar in this series, and this is one of the most interesting. The conquered Komarrans who don't want to become Barrayaran get a voice, and it's a reasonable one.

When Miles says to Ekaterin that he would like to be famous and have his father mentioned primarily as being his father, and she laughs, it's worth noting that for us he has that. We as readers are much more interested in Miles than in Aral.

The Betan/Barrayaran dynamic throughout the series is settled in *Memory* in favour of Barrayar, and the ways that's a male/female dynamic (even when internal to Miles, and oh, consider Bel in that context!) mean that in *Komarr* there has to be a new female angle. Ekaterin, as a female Vor Barrayaran, provides that.

Ekaterin strikes me as just a little too obviously planted as a mate for Miles. She may well be what he needs, now that he has decided to be his Barrayaran self, she's Vor, she's not a silly girl but a grown-up woman. Her decision to leave Tien just before he's killed is necessary and effective but his death makes things very tidy and easy. I like Ekaterin as herself, I don't like her when I see her as a prize for Miles. I've talked about how the universe, the text, is for or against Miles in different ways, and Ekaterin, Tien's death, the whole thing, seems like a little too much of the text being on Miles's side. In a conventional series he'd have married Elena, and he has spent a lot of time looking for a Countess Vorkosigan, but Ekaterin seems to come a little too patly to hand.

Komarr begins and ends with Ekaterin. She's in a much better position at the end than she was at the beginning. The thing that works best for me about her is the Vorzohn's Dystrophy. We've heard a lot about how Miles isn't a mutant, and how mutants are treated on Barrayar, so seeing an actual mutation and the shame and panic it causes is clever. Any normal person would get it fixed, the way it affects Tien is uniquely Barrayaran and Vor. Ekaterin has been supporting him long after love has gone because she gave her word. It takes an awful lot to get her to break it. Her act of leaving him is far braver than her actual act of heroism and saving herself, her planet and everything when she destroys the device on the space station.

Bujold talked about SF as being "fantasy of political agency" in the way romance is "fantasy of perfect love" and mysteries are "fantasies of justice." Thinking about this, the political agency plot of Komarr is just about perfect, but the personal and emotional plot isn't quite in step with it, so the climax and resolution are a little out of balance. It's great that Ekaterin saves herself and doesn't wait to be rescued by Miles, and it's even better that Miles (for whom rescuing people has been such a huge thing) is pleased about that, but the climactic moment of them sharing the same sense of sacrifice ("I'm Vor") is undercut by his babbling about his romances and her declaration, "Can I take a number." This needs resolution, which it doesn't get until the next volume. *Komarr* definitely does not contain a series ending. It has a whole (and very good) political plot but only half (or perhaps two-thirds) an emotional plot. It's a new departure for the series in that it isn't entirely self-contained.

46. She's getting away!
Lois McMaster Bujold's
A Civil Campaign

A Civil Campaign (2000) is another one that I don't think stands alone, as it is in many ways a continuation of the emotional and romantic plot of *Komarr* (1998). The two books are now available in one convenient volume as *Miles in Love*.

The Vorkosigan series began with books that looked like military adventure, developed unexpected depths, had a few volumes that look like investigative mysteries, and now this volume is an out-and-out comedy-of-manners romance. It's dedicated to "Jane, Charlotte, Georgette, and Dorothy" which I take to be Austen, Brontë, Heyer and Dunnett. The title is of course an homage to Heyer's *A Civil Contract,* though it bears no relationship to that story. If there's one Heyer to which it nods, it is *The Grand Sophy*.

There is a political plot, in the narrowest sense, maneuvering in council chambers for votes, and there's a scientific and economic plot about the invention of butter bugs, but the important heart of *A Civil Campaign* is all romantic.

I've complained about the covers before, but I think *A Civil Campaign* has the ugliest cover of any book in the house except the U.K. Vlad compilation. I took the dust jacket off the hard-cover, and I wince whenever I look at the paperback. If ever there was a case for a brown paper cover this is it. The colours are horrible, it's made of nasty shiny stuff, and the picture is unspeakable.

To get back to the text as rapidly as possible . . . The other books either use one point of view or alternate between two. *A Civil Campaign* has five points of view: Miles, Mark, Ekaterin, Kareen and Ivan.

There are a number of lovely things about *A Civil Campaign*. There are a lot of laugh-out-loud funny bits. There's Ivan's point of view. There's the couch scene. There are the twin problems of Rene Vorbretton, whose gene scan shows him one-eighth Cetagandan, and Lord Dono, formerly Lady Donna, Vorrutyer. There's Lord Vormuir and his daughters. There's Mark, though not enough of him. There's Kareen, torn between Barrayar and Beta and trying to figure out what she wants. There's Nikki calling Gregor, and indeed, a lot of Gregor, who seems to have grown up very happily. There's every Barrayaran character from earlier in the series, entirely making up for Komarr's lack of familiar characters.

It contains a good deal of embarrassment comedy (the dinner party in particular, which is excruciating) and rather more phys-ical comedy than I care for—the bug butter custard pie fight has not grown on me (if anything the reverse).

Uniquely for this series, it retcons. At the end of *Komarr,* Ekaterin asks to take a number. That's the resolution of the emo-tional arc of the novel. As of the beginning of *A Civil Campaign,* that resolution hasn't happened, and Miles is trying to woo Ekaterin in secret—in secret from her. This goes spectacularly wrong, as anyone but Miles would have predicted, and then goes right again. I find the going wrong much more convincing than the going right. This could just be me. I often have this problem with romance novels, where I find the descriptions of women falling in love adhere to emotional conventions that are as stylised as a Noh play and bear no relationship to anything I have ever felt or imagined feeling.

Miles's feelings for Ekaterin are no more or no less love than what he has felt for all his women since Elena, a genuine fondness, sexual passion, and a strong desire for a Lady Vorkosigan and a family. Miles always proposes—well, not to Taura, but he has proposed to every genetically human woman he's been involved with, however unsuitable. He pursues her, sometimes literally, he loves her, as he understands love, but he demonstrably can't give her space to let her be herself. He apologises, and he knows what he did, but he'd never have figured it out on his own and he'll do it again because that's who he is. Ekaterin's feelings for him are, as I said, beyond me. I liked her in *Komarr*, and I understood her horrible marriage to Tien. I can't get my head around her in *A Civil Campaign*. Miles gets the girl, finally. OK.

What I do find effective is that Tien's death, far from being the easy way out it seemed in *Komarr*, comes back to almost literally haunt them with the implications that Miles murdered Tien, which can't even be denied without revealing the whole plot. And speaking of hidden plots, Miles doesn't know the truth about the Sergyar war and the mountain of corpses Ezar buried Serg under. Aral mentions it was a lucky shot for Barrayar that killed Serg, and Miles just accepts that. The secret Cordelia fled to Barrayar to keep it a very closely held secret, still—when Illyan and Aral and Cordelia die, nobody will know it. Unless they've told Gregor? But the strong implication of that scene is that they haven't. That secret, not her love for Aral, is why Cordelia immured herself in Barrayar all this time. I was pleased to see Enrique mention that she was wasted on that planet. (Incidentally, I find Cordelia's love for Aral as we see it in her own POV utterly convincing.)

Meanwhile, Kareen loves Mark and wants to be herself, and Mark wants her to be. This pair are charming and I am charmed by them. Sure Mark needs more therapy and Kareen needs more Betan education, but they're growing up fine, and consistently with where we last saw them in *Mirror Dance*.

As for Ivan, he's just a delight, whether it's by running rings around him, or Miles accepting his refusal to help, or his disgust at being seconded to his mother for pre-wedding chores. Oh, and his romantic panic is also just right.

Barrayaran law, all we see of it, gives the perfect illusion of making sense, fitting with everything we have seen of it before, and with the human oddities that real legal systems have. That's quite an achievement. And how nice to see Lord Midnight mentioned again as a real precedent. And if it contrasts with the many forms the Escobarans have to fill in to extradite Enrique, well, we know about the runaround offworlders are given, from Calhoun back in *The Warrior's Apprentice*. You can't trust their word, bury them in forms. I love Nikki giving his word as Vorsoisson for the first time, too. In the best Heyer style, all the plots and plotting come together in a hectic climax where the obstacles go down like dominoes to reveal a happy ending. I mentioned the bug butter fight already, and I wish it wasn't there, it isn't necessary. The scene in the Council of Counts is terrific though. The bit with all the Koudelka girls finding such different partners is cute. And how nice to see Lord Vorhalas alive and well and as honourable as ever.

This is another potential ending for the series. Miles is betrothed, Mark is the next thing to betrothed, Gregor is married. I half-expected the next book to be set a generation ahead, with Aral and Cordelia dead and Miles and Ekaterin's children (and Mark and Kareen's) ready to get into trouble. The end of this book, with so many loose ends tied up so happily, would have made a good resting point. But with this kind of open series there's no reason ever to stop, as long as the characters keep interesting the author and there are new adventures to be had. There's no end, no climax that completes anything, just history going onwards. I think that's a strength and a weakness. It's certainly been a strength—the Vorkosigan saga has never been repetitive, and in doing new and different things it broke new ground—but it can also start to seem that it isn't headed anywhere. The things I like in this book (apart from the Ivan POV) are all little series background details, the kinds of things I call "sandwiches on space stations" as shorthand. (A friend and I once exchanged a lot of detailed emails with the title "Cheese Sandwiches in Cherryh.") If this had been the end of the series, I'd have been quite satisfied, but I don't think I'd have been as satisfied with this end as I would have been if *Memory* had been the end. But they're neither of them ends, and the series is ongoing.

47. Just my job:
Lois McMaster Bujold's
Diplomatic Immunity

Diplomatic Immunity (2002) is one of the most exciting books in the universe ever. The first time I read it, it gave me an asthma attack—those Cetagandan bioviruses are so effective, they incapacitated me through the eyes, in text! It almost did the same this time, it was only remembering that it did last time and breathing carefully that got me through the incredibly tense bit.

I don't think there's anything else I can safely say about it without spoilers, not for it but for the rest of the series. It would be a perfectly reasonable standalone book, or place to start, I think. It probably helps if you've read *Cetaganda* and *Falling Free,* and a fair sprinkling of the others, and it would certainly contain spoilers for them, but it wouldn't be a problem for enjoying what's going on and having fun.

Miles and Ekaterin, married for a year, go off for a galactic honeymoon while twin babies are being cooked up in uterine replicators. On their way home they're diverted to Quaddiespace where mysterious things have detained a Komarran trade fleet and its Barrayaran escort. Miles is designated to deal with the problem. He meets Bel Thorne, now living with Nicol from

"Labyrinth," investigates the problems and finds out they're being caused by a Cetagandan Ba, disguised as a Betan herm under the common Betan name Dubauer (very clever bit of misdirection there, because I instantly started thinking he must be related to poor Ensign Dubauer from *Shards of Honor*) who is trying to steal a load of Cetagandan haut babies and start his own empire, while starting a war between Cetaganda and Barrayar as misdirection. Miles and Ekaterin manage to stop the war, but not without much tense excitement and bioweapons, and Miles being infected by being too clever for his own good. There's some excellent broadening of the scope of the problem.

This is only the second time I've read *Diplomatic Immunity,* the first time since it came out in 2002 and we all read it in relays. Most of these books I know backwards and forwards, but I'd forgotten the details of *Diplomatic Immunity* until they came back to me while I was reading.

This is another surprising departure for the series. It's a mystery, which isn't surprising, but it's galactic, which is, and there's almost a war. We thought Miles had put away the Little Admiral for good, but here we have him signing off "Nai—Vorkosigan out!" in a top-speed full-steam-ahead crisis. Naismith is still there for Miles to draw on when he needs to be him. It's not a Dendarii Free Mercenaries adventure, but it's much closer to *The Vor Game* than it is to *Komarr.* After all these books centred on Barrayar and Barrayaran problems and politics and interactions with Komarr, we're suddenly back in space, and the problems turn out to be Cetagandan.

What's wrong with it is the end. The book is going along at a zillion miles an hour, and I am hyperventilating (or, this time, deliberately stopping for chocolate to avoid hyperventilating) and everything is going along fine and then . . . it pulls back. It's like the end of *Mansfield Park.* The text withdraws into tell-mode. Miles succumbs to the sickness, and Ekaterin deals with the crisis, but we don't see it, we hear about it later. We get caught up with the plot, we do not get to see it firsthand, which, after the extremely close tension up to that point, is just weird. The epilogue is fine, and the rewards and medals from the Cetagandans are fine as well, I suppose, but there's a big hole in between Miles passing out on the ship and there.

This could very easily have been plugged by giving us some Ekaterin point of view, and Bujold has not been stingy with Ekaterin POV in the last two books. Indeed, the whole of *Diplomatic Immunity* could have been enhanced with some Ekaterin alternating chapters, like *Komarr*. How is marriage to Miles settling down from Ekaterin's POV? Ekaterin goes shopping with Bel and they talk about Miles. Ekaterin looks at quaddie hydroponics. Ekaterin deals with Admiral Vorpatril and the Cetagandan Empire. It could have been so cool! It would have made such a great intercut with Miles trying to solve the problems and then it getting all so exciting. Unfortunately, thinking about this Ekaterin-shaped shadow makes the book feel to me as if it has an Ekaterin-POV-shaped hole in it, and that's why I hadn't re-read it, despite having re-read several other bits of the series on different occasions since then.

The book ends with Aral Alexander and Helen Natalia being decanted. Would this make a good series end? Well, it has been the de facto series end for the last seven years, and it certainly isn't leaving anything trailing, but it definitely doesn't feel like a good conclusion—both *Memory* and *A Civil Campaign* come with better places to stop.

48. Every day is a gift:
Lois McMaster Bujold's
"Winterfair Gifts"

All right, I can take a hint. I could have ignored the number of people here asking me if I was going to write about "Winterfair Gifts" but when the author herself sends me a copy? Thanks again, Lois!

"Winterfair Gifts" comes chronologically between *A Civil Campaign* and *Diplomatic Immunity,* but it was published last, and thus despite myself I stick to my goal of reading in publication order. It's a novella, not a whole book, and I think it's weaker for not having the strengthening themes and context that being part of a novel would have given it—Bujold is generally best with room to stretch herself. (If there are authors, Ted Chiang, John Varley, Robert Reed, whose most natural length is the short form, and others whose most natural length is a novel, are there others whose most natural length is a fourteen-book series?) It's from the point of view of Miles's armsman Roic, who first appeared in *A Civil Campaign* and who is a major character, though not a point-of-view character, in *Diplomatic Immunity.*

I wouldn't recommend starting with it. But I can't see that it would do any harm either.

This story is set around Miles and Ekaterin's wedding. It's another romance, and it was written specifically to be published in a genre romance anthology. It's a romance between Roic and Taura, around the wedding, and around a plot to hurt Miles by killing Ekaterin on her wedding day by giving her poisoned pearls, and trying to frame Quinn. This story got snarled for me by my going to a reading at Minicon at which Lois read the first half. I then had to wait months and months for the second half, during which time I deduced the shape of what had to happen in it, and figured out that Quinn hadn't done it. I'm pretty good at doing that if you give me half a story, which is why it's a terrible idea to give me half a story. Give me a whole story and I'll swallow it whole. I no longer go to readings at cons for this very reason. Re-reading it now, I notice it doesn't actually have pacing problems, they were an illusion caused by this. It's well paced, like all Bujold except the very end of *Diplomatic Immunity*.

The romance is sweet and nicely done. Taura and Roic are convincing, Taura's philosophy is just what one would expect, and the obstacles of Roic's prejudices against mutants and female soldiers go down very nicely. It's also a nice touch that she's as much taller than him as normal women are to Miles. (Normal tall women. I'd only be a couple of centimetres taller. But Miles likes tall women.) I'm not sure how readers of genre romance would see it, as it isn't a "here is the destined One Person" romance but a "gather ye rosebuds" one, and much the better for that in my opinion. I hope they liked it, as I hear there are a lot of them and they buy a lot of books.

Roic's POV is great. I like his hesitancy about having been a (heroic) policeman instead of a military man, like the other armsmen. I like the way this plays into *Diplomatic Immunity,* where Miles finally assures him he's glad that Roic is the one he brought. And it's an interesting point of view, too, proletarian Barrayaran, Vorkosigan district, entirely impressed with Miles

165

but more so with Aral, easily embarrassed, quite different from anyone else we've seen.

The wedding. Well. On the sandwich level, I was just as delighted as Nikki was to see Arde Mayhew, and I was upset that Mark and Kareen didn't get home. I liked Quinn sending the cat blanket. I liked Elena calling her daughter Cordelia. I liked the ice garden. I love Lady Alys using Roic as a reaction test to how Taura looks, and also that she looks great. I didn't like Ekaterin being so nervous or Miles thinking she wanted to back out. I like Ekaterin saying of the poisoned pearls: "I'd have worn them as a courtesy to your friend, I'll wear them now as a defiance to our enemies." That's the spirit. Maybe she can keep up with him. I do hope so.

The plot seems a little rushed. But that's not much of a problem. All in all it's a charming little story with a lot of nice shout-outs to fans that shouldn't spoil the flow for new readers. It's minor in the context of the series, but it is an interesting perspective and very nice to see Miles and Ekaterin settled. As an end for the series—nope. It's too slight to bear the weight of that. But it's a lot of fun to read.

49. Choose again, and change: Lois McMaster Bujold's Vorkosigan saga

The Vorkosigan saga began to be published in 1986, there are thirteen volumes so far, the most recent one published in 2002, and there's a new one being written. It's a series of stand-alone volumes that you can start almost anywhere, a series where very few of the books are like each other, where the volumes build on other volumes so that you want to read them all but you don't need to for it to make sense. It's science fiction, specifically space opera set in societies where the introduction of new technologies is changing everything. Some volumes are military science fiction, some are mysteries, one is a romance (arguably two), some are political and deal with the fates of empires, others are up-close character studies with nothing more (or less) at stake than one person's integrity. It's a series with at least three beginnings, and with at least two possible ends, although it is ongoing. Lots of people love it, but others despise it, saying that technologies of birth and death are not technological enough. As a series, it's constantly surprising, never predictable, almost never what you might expect—which may well be what has kept it fresh and improving for so long.

I started it first in the middle, went back to the beginning, read the books in entirely random order until I was caught up, and subsequently read the books as they came out. My shelves started off with scruffy secondhand British paperbacks, graduated to smarter new British paperbacks, then new U.S. paperbacks, then U.S. hardbacks. Over time I've replaced the secondhand British paperbacks (except for *Shards of Honor*) and for this re-read where I've been reading really fast and carrying the books around with me, I replaced my hardcovers with paperbacks. (I'd never buy hardcovers if it wasn't for impatience. I often end up buying a hardcover and then replacing it with a paperback. When we finally get print on demand, I'm going to demand trade paperbacks instantly at hardcover prices.) I first started reading them in the early nineties and I've re-read them often in the two decades since, but always in internal chronological order. I started reading with *Brothers in Arms* and got hooked on *Shards of Honor*.

And I've been re-reading them non-stop for a fortnight now. I've done 13 posts about them in 15 days. I've been so entirely immersed in them, I had a terrific dream about the Third Cetagandan War the other night. I started reading them in publication order to consider them as a series that improves as it goes on, and I've been thinking about them as a series and as a whole.

I find them remarkably easy to be entirely absorbed in, and surprisingly hard to stand away from and analyse. Some of these posts I've managed it, others I've just burbled. Gossiping about the characters is easy.

I have a theory that that's one of the functions of long-running series. It's not just art, which is between you and the artist, it's also gossip, between you and other people. Certainly I have discussed these books a lot. With a long series where details and information and events reflect on other volumes, there's more to discuss because there's more context. There's more gossip. The Vorkosiverse is very open to gossip, about the characters, about the history, about the details. Consider the discussion about the Escobaran replicators still going on a week after I posted about *Barrayar*. People care about the characters, and the history, and it all fits together well enough that you can trust it.

Bujold has said she reserves the right to have a better idea. Nevertheless, she does remarkably little changing things—you get occasional things, like "Luigi Bharaputra" losing the "and Sons"—but mostly the universe can be trusted to stay where she put it. When you get more history it almost always appears to be fractally opening out from what you already knew.

There are good things with long series, where little things from early on get picked up and built on, or just mentioned. Miles never stops missing Bothari. Elena is visiting her mother. Ivan isn't an idiot. Occasionally, I noticed a tech thing where the real world has moved faster than you'd expect. In *Komarr,* Miles uses (and snoops on) Ekaterin's comconsole. Yeah, I used to borrow other people's computers to check my mail in 1998 as well. There's surprisingly little of this, considering that a lot of books written in the late eighties have been entirely left behind by widespread home computers, the Internet, and ubiquitous mobile phones.

Some people who started reading late in the order of the published series say they like Lord Vorkosigan more than Admiral Naismith, others have other opinions. I've always liked the duality in Miles, the multiplicity in Mark, the complexity of the universe.

As I was finishing *Diplomatic Immunity* the other day and considering whether it made a good end for the series, I realised that I had no idea what the new book would be about. No idea who it would be focused on, when it would be set, or even what subgenre it would be in. She could do anything with this series. I'd rather thought she'd moved beyond it, with the Five Gods books and the Sharing Knife books, but I'm really pleased she's coming back to it—or going on to it, as Elena says in *Memory*: You don't go back, you go forward.

The titles of all these posts have been quotes from the books, and the quote for this post comes from *Brothers in Arms*, and it's what Miles says to Mark when Mark is terrified and stuck and totally in control of Miles, who is strapped to a chair at the time. Mark says who and what he is, and Miles tells him to choose again, and change. (Someone else in that situation might beg him to, Miles pretty much orders him to.) The series seems to have taken that advice, it makes new choices, it changes, it goes on from where it is and becomes something different.

So I was thinking what I'd like to be in the new volume, *Cryoburn*, due out in fall 2010, and I decided that I wanted it to utterly surprise me.

50. So, what sort of series do you like?

I love series because when I love something I want more of it. Sure I'll buy an utterly new book by an author I like, but I also want to find out what happened to the characters I already know I care about. I never realised quite how much genre readers love series until I got published though. People are always asking me if I'm writing a sequel to *Tooth and Claw* (No!) and if I'll write any more of the Small Change books (No!). Some people really don't want to let go. And of course I'm the same, when I heard Bujold was writing a new Miles book I bounced up and down for hours.

So, fine, everyone loves series. But what kind of series do you like? *The Lord of the Rings* isn't a series, it's one long book published in three volumes for technical bookbinding reasons. Cherryh's Union-Alliance books are a series, they're all independent stories with their own plots and their own characters, but set in the same universe. Away from those extremes there are Bujold's Vorkosigan books and Brust's Vlad books where the books are about the same characters but are all independent stories and you can start pretty much anywhere, and in contrast Sarah Monette's Doctrine of Labyrinths books and Daniel Abraham's Long Price Quartet where the individual books have their own story arcs but the later volumes really aren't going to make as much sense if you haven't read the earlier volumes.

So, there's style one, *The Lord of the Rings,* one book with extra pieces of cardboard.

There's style two, Doctrine of Labyrinths, where you have volume closure but need to read the books in order.

There's style three, Vlad and Vorkosigan, where the cumulative effect of reading all of them is to give you a story arc and more investment in the characters, but it doesn't really matter where you start and whether you read them in order.

And there's style four, Union-Alliance, where the volumes are completely independent of each other though they may reflect interestingly on each other.

I've been thinking about this because just as I've been thinking about the Vorkosigan books and the way they're a series, Sarah Monette made a post in her LiveJournal in which she talks about the way her books have not had a series name or numbers attached to them, and how the reviews of the fourth book, *Corambis* (2009), seem to assume that it's a bad thing that it's part of a series and you need to have read the others for it to make sense. And she goes on to ask some interesting questions about the marketing decisions made with those books.

Personally, I like all four kinds of series, as you can tell by the way I can come up with examples of all of them off the top of my head and from my own bookshelves. What I can't stand is when I pick up a random book in a bookshop or the library and it's part of a series and that isn't clearly indicated anywhere on it. I've picked up random volumes that are clearly part of a series in style one or style two, read a bit, been utterly confused, and never looked at the author again. I hate this. But Sarah says this is what marketing specifically required:

(M)y editor told me that we couldn't put Book One of the Doctrine of Labyrinths on the cover or in the front matter. Marketing wouldn't let us.

She explained their reasoning to me:

> If a person buys a book and then discovers it is part of a series, they are more likely to buy the other books, whereas if a person picks up a book in a bookstore and sees it's Book Two, they won't buy it. (I think there's a self-defeating flaw in this reasoning, since it assumes that Book One will not be near Book Two on the bookstore shelves, but that's neither here nor there.) Never mind the fact that a person who buys a book only to discover it's Book Two is likely to be an unhappy person, and never mind that, since the damn thing ISN'T LABELED as Book Two, the person has no immediately obvious and easy way of figuring out either which series it's a part of, nor which books in the series come BEFORE it. . . . Marketing said, Thou Shalt Not Label The Books Of Thy Series, and lo, the books were not labeled.

Crazy for a style one or two series. But it's going to work fine with a style three or four series.

Now, the Vorkosigan books (style three) are very good about this. They don't say "Volume X of Y" on them, but they don't need to. But they do have a timeline in the back that tells you precisely how to read them in internal chronological order. When I randomly picked up *Brothers in Arms* in the library many years ago, I could tell it was a series book and read it anyway.

I wonder if publishers and marketing people are sometimes mistaking a style one or two series for a style three or four series, or mistaking what works for a style three or four series as something that ought to work for all series. Or maybe they want every series to be a style three series—in which case, they should perhaps mention this to their authors. Certainly nobody has ever said this to me, and my first two published books were a style one, and it looks as if nobody has said it to Sarah either. And are style three series what readers want? I mean I like them, but as I already said, I like all these kinds of series.

51. Time travel and slavery: Octavia Butler's Kindred

The immediate effect of reading Octavia Butler's *Kindred* (1981) is to make every other time travel book in the world look as if it's wimping out. The Black Death in *Doomsday Book*? Wandering about your own life naked in *The Time Traveler's Wife*? Only *Days of Cain* and *The Devil's Arithmetic* can possibly compete. In *Kindred,* Dana finds herself repeatedly going back from her own happy life in Los Angeles in 1976 to a plantation in Maryland in 1815. And she's black, a fact given away by every cover and blurb I've ever seen about the book but actually cleverly concealed by the text for quite a time, so that if you'd managed to read it with nothing between you and the words it would be something you'd be worried about until it is confirmed.

In 1815, without papers, a black woman is automatically assumed to be a slave, and treated as a slave.

This is a brilliant book, utterly absorbing, very well written, and deeply distressing. It's very hard to read, not because it's not good but because it's so good. By wrenching a sheltered modern character like Dana back to the time of slavery you get to see it all fresh, as if it's happening to you. You don't get the acceptance of characters who are used to it, though we see plenty of them and their ways of coping, through Dana's eyes. There's no getting away from the vivid reality of the patrollers, the whip, the woman whose children are sold away. Horrible things happen to Dana, and yet she is the lucky one, she has 1976 to go back to, everyone else has to just keep on living there going forward one day at a time.

This is fantasy time travel, not science-fictional. There's no time machine, no escape mechanism, very little recovery time. Dana figures out that she's being pulled through time by Rufus, who when she first meets him is just a little boy. She learns that he is her ancestor and that she's going through time to save his life. But there's no real explanation, we all have ancestors, and that doesn't happen to everyone. I think the book is stronger for not trying to explain, for letting that be axiomatic. Once it is accepted that Rufus is calling her through time, the other things, the rate at which time passes in 1815 as against 1976, the things that make Dana transfer between them, the link—all work science fictionally with precise reliable extrapolation.

Most genre stories about time travel are about people who change things. But we're a long way from Martin Padway here. Dana doesn't even try. She has an unlimited ability to bring things she can hold from 1976, aspirins and antiseptic and a book on slavery that gets burned, and her husband, Kevin, who gets stuck in the past for five years and brutalised by it. Kevin doesn't try to change the past either, and with less excuse, as he doesn't have the inherent disadvantage of being mistaken for a slave. Kevin acts as a safe house for escaping slaves, but that's something people of that time did. He doesn't try to invent penicillin or even railroads. But this is a thought after the book—the reality of the book is sufficiently compelling that you don't question it while you're in it. The details of the early-nineteenth-century plantation are so well researched they feel unquestionably real, in all their awful immediacy.

I think Butler idealises 1976 quite a bit, to make it a better contrast for 1815. The thing that really made me notice this was Dana's inability to code-switch. She acts, in 1815, as if she's never met anyone before who has a problem with black people talking in formal English, which surprised me. She's led a fairly sheltered life, and she's married to a white man, but you'd think that doing the kind of temp jobs she does to make a living while she writes she'd have run into more kinds of prejudice than are mentioned. On this reading, I wondered if Butler had deliberately made Dana a kind of Hari Kumar, a character who is white in all but appearance who is then suddenly forced to confront the reality of being judged by that appearance and forced into a very unwelcome box by it. If that was Butler's choice—and the concealment of Dana's skin color for the first thirty pages of the book seems to be another piece of evidence for this—I wonder if she might have done it to make it an easier identification for white readers, not to stir up present-day issues but to get right to what she wanted to talk about.

52. America the Beautiful:
Terry Bisson's
Fire on the Mountain

After reading *Kindred,* I wanted to read something where the slaves were freed, and not just freed a bit, but freed a *lot*. So that would be Terry Bisson's *Fire on the Mountain* (1988). It's an alternate history, and an alternate U.S. Civil War where John Brown's raid on Harper's Ferry is successful. The book is set a hundred years later in 1959 on the eve of the first manned Mars landing, but it also contains letters and a diary from 1859.

Terry Bisson is one of those brilliant writers who is inexplicably uncommercial. He has the gift of writing things that make me miss my stop on the metro because I'm so absorbed, but I almost never meet anyone who reads him. My very favourite book of his is *Talking Man* (1986), an American fantasy. *Fire on the Mountain* runs it a close second. It got wonderful reviews—they're all over this Ace paperback I bought new in 1990. His short work wins awards, and I'll buy SF magazines if he has a story in them. I think he's one of the best living stylists. But all he has in print are three admittedly excellent collections.

It's hard to write stories in Utopia, because by definition story-type things don't happen. In *Fire on the Mountain* Bisson makes it work by the method Delany and Kim Stanley Robinson have also used, of having a central character who isn't happy. (You can convey dystopias well by the opposite method of having characters who are perfectly cheerful about them. But dystopias are easier anyway.) Yasmin's husband died on the first Mars fly-by mission five years ago. He's a hero to the world, but she can't get over not having his body to bury. The new Mars mission, which is taking his name on a plaque, is breaking her heart every time she hears about it on the news. She's an archaeologist who has been recently working at Olduvai. She's now going to Harper's Ferry with her daughter Harriet to take her great-grandfather's diary to the museum there. The book alternates between her trip, her great-grandfather's diary of how he escaped slavery and joined the rebellion, and the 1859 letters of a white liberal abolitionist.

This is, like all Bisson's work, a very American book. It's not just the history, it's also the wonderful sense of place. I found myself thinking of it when I went on the Capitol Limited train down through Harper's Ferry last summer, the geography of the novel informed the geography out of the train window. At one point I realised I'd just crossed the bridge that is destroyed in the book—but that wasn't in real life. That was the turning point of history—in Bisson's novel, Tubman was with Brown and they burned the bridge, and everything was different afterwards. In Bisson's 1959, the South, Nova Africa, with its N'African inhabitants, black and white, and the North, the United Socialist States of America, are at peace, the border seems a lot like the way the border between the US and Canada used to be. (Speaking of Canada, Quebec is mentioned separately from Canada and must have gained independence somehow, or maybe Confederation happened differently. Unsurprisingly, Bisson doesn't go into detail.)

I like the characters, all of them, the 1859 and the 1959 ones.

The minor characters are done very expressively with just a little description going a long way:

> Harriet was at the Center, Pearl said, working on Sunday, was that what socialism was all about, come on in? Not that Harriet would ever consider going to church, she was like her Daddy that way, God Rest His Soul, sit down. This was the week for the Mars landing, and Pearl found it hard to listen to on the radio until they had their feet on the ground, if ground was what they called it there, even though she wished them well and prayed for them every night. God didn't care what planet you were on, have some iced tea? Or even if you weren't on one at all. Sugar? So Pearl hoped Yasmin didn't mind if the radio was off.

and the book's style moves seamlessly from that kind of thing to:

> Dear Emily, I am writing to tell you that my plans changed, I went to Bethel Church last night and saw the great Frederick Douglass. Instead of a funeral, I attended a Birth. Instead of a rain of tears, the Thunder of Righteousness.

I like the way the history seems to fit together without all being explained. I like the shoes from space that learn your feet, and the way they are thematic all the way through. I like the way the people in 1959 have their own lives and don't think about the historical past any more than people really do, despite what Abraham thought when he wrote for his great-grandson, not guessing it might be a great-granddaughter. I like the buffalo having right of way across highways and causing occasional delays. I like the coinage N'African, and I like that almost all the characters in the book are black but nobody makes any fuss about it. (They didn't put any of them on the cover, though.) There's one heavy-handed moment, when a white supremacist (the descendant of the white abolitionist doctor) gives Yasmin a copy of a 1920s alternate history *John Brown's Body,* a book describing our world. They don't think much of it, and you can understand why. Their world is socialist, green, more technologically advanced—it's 1959 and they have space manufacturing and a Mars mission, as well as airships (of course!) and green cars—and still has herds of buffalo and nations of First Nations people. Texas and California rejoined Mexico. Ireland won independence in 1885. It's been a struggle, and it feels complicated, like history, but not many people would prefer the racism, class problems and injustice of our world. Yet it isn't preachy, except for that one moment.

I've heard it said that the U.S. obsession with their Civil War, and the large number of alternate histories featuring it as a turning point, arise out of a desire to have slavery back. I think even the South Triumphant novels are more often Awful Warnings than slaver panegyrics, and *Fire on the Mountain* puts the whole thing in a different light. People want to do the Civil War again and get it right this time. The book may be a little utopian, a little naive, but it's a beautifully written story about a nicer world, where, in the background, people are landing on Mars. In 1959.

53. Susan Palwick's Shelter

There's a certain kind of book that's almost a subgenre: the important book. The sort of book that everyone is talking about even if they hate it, the sort of book that gets reviewed everywhere and appears on award lists and gets discussed and is influential on the genre and other writers. *Anathem* is one of last year's and so is *Little Brother* (2008). If you're reading this, then it's quite likely that you've read them and even more likely that you've heard people talking about them and you plan to read them, or you very strongly plan not to read them because what you've heard has put you off. Sometimes, though, there will be a book that seems to me like it ought to be an important book and then for some inexplicable reason practically nobody agrees with me. It comes out, it does OK, but it doesn't get the attention I feel it deserves. Some people like it, but it never becomes something everyone is talking about. I've talked about a couple of these here, *Random Acts of Senseless Violence* and *Lady of Mazes*. Susan Palwick's *Shelter* is another. It came out in 2007 and I read it instantly, because I love Palwick, and I wrote about it on my LiveJournal and then—nothing. Nobody else was excited about it, it didn't get nominated for anything, though I nominated it for a Hugo. *Shelter* is very well worth your attention.

It's set in a near-future San Francisco, it covers twenty years of history, and it deals with a world in which a whole pile of current trends and new technology intersect in complex and fascinating ways with people's lives. As you'd expect if you've read Palwick's fantasy novels *Flying in Place* (1992) and *The Necessary Beggar* (2005), it has solidly drawn characters and the world feels very real. What you might not expect is how well she does the science-fictional extrapolation.

There's a major plague known as CV, "caravan virus," that mutates fast and has many strains. It kills lots of people, and the ones who survive have to cope in isolation with robot ("bot") nursing and people interacting with them only in whole-body protective suits. Two little girls survive the virus: Meredith, rich and white, and Roberta, poor and black. They also represent the two extremes of selfishness and altruism—and this is a world where altruism has been medicalised and Roberta spends a lot of time in therapy and in fear of mindwipe because of her "problem." Their lives are intertwined from that childhood illness through their connection to Meredith's father, the uploaded Preston, and to Meredith's troubled adopted son. When mental problems are routinely treated with mindwiping, what do you do if you discover someone you love is beginning to develop them? How can you ask for help when you know what sort of help you're likely to get?

The book opens with the third narrator, House, an AI convinced it isn't an AI. AIs are illegal in the US because they're defined as legally persons, and therefore owning them is slavery. There's also the AI terrorism problem. . . . House's point of view is done beautifully. It feels entirely real, entirely immersive, and you can really believe the way it reasons its way through decisions. The book begins in the "present" of the story, during a very severe storm (global warming has deteriorated), and goes back to the earlier events that led to the world and the relationships we're given at the beginning. Palwick directs our sympathies as a conductor directs a symphony. The twenty years of history and events we're shown, from different points of view, build up a picture of a future that has clearly grown from our present. Every detail has second-order implications—you have bots doing the cleaning, so you have people afraid of bots, and people who think doing your own cleaning is a religious act, and you have sponge bots trying to stem a flood as a metaphor for people unable to cope.

This is also the kind of SF you can put up against *Middlemarch* as character study; it's really a story about people. But the people are in situations they can be in only given the science-fictional premises of the story—damaged by the isolation, worried about mindwipe, trying to fake not being altruistic, coming up with new kinds of art, trying to cope with an uploaded, ubiquitous, but not necessarily benign father.

I also liked it that Roberta was a lesbian and this was an undramatic fact—well, breaking up with her girlfriend was dramatic, but the fact of her orientation was no more significant than Meredith's heterosexuality. It's refreshing to have major characters with non-heteronormative sexuality without the book being about that.

One thing I found weird and unconvincing was that Gaianism had become the mainstream religion of the US, displacing Christianity which still exists as a minority thing. I don't see Christmas celebrations being replaced by Solstice ones anytime as soon as *Shelter,* and while I understand the purpose of the Gaian temple and how much better that worked for the story than a church would have, I didn't see anything that would have made Christianity be all but forgotten. I kept worrying at this detail because the general level of worldbuilding and world-holding-together is so good that this niggled.

This was actually my third reading of *Shelter,* because I read it straight through again as soon as I'd finished it. The harrowing parts of it, and the ethical dilemma that lies at the heart of it, don't get any easier to read. But it remains a wonderful book, a shining example of what science fiction can be when it tries.

54. Scintillations of a sensory syrynx: Samuel Delany's Nova

I've talked before about how my least favourite books by an author can end up becoming my favourites because they stay fresh while I read the others to death. I can't imagine how it is that I ever didn't like *Nova*. It was published when I was four years old, in 1968 (and it's in print!), and I read it when I was fifteen, and twenty, and twenty-five (I read everything on the shelves in alphabetical order when I was twenty-five) and I don't think I've picked it up again until now. I was clearly too young for it those earlier times. Maybe this is a book you have to be forty-four and a half to appreciate. (Though Delany would have been twenty-four, twenty-five when he wrote it.) Reading it now I have vivid impressions from those earlier reads, images from it that have stuck with me for twenty (twenty-five, thirty) years but I'd also forgotten it enough that it was like reading an exciting new book, a new science fiction Delany! People have been saying often enough over the last twenty-five years when I've talked about Delany, "And *Nova*!" and I've always had half a mental hesitation in agreeing, because I knew I hadn't enjoyed it. I was an idiot! This is one of the best of Delany's early works. And yet, reading it now, and thoroughly enjoying it, I kept

186

trying to find the book I knew I hadn't liked in this new book that I did.

It's a thousand years in the future, and humanity is scattered over the universe, with many colonized planets. There are three main political units: Draco (including Earth), the Pleiades Federation, and the Outer Planets. The transuranic element Illyrion is what powers the incredibly fast FTL spaceships, and keeps the balance of power among the three groups. Lorq Von Ray of the Pleiades has a feud with Prince and Ruby Red, of Draco, and is decided to get seven tons of Illyrion from the heart of a nova. But although all this is true, it isn't quite that kind of book—it's about the dignity of labour and a post-scarcity (except of Illyrion) post-cleanliness society, but it's mainly about a gypsy boy called Mouse and his sensory syrynx, and tall Katan who comes from the moon and likes moons better than planets, and the twins Idas and Lyncaos, one black and one albino. It's a grail quest story, and a grudge story, and it's a story where the shape of the darkness between what's said makes a pattern to match the visible pattern of the story—and maybe that's what I didn't like about it? Maybe I couldn't see it in enough dimensions the last time I read it?

As always with Delany he has thought a lot about the implications of his future, the technology and the economics are all worked out and then mentioned only as they are relevant. It has aged pretty well, it doesn't feel more than forty years old except sometimes when it talks about humanity living spread out on a number of worlds by the end of the twentieth century (I wish!) and when it talks about Pluto as the solar system's outer edge and Triton as her most distant moon. We're all still stuck on Earth, but we have found a lot more moons since 1967, not to mention the Oort cloud. I never thought the local geography of the solar system I learned as an SF-reading teen would seem so quaintly obsolete.

There are a lot of science fiction futures with faster-than-light drives, but I wonder if *Nova* has the fastest one of anything? They zip about between stars as Americans go between cities, for parties. It takes five hours to go from Alkane in Draco to the Dim Dead Sister in the Pleiades. There are no slow transits of systems, no time lost in hyperspace, no relativisitic problems, no gravitational problems, just whizzing along jacked in (1968 . . . anticipating some of cyberpunk) and landing directly on the planet when you get there. There's a whole apparatus and paraphernalia of SF furniture missing. (Maybe that was my problem?) It's weird though, it's as if SF as a whole has decided on the speed of space travel not because of physics but because of the way other SF has done it, and Delany ignored that. In place of it there's this very fast moving universe where worlds are big places and there are lots and lots of them and the characters zip between them excessively fast but without the reader losing the sense of places and distance.

There's also a mythical dimension. This was one of the things that bothered me before. I felt I wasn't getting it, and that it unbalanced the actual story. It's stated overtly to be a grail quest, which makes Prince with his missing arm the Fisher King . . . or does it? Is Mouse with his one bare foot Jason—but so many of them have one bare foot. The mythical resonances are there, but they tangle. Is Lorq Prometheus, stealing fire to give to mankind? Is blind Dan falling in the chasm the Tarot Fool? One of the things I always remembered about *Nova* is that Mouse's gypsy lack of belief in the tarot is seen as old-fashioned superstition—and they're on a starship. The characters are clearly huge figures of mythical significance, but what figures, and in what system? I've never been sure. This read, it didn't matter, their significance wasn't more than appropriate, that they were themselves enough to carry it. The allegory may have been there but it never broke through the surface enough to disturb me.

Katin is trying to write a novel, though the art form is obsolete. He's been making notes for years, but hasn't written any of the novel yet. Mouse learned to play the sensory syrynx in Istanbul when he was a boy, and he can create three-dimensional scenes and beautiful music, and he does, frequently, in different styles and for different people. Katin is over-educated and Mouse under-educated, or they have educations orthogonal to each other. Katin explains things to Mouse, and through him to the reader. But it's Mouse who knows the songs and the stories and knows how to make them real with his syrynx. These two with their different takes on creativity seem more important to me than Lorq Van Roy and his quest for Illyrion—he just wants it to defeat his enemies and protect himself and his worlds. They want to find ways of telling significant stories in the moment they find themselves in. Their story is about being alone and wanting to create, which doesn't balance with the story of stealing fire.

Nova is a space opera set in a far future that has a working class, that has people of all colours and lots of different cultures, that's plausibly a future we could get to, or could have got to from 1968, with real hard science and mythic resonance—and I'm glad I didn't like it before so that I come to it fresh now.

I wish Samuel Delany would write more SF. I know there's a theory that he wrote SF because he couldn't write openly about the experience of being gay, and now he can, and I like his mimetic novels and memoirs but . . . science fiction is what I really like to read, and I just wish he'd write more SF anyway.

55. You may not know it, but you want to read this: Francis Spufford's Backroom Boys: The Secret Return of the British Boffin

Backroom Boys: The Secret Return of the British Boffin (2003) is about the history of technology and society. I keep wanting to say it's thought-provoking and full of nifty information, but what I really want to say is that it's unputdownable.

It's about six engineering projects that have taken place in Britain since WWII. It's very time and place specific, and very specific to its six subjects too, but nevertheless I recommend it to anyone who wants to write science fiction and most people who like to read it. This is a history book about how science and engineering are embedded in culture, arising almost organically from the cultural matrix of their time. And it's written fluidly and amusingly, with prose that makes it a joy to read and re-read. I read it the first time because it had been recommended to me as interesting and I thought (quite correctly) that it would also be useful for worldbuilding. But I read it again because reading it is such a joy.

The projects range from rockets through Concorde to computer games, cell phones, and the Human Genome Project, and they're all described with good-humoured understanding and sympathy and in the complete context of their time and the people involved with them. Also, they're full of charming anecdotes and amusing asides, and unexpected angles of seeing things.

The first project covered is the Blue Streak/Black Knight rocket project of the forties and fifties, which succeeded in putting one satellite into orbit once. It begins with a description of a meeting of the British Interplanetary Society which was interrupted by a V2 rocket, at which the members cheered. Later there's an amazing glimpse of some of our cultural heroes:

It was at about this time that an encounter took place between two outlooks almost equally marginal to the spirit of the time in Britain. Arthur C. Clarke, by now a well established science fiction writer as well as the author of the pioneering paper on satellite communications, had been growing increasingly irritated by the theological science fiction of C.S. Lewis, who saw space travel as a sinful attempt by fallen humanity to overstep its god-given place. [. . .] Clarke contacted Lewis and they agreed to meet in the Eastgate Tavern, Oxford. Clarke brought Val Cleaver as his second, Lewis brought J.R.R. Tolkien. They saw the world so differently that even argument was scarcely possible. As Orwell said about something completely different, their beliefs were as impossible to compare as a sausage and a rose. Clarke and Cleaver could not see any darkness in technology, while Lewis and Tolkien could not see the way in which a new tool genuinely transforms the possibilities of human awareness. For them, machines at the very best were a purely instrumental source of pipe tobacco and transport to the Bodleian. So what could they do? They all got pissed. "I'm sure you are all very wicked people," said Lewis cheerfully as he staggered away, "but how dull it would be if everyone was good!"

You couldn't make it up.

The strangest thing about this book is how directly relevant it is to my life. There's a section about the computer game *Elite*. I played that! (Along with everyone else with a computer in the late eighties.) And a friend of mine was in the room when the designers brought the first demo of it to Acornsoft! As for the Human Genome Project stuff, my husband barely misses being name-checked. It talks about how the cell network was set up in Britain and how the cells were mapped, but it also talks about how contracts to re-sell were shared among many tiny distributors. That was one of my first jobs, when I was in university, selling cell phones part-time when they were car phones. (I still don't own one.) It's fascinating to think that this book touches even my unscientific untechnical life at all these points, and for practically everyone who grew up in Britain between 1945 and 2003 I think it would touch it somewhere—because science and engineering run all through society, which is one of the book's points.

The "boffins" and "backroom boys" of the title are the unglamorous engineers who get things done invisibly. The men (and they are mostly men, with a few women visible as it comes closer to the present time) in this book are definitely that. Few people would be familiar with their names. But that's the point, they don't need that to be significant to our lives.

This is a book about Britain, but I think it would be no less interesting to North American readers, if slightly more exotic.

Imagine Romford. No, go on, imagine Romford; or if you can't quite bear that, at least imagine the approach to

192

Romford in the north-eastern corner of London where thinning city is shading over into built up Essex.

It's funnier if you do shudder at the thought of imagining Romford, but even if you've never heard of Romford, you can treat it as a voyage of discovery.

It's remarkably interesting and a surprisingly fun read.

56. Faster Than Light
at any speed

When I read *Nova* I noted how unusually fast the faster-than-light was. The ship goes from Alkane to the Dim Dark Sister in five hours, and from the Pleiades to Earth in three days. These are cars-in-the-US velocities, the whole inhabited galaxy is about as far apart emotionally as New York and San Francisco. And they land directly on the planets too, and can be used on the planet to whizz around to the other hemisphere.

Normally in science fiction, faster than light has a speed that has nothing to do with Einstein and everything to do with self-referentiality and the way other science fiction has done it—faster-than-light ships go at the speed of sailing ships, taking months to go between stars. There are wormholes or Jump or something letting them go faster than light, but it takes months of the crew's real time. And when they get there, they can't land on planets, any more than sailing ships can (outside of Dunsany) sail on land, they need space stations to be their ports, and they need dedicated career sailors and officers.

There's nothing wrong with doing the Napoleonic Wars in space, as Honor Harrington does, and the *Midshipman's Hope* books, and perhaps Dread Empire's Fall too. And if that's what you're doing, it's reasonable that your ships work that way. But there are a lot of books where there isn't an explicit analogy, where the ships aren't even naval vessels but commercial shipping. Cherryh's Union-Alliance and Chanur, Bujold's Vorkosigan books, Elizabeth Moon's Vatta's War books and her Aunts in Space series, Larry Niven's Known Space, George R. R. Martin's *Dying of the Light* universe. That's a lot of really different kinds of books that have this kind of "standard" FTL.

I don't know where it comes from. Was there some ur-novel that did it at this speed and everyone copied it? If so, what? Was it *Citizen of the Galaxy*? Or was it from the influential role-playing game *Traveller,* or even the influence of *Star Trek*?

And what's the appeal? Is it that it gives you lots of time in space, in a contained environment where adventures can happen, coming to planets as ports at usefully specified intervals? Because I can see how it's plot-useful, but there isn't any natural law saying that this is how FTL will work.

There are a few books with notably slow FTL. Ken MacLeod's *Cosmonaut Keep* series, and David Zindell's *Neverness* series, but it's very unusual. And then there's the ever brilliant Vernor Vinge who always thinks about what he's doing, with a whole range of speeds of faster than light in *A Fire Upon the Deep,* and "nearly as fast as light, plus coldsleep" in *A Deepness in the Sky.*

I think at this point, if you're writing anything with FTL, it would be worth considering other models than the sailing ship. Delany did long car-trip distances. We could also consider commercial planes, getting us around North America in a few hours, and across the world in half a day. And there are always trains, either long distance or commuter rail—and how about freighters as long-haul trucks? I don't mean copy them slavishly, just take the internalised emotional truth of the way they work and try it on a larger scale. Never mind leaving Earth and putting in at Madeira's Star for water in a month's time, how about leaving

Earth and spending seven hours in cramped seats eating awful food and ending up in Andromeda. It doesn't mean people would do it all the time, how often do you cross the Atlantic, after all, and anyway, a universe where people did it all the time would be an interestingly different universe. Best of all, how about something that isn't an Earth model, something that will make me look up from the book and say, "Wow, wow, you'll never believe the way they did faster than light in this one!"

57. Gender and glaciers: Ursula K. Le Guin's The Left Hand of Darkness

The Left Hand of Darkness is one of those books that changed the world, so that reading it now, in the world it helped grow, it isn't possible to have the same experience as reading it in the world it was written in and for. *The Left Hand of Darkness* didn't just change science fiction—it changed feminism, and it was part of the process of change of the concept of what it was to be a man or a woman. The battle may not be over. What I mean is that thanks in part to this book we're standing in a very different place from the combatants of 1969. Almost all books that do this kind of historic changing are important afterwards as historical artifacts, but not as stories, and they get left behind by the tide and end up looking quaint. Ninety percent of the discussion I've seen of *The Left Hand of Darkness* is about the gender issue, about the Gethenians and their interesting states of kemmer (of either gender for a few days a month) and somer (neuter for the majority of the time). But what makes it a book that continues to be great and enjoyable to read, rather than a historical curiosity, is that it's a terrific story set in a fascinating culture, and the gender stuff is only part of that.

The Left Hand of Darkness is the story of how the Terran Genly Ai comes to the planet Gethen to persuade Gethen to enter the Ekumen, the community of worlds. And it's the story of the Gethenian Therem Harth rem i'r Estraven who recognises something larger than the horizons he grew up with. And it's the story of the journey these two people take together. The book is written in such a way that you have Estraven's journals written at the time and Genly's report written later and various poems and folktales and stories of Gethen inserted in the text at appropriate points, so that the world is not only a character but one of the most important characters. I love the world, I love Karhide at least, the country and the people and how different it is from its government, and the religions. The planet is in an ice age, and the adaptations to the climate have shaped the cultures of the planet at least as much as the gender thing has. They're like real cultures, with real oddities, and the way the story is told enhances that. If you haven't read it, and if you've always seen it mentioned as a worthy feminist classic with weirdly gendered aliens, you might be surprised by this interesting story of the discovery of a planet and a journey across the ice. It is a living breathing story that happened to change the world, not a dry text with a message.

The book is set in the same universe as a number of Le Guin's other books, many written much earlier. It has the same furniture, the ansible, the Nearly as Fast as Light ships, the long ago Hainish experimental colonization of planets with tweaked humans—were they trying to make their own aliens? The previously worked out background doesn't give the book any problems, it makes it seem more solidly rooted.

We don't see any of the other planets, the book is firmly focused on Gethen, also known as "Winter." There is one narrative voice from an earlier report on the planet that's a woman from Chiffewar, but the non-Gethenian we are given to identify with is Genly Ai, a black man from Earth. We're not given his cultural context on Earth, though his dark skin, darker than most Gethenians, is mentioned. Neither "Genly" nor "Ai" are names I'm familiar with. A quick Google search finds me a town called Genly in Belgium, a factory in China, and people in the Philippines, China and India—Ai is regrettably unsearchable. Rene Walling suggests that it's the French "Jean-Louis" with the Japanese surname Ai, and he's from Montreal. In any case, whatever his ethnic background, Genly is our "normal" character, our filter, the one who is a gender we recognise and from a planet we're familiar with. He's our "unmarked" character, if you like. I think that's cool, even though we don't hear anything from him that makes his ethnicity other than "Terran." His sexual preference—heterosexuality—is mentioned, and his gender essentialism is very much dated from the world the book was written in, not the world in which it is now read.

The character I'm ridiculously fond of is Estraven. I've loved him since I was a teenager. He's not a man or a woman, he's in exile always and everywhere, and he always sees the big picture and tries to do what he can. He tries to be as good a person as he can, in difficult circumstances. He's one of my favourite characters in all of fiction, and when people play that "who would you invite to dinner" game, I almost always choose him, immediately throwing all hope of gender balance out of the window. I cry when he dies, and at the end of the book, every time. I don't know if I'd react so strongly to Estraven if I read the book for the first time now. His backstory, which is revealed so beautifully slowly, is one of the beauties of the book. His name reflects the levels of culture we have in Karhide, friends and hearth-brothers call him Therem, acquaintances call him Harth, and Estraven is his landname, which would be used where we use a title—yet when he learns mindspeech, up on the glacier, it is as Therem that he manages to hear it, and he hears it in his dead brother's voice—the dead brother with whom he had a child. Poor Estraven, so tragic, so clear-sighted, so perfectly and essentially of his world and culture!

It's a commonplace of SF for planets to have only one country and culture. Le Guin should be commended for mentioning four or five on Gethen and showing us two. However, there's a Cold War legacy in the way Karhide and Orgereyn are opposed, and Orgereyn is totalitarian, with its units and digits and work camps. I feel Orgereyn only really exists to give Genly and Estraven something to escape from, but I love their escape so much that I don't care. I think it's done pretty well, certainly Genly's subjective experience of it, but I don't think Orgereyn is as developed or as well thought through as Karhide.

The "tamed hunch" of the fastnesses, and the "mindspeech" of the Ekumen are both dealt with science fictionally rather than fantastically, but are "psi powers" of a kind rather unfashionable these days. Le Guin writes about them believably and interestingly, and I think they enhance the book by being there and providing more strangeness.

The heart of the book is the journey across the glacier, two people, from different worlds, manhauling a sledge across vast distances. There are echoes of Scott's Antarctic expeditions—for me, echoes the other way around, because I read *The Left Hand of Darkness* first. She took these quintessentially useless and particularly masculine endeavours and made them over into something else entirely. She was clearly fascinated with polar exploration—she has a short story in *The Compass Rose* about women from South America getting to the South Pole first and not marking it or telling anyone. Here there's a reason for the winter journey. So that's another gender subversion.

The Gethenians have a concept they call "shifgrethor," which is like pride. You waive shifgrethor for someone to tell you something directly, otherwise you sidle around to avoid offending them. This is notably different from Earth notions of offending pride only in how conscious they are of it, of what is sayable and unsayable, of having a mechanism for waiving it. I think it's one of the more interesting gender things—much more interesting than that they don't fight wars—that they have this set of shifting privileges and offendable pride and that they're aware of it. They're touchy in a very alien way, and I think that's really effective.

Le Guin has written essays since about the assumptions she made in writing the book. She also wrote the story "The Winter King" where she uses "she" as the pronoun for all Gethenians, rather than "he" as she does in the book, and the later story "Coming of Age in Karhide." Both of these explicitly feminise the Gethenians. They're interesting, as are her writings about the book, but they're afterthoughts from a different world.

It is light that is the left hand of darkness, and darkness the left hand of light, as in the yin-yang symbol, in which dualities are united. *The Left Hand of Darkness* is a book about making whole. It's also a book about what it means to be a good person and where gender is significant in that. But mostly it's about the joy of pulling a sledge over a glacier between two worlds.

58. Licensed to sell weasels and jade earrings: The short stories of Lord Dunsany

The first time I ever heard of Lord Dunsany was when my friend Jez Green read his story "Idle Days on the Yann" at one of my story parties. Although I'd never read it before, hearing it was like hearing something I'd read as a child, or before I was born, and the process of discovery was like a process of rediscovery. I've never felt that with any other writer—they were always new when they were new, but not Dunsany. And when I do re-read him, it's recursive. In Tolkien's "Leaf by Niggle" he talks about going into distances that continue to hold their charm as distance and never become mere surroundings, and that's the best description of reading Dunsany I can think of.

Dunsany wrote in the early part of the twentieth century. When I tried to find more Dunsany in the early nineties he was about as out of print as it is possible for anything to be. His short stories had been reissued in Ballantine editions by Lin Carter in the seventies, and I eventually managed to get hold of these secondhand in one of those little bookshops that you just know wouldn't be there if you ever went back to it. Fortunately, this situation has improved, and right now tons of Dunsany is available. *Time and the Gods* is an excellent big collection from Gollancz, and *Wonder Tales* and *In the Land of Time* are also in print. Besides these, there are a number of e-editions, and lots of his early stories are available free on Project Gutenberg. So right now it's easy to get hold of Dunsany. But why would you want to?

Lord Dunsany wasn't writing fantasy, because what he was writing was defining the space in which fantasy could later happen. He was influential on Lovecraft and Tolkien. There's a whole strand of fantasy—the Leiber/Moorcock/Gaiman strand—that's a direct descendant of his. But though he has always had a small enthusiastic fan base, it was possible for me to miss him entirely until the early nineties, and for lots of other people to miss him for even longer. I think this may be because he didn't write many novels, and the novels he did write aren't his best work. His acknowledged masterpiece novel, *The King of Elfland's Daughter,* is probably best described as good but odd. He isn't at his best writing characters, which gets peculiar at novel length. What he could do, what he did better than anyone, was to take poetic images and airy tissues of imagination and weight them down at the corners with perfect details to craft a net to catch dreams in. It's not surprising he couldn't make this work for whole novels, when as far as I know, nobody else has ever quite made it work in prose. If it is prose. It's some of the most poetic prose ever written, quite enough to get anyone drunk on words.

Take this for example:

> He opened a little, old, dark door in the wall through which I went, and he wheezed and shut the door. The back of the shop was of incredible age. I saw in antique characters upon a mouldering board, "Licensed to sell weasels and jade earrings." The sun was setting now and

shone on little golden spires that gleamed along the roof which had long ago been thatched and with a wonderful straw. I saw that the whole of Go-by Street had the same strange appearance when looked at from behind. The pavement was the same as the pavement of which I was weary and of which so many thousand miles lay the other side of those houses, but the street was of most pure untrampled grass with such marvellous flowers in it that they lured downward from great heights the flocks of butterflies as they traveled by, going I know not whence. The other side of the street there was pavement again but no houses of any kind, and what there was in place of them I did not stop to see, for I turned to my right and walked along the back of Go-by Street till I came to the open fields and the gardens of the cottages that I sought. Huge flowers went up out of these gardens like slow rockets and burst into purple blooms and stood there huge and radiant on six-foot stalks and softly sang strange songs. Others came up beside them and bloomed and began singing too. A very old witch came out of her cottage by the back door and into the garden in which I stood. (from "The Shop in Go-By Street")

It's the weasels and the jade earrings that make it real and fantastical at once. It's whimsy, but it isn't ever empty whimsy. Or here again:

In a wood older than record, a foster brother of the hills, stood the village of Allathurion; and there was peace between the people of that village and all the folk who walked in the dark ways of the wood, whether they were human or of the tribes of the beasts or of the race of the fairies and the elves and the little sacred spirits of trees and streams. Moreover, the village people had peace among themselves and between them and their lord, Lorendiac. In front of the village was a wide and grassy space, and beyond this the great wood again, but at the back the trees came right up to the houses, which, with their great beams and wooden framework and thatched roofs, green with moss, seemed almost to be a part of the forest. (from "The Fortress Unvanquishable, Save for Sacnoth")

Sacnoth is a magic sword. It's the moss on the roofs and the tribes of the beasts that anchor this, and all of it looks forward to the actual fantasy it prefigures. And here:

The Gibbelins eat, as is well known, nothing less good than man. Their evil tower is joined to Terra Cognita, to the lands we know, by a bridge. Their hoard is beyond reason; avarice has no use for it; they have a separate cellar for emeralds and a separate cellar for sapphires; they have filled a hole with gold and dig it up when they need it. And the only use that is known for their ridiculous wealth is to attract to their larder a continual supply of food. In times of famine they have even been known to scatter rubies abroad, a little trail of them to some city of Man, and sure enough their larders would soon be full again. (from "The Sword of Welleran")

It's the "well-known" and the prosaic different cellars—I think you have to read a whole story to fully appreciate what he was doing, but these paragraphs are enough to give you a taste of the style and the form.

He really isn't like anyone else at all—the closest in my

opinion is Cordwainer Smith, who was writing SF, but who did the same sort of thing with assumptions and details and a long perspective.

Dunsany was a contemporary of Wells's, but when we read Wells now we can see what he was writing was actual science fiction, like the science fiction we write now. You can't do that with Dunsany and fantasy, but in a way that makes him even more interesting. He isn't a father of fantasy but a grandfather or a fairy godfather. I tend to read, or even re-read, one Dunsany story at a time, but the images in them stick with me forever, which is how I know I didn't really read them as a child, because I couldn't have possibly forgotten them.

Give him a try, you'll be glad you did.

59. The Net of a Million Lies: Vernor Vinge's A Fire Upon the Deep

Any one of the ideas in *A Fire Upon the Deep* (1992) would have kept an ordinary writer going for years. For me it's the book that does everything right, the type example of what science fiction does when it works.

There's a universe where not only technology but also the very ability to think increases with distance from the galactic core, and the universe is divided into "zones of thought." In the "Slow Zone" you can't have true AI or FTL. In the "Beyond" you can have those things, but nothing that takes more than human-level intelligence. In the "Transcend" you have singularities and godlike beings, and above that, who knows? There's an ancient godlike evil known as the Blight lurking at the edge of the Transcend, the level where it's possible to become a Power. Humans poking around wake it up and trigger a catastrophe. Their escaping ship, which might contain the seeds of the Blight's destruction, rushes to the bottom of the Beyond, where it lands on a planet where the inhabitants, the Tines, are pack minds, at a medieval tech level. Meanwhile, Ravna, a human librarian at Relay, and Pham, a human rescued from the

Slowness and patched together by a Power, start a rescue mission.

You could have lots of great stories set in the Beyond, with its solar systems full of uneasily co-existing alien civilizations. You could have stories set in the Slowness—Vinge later outdid himself with one, *A Deepness in the Sky*. You could have long series of books set on the Tines world, especially about first contact with them when humans get there. The interstellar newsgroups could themselves have sustained trilogies. What Vinge gives us of his universe is like what Tolkien says of Middle Earth, "an account . . . of its end and passing away before its beginning and middle had been told." *A Fire Upon the Deep* is the story of an absolutely fascinating universe and of how it came to an end.

The book alternates between the big events happening in space and the small events happening on Tines World. It never fails to leave one story at a point where you want more of it, and never fails to be enthralling with the other story. There are two stories on the planet—Jefri and Johanna are separated and dealing with two entirely opposed groups of aliens. Tines World has nations and climates and history and philosophies, as well as fascinatingly bizarre aliens. And for those aliens, the human language, Samnorsk, and human history and technology as revealed by the child's toy dataset they have from the human children, is new and universe changing, while we know that humans are trivially unimportant in the larger scale of things and that Samnorsk is a minor unimportant language. There's a good cognitive dissonance with that.

Vinge does really well at making the wider universe seem real, even though we don't see all that much of it. We have what Ravna takes for granted, and what she has to explain to Pham. We see the newsgroups and get to know some of the posters— like the Aphranti Hegemony ("Death to Vermin") and Sandor at the Zoo. We see a little of Relay and a little of Harmonious

Repose, but it's surprising how much detail is evoked with so little. The Beyond feels solid, with its layers of translation and weird aliens—ones that walk on tusks, and ones like potted plants, and Twirlip of the Mists, who sounds demented but is always right.

He does a lot with evocative names and casually mentioned references that get nailed down by being referenced from different directions—for example the planet from which humanity emerged from the Slowness, Njora, is mentioned in the context of the fairy tale "Age of Princesses" several times by the kids on Tines World comparing the Tines tech, and there's a reference to the fountain flowing on Straum to say humanity would never forget its origins, not to mention the Straumli forests with mechanical copies of Njoran wildlife, and then on the ship (the *Out of Band II,* great name) when Pham makes the illusion of a castle Ravna thinks that in the Age of Princesses the castles were in tropical swamps so they didn't have fireplaces. That's just one tiny thing, but everything is as well sourced as this, and all the information is delicately inclued, dropped in smoothly. The details build up a picture that's consistent and interesting, and some of the details are major clues you can't recognise the first time through.

I read *A Fire Upon the Deep* from the library pretty much as soon as it was published in 1992. I was already looking out for Vinge; I'd enjoyed *The Peace War* and *Marooned in Realtime* a few years before, though I was very impressed with how much better this was. I bought the Millennium paperback I now own as soon as it came out in 1993. So I'd read it at least twice before I got online in May 1994. The thing about that was that when I saw Usenet, I immediately recognised it from Vinge's "Net of a Million Lies." I can't thank Vinge enough for educating me in how Usenet worked so that I could plunge right in and not make too much of a fool of myself. It's weird that blogs, which didn't come along until much later, work like the net in *Ender's Game,* which I first read on New Year's Day 1986.

A Fire Upon the Deep remains a favourite and a delight to re-read, absorbing even when I know exactly what's coming. *Deepness* is a better novel, but *A Fire Upon the Deep* is more fun.

60. The worst book I love: Robert A. Heinlein's Friday

On a miserably wet Saturday morning in 1982, when I was young and desolate, I went into the library, as I always did, without very much hope. As I reached the New Books section there, entirely unexpectedly, was *Friday*, a new Heinlein book. It was not just as if the sun had come out, it was as if the sun had come out and it was an F-type star and I was suddenly on a much nicer planet.

Friday is one of Heinlein's "late period" novels. The general rule if you haven't read any Heinlein is to start with anything less than an inch thick. But of his later books, I've always been fond of *Friday*. It's the first-person story of Friday Jones, courier and secret agent. She's a clone (in the terms of her world an "artificial person") who was brought up in a crèche and who is passing as human. It's a book about passing, about what makes you human. I think it was the first female out-and-out action hero that I read. It's also a book about being good at some things but with a large hole in your confidence underneath. No wonder I lapped it up when I was seventeen!

What's good about it now? The whole "passing" bit. The cloning, the attitudes to cloning, the worry about jobs. The

211

economy. It has an interesting future world, with lots of colonized planets, but most of the action taking place on Earth—that's surprisingly unusual. There's a Balkanized US and a very Balkanized world come to that, but with huge multinational corporations who have assassination "wars" and civil wars. There's a proto-Net, with search paths, that doesn't have any junk in it—that's always the failure mode of imagining the Net. It was easy enough to figure out you could sit at home and connect to the Library of Congress, but harder to imagine Wikipedia editing wars and all the baroque weirdness that is the Web.

Friday's point of view works for me as someone with severely shaken confidence, and as always with Heinlein it's immersive. Reading this now I can feel myself sinking right in to *Friday* without any problem. There's a complex multi-adult family, not unusual in late Heinlein, but this one disintegrates in a messy divorce, which is unusual and well done as well. And it's a fun read, even if it's ultimately unsatisfying.

What's wrong with it is that it doesn't have a plot.

Even at seventeen I couldn't love it uncritically. I can't think of any book for which I have expended more energy trying to fix the end in my head. It's practically a hobby. For years I would tell myself I'd re-read it and just stop when the good bit stops and skip the end—though I have to say I've never managed it. Heinlein's ability to write a sentence that makes you want to read the next sentence remains unparalleled. But the book as a whole is almost like *Dhalgren*. Every sentence and every paragraph and page and chapter lead on to the next, but it's just one thing after another, there's no real connection going on. It has no plot, it's a set of incidents that look as if they're going somewhere and don't ever resolve, just stop. It doesn't work as an emotional plot about Friday growing up, though it's closer to working as that than as anything else. (Even as that—well, I really have problems with the way she forgives the rapist, if that's supposed to be maturity.) It really doesn't work on any of the other levels you can look at it on.

Heinlein wrote about how he wrote in several places—*Expanded Universe* and some letters in *Grumbles from the Grave*. From this it's quite clear that he worked hard on the background and the characters but that he let his backbrain do the plotting. There are comments like, "There were Martians in *The Door into Summer* for a few pages until I realised they didn't belong so I took them out." (Paraphrased from memory.) As he got older, it's clear that he lost some grip on that ability to tell what didn't belong. *Friday* is an example where you can see this in action. It sets things up that it never invokes, most notably Olympia and the connections back to the novella "Gulf." It starts hares both in the human plot and the wider plot, and loses track of them. You can see how he did it, and you can imagine how he would have pulled it together, and what he might have gone back and fixed.

Even as it is, I love it for its moments of clarity and beauty. I wouldn't be without it. I taught myself almost all I know about how to plot by lying awake trying to fix the end of *Friday* in my head.

61. India's superheroes: Salman Rushdie's Midnight's Children

Saleem Sinai, the first-person narrator of *Midnight's Children* (1981), was born in the very moment of India's independence in 1947. The conceit of the book is that he, and other children born in that first hour, have astonishing magical superheroic powers. The story is bound up with Indian independence, not just after 1947 but also before—the story of how Saleem's parents meet is one of the best bits—and how Saleem's telepathic powers are at first a blessing and later a curse. What makes it great is the immense enthusiasm of the story and the language in which it is written. It isn't Rushdie's first novel, that would be the odd and openly science-fictional *Grimus*. But it has the kind of energy and vitality that a lot of first novels have. Rushdie's later novels are more technically accomplished but they're also much drier. *Midnight's Children* is a book it's easy to sink into. And the prose is astonishing:

> I was born in the city of Bombay . . . once upon a time.
> No, that won't do, there's no getting away from the date.
> I was born in Doctor Narlikar's Nursing Home on

214

August 15th 1947. And the time? The time matters too. Well then, at night. No, it's important to be more . . . On the stroke of midnight, as a matter of fact. Clock-hands joined palms in respectful greeting as I came. Oh, spell it out, spell it out, at the precise instant of India's arrival at independence, I tumbled forth into the world. There were gasps, and outside the window fireworks and crowds. A few seconds later my father broke his big toe, but his accident was a mere trifle when set beside what had befallen me in that benighted moment, when thanks to the occult tyrannies of the blandly saluting clocks I had been mysteriously handcuffed to history, my destinies indissolubly chained to those of my country. For the next three decades there was to be no escape. Soothsayers had prophesied me, newspapers celebrated my arrival, politicos ratified my authenticity. I was left entirely without a say in the matter.

This is a very Indian book. Not only is it set in India, written by an Indian writer in an Indian flavour of English, but the theme is Indian independence as reflected in the life of one boy and his friends. Even the superpowers are especially Indian, connected to Indian mythology rather than to the Western myths that give us the American superheroes. But it is also extremely approachable, especially for a genre reader. It was written in English (one of the great languages of modern India . . .) and by a writer steeped in the traditions of literature in English. *Midnight's Children* is usually classified as a kind of magical realism, but Rushdie has always been open about enjoying genre SF and fantasy; he knows what he's doing with manipulating the fantastic. The powers are real, in the context of the story. It isn't allegory. There's no barrier of translation here or problem with different conventions.

Midnight's Children invites you to immerse yourself in India the way you would with a fantasy world—and I think that was partly Rushdie's intention. He was living in England when he wrote it. He has talked about how writers like Paul Scott and E. M. Forster were untrue to the real India, and with this book I think he wanted to make his vision of India something all readers, whether they start from inside or outside that culture, could throw themselves into. I don't think his intention was to teach Indian history, though you'll certainly pick some up from reading it, so much as to demonstrate the experience of being plunged into Indian history, as Saleem is plunged into it at birth.

If it weren't so brilliantly written, it would fall flat on its face. As it is, it has become a classic—it won the Booker Prize when it was published in 1981, and the "Booker of Bookers," as the best Booker winner ever, twenty-five years later. It's still in print and still being read, but largely as mainstream literature. It's not much discussed as a genre work. I do think it has had influences on genre though, notably on Martin's *Wild Cards* series. Both were clearly influenced by the comic book superheroes of earlier decades, but I think the Jokers in the *Wild Cards* books, the people with minor useless superpowers, may have come from Rushdie:

> The closer to midnight our birth times were, the greater were our gifts. Those children born in the last seconds of the hour were (to be frank) little more than circus freaks: a bearded girl, a boy with the fully operative gills of a freshwater mahaseer trout, Siamese twins with two bodies dangling off a single head and neck—the head could speak in two voices, one male one female, and every language and dialect spoken in the subcontinent; but for all their marvellousness these were the unfortunates, the living casualties of that numinous hour.

216

In any case, this is a delight to read, bursting with characters and description and the excitement of a whole real complex country sprinkled with magic.

62. A funny book with a lot of death in it: Iain Banks's The Crow Road

I bought this particular copy of *The Crow Road* in Hay-on-Wye. Abacus had done nifty patching B-format paperbacks of all Banks's novels, all with metaphorical covers, the mainstream books in black and white and the SF coloured. (I'm sure they were thinking something when they made that decision, but it's too obvious to be interesting.) Emmet had all the other ones in matching editions, but had lost his *Crow Road,* and meanwhile they'd come out with new ugly covers. So I was in Hay-on-Wye, town of books, and I was writing *Tooth and Claw* and reading Trollope. In one of the secondhand bookshops there I bought fifteen Trollope novels and *The Crow Road*. The shop assistant looked at me oddly. "That's a bit different!" she said.

"Well," I said, "I suppose it is a bit different in that it's set in 1990 rather than 1880, but they're all books with a strong sense of place and time and family, where the boy gets the girl in the end and the family secrets are unraveled. I'll grant you the Banks has a bit more sex."

This somehow didn't stop her looking at me oddly. I think there may be a lot of people out there whose reading tastes are incredibly narrow. My main question on re-reading *The Crow Road* now is to ask why people don't write SF like this. SF stories that are about people but informed with the history that is going on around them. More specifically, why is it that Iain Banks writes these mainstream books with great characters and voice and a strong sense of place and then writes SF with nifty backgrounds and ideas but almost lacking in characters? The only one of his SF novels that has characters I remember is *Use of Weapons*. There are lots of writers who write SF and mainstream, but Banks is the only one whose mainstream I like better. Mystifying.

The Crow Road famously begins:

It was the day my grandmother exploded. I sat in the crematorium, listening to my Uncle Hamish quietly snoring in harmony to Bach's Mass in B minor, and I reflected that it always seemed to be death that drew me back to Gallanach.

"The crow road" means death, and "he's away the crow road" means that someone has died. The book begins with a funeral, and there are several more, along with a sprinkling of weddings and christenings, before the end. It's also the title of a work of fiction Rory's working on at the time of his death. Rory is Prentice's other uncle, and Prentice is the first-person narrator of a large proportion of the novel. This is a family saga, and if you can't cope with a couple of generations of McHoans and Urvills and Watts, you won't like it. I'd also advise against it if you loathe Scotland, as all the characters are Scottish and the whole novel takes place in Scotland. Oh, and they drink like they have no care for their livers. But if you don't mind these little things, it's a very good read.

The present tense of the story is set very precisely in 1989 and '90—coincidentally, the exact same time as Atwood's *The Robber Bride,* which I read last week. The First Gulf War is mentioned in both books. One of the characters in *The Crow Road* goes to Canada, but when I wonder if she'll encounter the characters from *The Robber Bride,* my brain explodes. Toronto and Gallanach—or maybe just Atwood and Banks—are clearly on different planets. And yet there are similarities. Both books have a present and long flashbacks into the past—*The Crow Road* goes back to Prentice's father's childhood. Still, different planets. Different assumptions about how human beings are.

So, why do you want to read *The Crow Road*? It's absorbing. It's very funny, with humour arising from situation and characters. (There's an atheist struck by lightning climbing a church.) There's a family like my family, which isn't to say realistic. There are the sort of situations you have in real life but so rarely in fiction, like the bit where the two young men are digging their father's grave while the gravedigger sleeps, and they wake him up by laughing, and he's appalled. There's a mysterious disappearance that might be murder. There's True Love, false love, skullduggery, death, birth, sex, cars, and Scotland.

> The land around Gallanach is thick with ancient monuments; burial sites, henges, and strangely carved rocks. You can hardly put a foot down without stepping on something that had religious significance to somebody sometime. Verity had heard of all this ancient stoneware but she'd never really seen it properly, her visits to Gallanach in the past had been busy with other things, and about the only thing she had seen was Dunadd, because it was an easy walk from the castle. And of course, because we'd lived here all our lives, none of the rest of us had bothered to visit half the places either.

It isn't in any way a genre novel, but it's great fun and so very good.

63. More dimensions
than you'd expect:
Samuel Delany's Babel-17

Babel-17 was published in 1966, the year in which I learned to talk. I didn't read it until I was a teenager, and it's been in my regular rotation ever since. It's set against a background of galactic conflict, huge wars between sections of humanity and their various alien allies. "Babel 17" is a code, or an alien language, that the military can't break. They call in a retired codebreaker-turned-poet called Rydra Wong, who goes off with a ship of misfits to adventure near the front lines, be captured, find allies in unexpected places, and discover the truth about Babel-17.

The thing about the description in the paragraph above is that it's all true and yet it's really not that kind of book. All those things happen, but they're not what the book is about. It is about the strong Sapir-Whorf hypothesis, the (now disproved, but cutting-edge linguistic theory at the time the book was written) idea that language shapes perception to such an extent that thinking in a different language gives you a different perception. It isn't true, but it's a lovely speculation for science fiction, and in *Babel-17* you have people whose brains are literally repro-grammed by language, and moments where changing language to think about it shows you the weak points in a structure. It might not be the case that speaking a language without the word "I" gives you no concept of self, but how very interesting to play with a character like that.

But it isn't the kind of science fiction that's all about the ideas either. There are exciting adventures and wonderful characters and fascinating worldbuilding and testing scientific ideas to destruction, which as a set of things is pretty much a definition of science fiction. But it's a very unusual book.

There are a lot of common tropes of SF in *Babel-17* that are treated in a way that's not just unusual for 1966 but that remain unusual now.

I mentioned there's a war. Later in the book there's combat and even action scenes. But the first mention of the war we have, the first image of it, is of the blockade of planets and the consequent starvation and cannibalism. Everyone in the book has lived through that. It's part of all their histories, whether they're talking about it or not, it's always informing their actions and motivations. This is so like real war and so little like the conventions of writing military SF that I can't think of anything else like it. And this is part of the background, not the focus of the book.

Rydra is telepathic, which is a fairly common attribute for a science fiction heroine. But it's a weird form of telepathy that makes her unhappy and which she denies for as long as she can. She's also a plausible great poet—Delany uses some of Marilyn Hacker's poetry as examples, which helps. (Generally with a character who's presented a great poet, it's better not to show their work unless you have some great poetry at hand.) Delany makes the choice to show us Rydra from the outside and from several different points of view before we get into her head, which works astonishingly well at giving us a picture of her complexity. She's a surprisingly three-dimensional character.

222

Also, and I almost didn't say this, she's a woman. She's the protagonist, she's a space captain and poet, she's competent and active, she makes her own choices and rescues herself and saves the world, and she's a woman, and it was 1966.

There are interesting family structures. Triples—marriage, close work, and living arrangements among three people—are common. Rydra is a surviving member of one, other members of her crew are in one. This is never anything but an accepted piece of background. There's also a scene where a very straight man has a sexual encounter with a (technological rather than supernatural) ghost. There's a clearly implicit background of a complex set of sexualities and relationship shapes that fit within the future culture.

The background is unusually dense, as always with Delany, with layers and implied further layers and texture. There are multiple cultures, even within the one side of the conflict we see, there are people of all colours, shapes and sizes and social classes. There are castes and classes, there's also the sense that working people actually work, with a notion of things they actually do. There is also body modification for fashion and lifestyle reasons (solid roses growing from your shoulder, like a tattoo) that have social significance as class and status markers. It's projecting the sixties, but not at all as you'd expect, and it falls into its own shapes and makes a unique future.

If *Babel-17* were published now as a new book, I think it would strike us as great work that was doing wonderful things and expanding the boundaries of science fiction. I think we'd nominate it for awards and talk a lot about it. It's almost as old as I am, and I really think it would still be an exciting significant book if it were new now.

64. Bad, but good: David Feintuch's Midshipman's Hope

Midshipman's Hope is unashamedly reminiscent of both Forester's Hornblower books and Heinlein's *Starman Jones*. A lot of the worldbuilding is there explicitly to load the deck to get the result Feintuch wants—a Napoleonic space navy where adolescents go into space with ridiculous amounts of responsibility and angst about it. It could be an Oliver Optic novel! The majority of the book is about how Nicholas Seafort, a seventeen-year-old midshipman on *Hibernia*, a ship headed on a three-year interstellar cruise, is forced by circumstances and his own honour into situations where he has to make awful choices which always turn out to be right. The book is written in first person, so we spend it nose to nose with Seafort, his angst, his nightmares, his funk, his utter inability to forgive himself or unbend for an instant. And that's what's good about it. It's ludicrous really—later in the series he eventually gets to a point where the only way for him to get more responsibility to angst over and a higher position he isn't qualified for would be if he was suddenly forced to be God—but it's compelling nevertheless.

I read it in the first place because the late Mr. Feintuch used to post on rec.arts.sf.written, and he made it sound like something I'd like. And it is something I like. I've read the whole series. Indeed, everyone in our house read it, to the point where we affectionately refer to the series as *Midshipman's Mope*. But if it's so awful, why did I keep it, and why am I reading it again? Isn't that an interesting question?

At a Fourth Street Fantasy Convention, the question was raised as to why people read bad books. Sharyn November, the editor of Penguin's YA Firebird line, replied that everyone wants Cheetos sometimes. The problem with that answer is that it doesn't really model what I do—and I'm generalising from one person here, but then, as Steven Brust says, everyone does that. If it was a case of "everyone eats Cheetos sometimes," the requirement for something undemanding, then almost anything undemanding would do. Now I do from time to time want things that are undemanding for their undemandingness, but I always want specific things. It's not a case of "anything undemanding would do." I want things that scratch particular itches.

When I think of my comfort re-reads they all tend to be things where everything comes out all right in the end—children's books, romances, and military stories. The characters in these sorts of books tend to be justified in what they do. There's a certain black and white nature to everything. They tend to be series, so I can really soak myself in them, or if not series then at least a lot of books to the same formula. If I'm comfort reading I don't read one Noel Streatfeild or Georgette Heyer or W. E. B. Griffin, I read typically five or six. The other thing they have in common is that while the prose might be clunky, the characters might have only two dimensions and the plots when examined may be ridiculous, they're really good on the storytelling level. They may look contrived when you step away from them, but while you're immersed, you can care. Indeed, you're allowed to care, encouraged to care. They're manipulative in some ways,

225

but you feel that the author is buying what they're selling, they're button-pushing, but they're honest. They're the author's buttons too. Heyer may be laughing just a little at her heroine, and inviting you to laugh with her, but the text is also deeply invested in the reality of social anxiety and true love. And they're not interchangeable. If I want military training and male camaraderie, then giving me waltzing at Almacks doesn't cut it, and vice versa.

Now this probably doesn't help with why other people read bad books at all, as lots of people don't re-read much if at all. But it might be why they keep on reading new volumes in a bad series. They know what they're getting, it's honest, you're invited to care about the characters, who will be justified in their main actions, and the storytelling is good.

Midshipman's Hope definitely fits all this. I picked it up this time because I was trying to think about why I read bad books, so I wasn't pining for a rigid navy in space, or for aliens and planets, which are definitely elements that make me forgive a lot of flaws. By about a third of the way in, though, the book had entirely grabbed me. I didn't want to put it down, even though I knew what happened, I wanted to go through that dance again with poor old unforgiving Seafort as he does everything wrong and hates himself and it all turns out to have been right. I didn't go on to re-read the rest of the series. But if I'd been at home and they'd been there, I might well have, even knowing everything I already know about them.

(The future slang in the later books irritates me, and the fact Seafort comes from Cardiff, which is mildly irritating in *Midshipman's Hope,* because he's so totally American, becomes actively annoying later where Feintuch demonstrates he knows nothing about the geography and culture. I'm writing this post in Cardiff. It's a city that has changed a lot in my lifetime. I'm sure it'll change a lot more by 2194, but I think it would take a lot longer than that to change into the U.S. Midwest. I wonder if there are people in the Philippines who grump like this about Juan Rico?)

However and notwithstanding, if you're looking for a book about a boy with an uncompromising sense of honour who gets piled with too much responsibility, and that has spaceships and aliens and strong narrative drive and undeniable sincerity, and if you can put up with a handful of ludicrous coincidences pushing the plot along, then *Midshipman's Hope* is definitely the book for you.

65. Subtly twisted history: John M. Ford's *The Dragon Waiting*

It's so easy to talk about how clever *The Dragon Waiting* (1983) is that it's easy to lose sight of what good fun it is, so I wanted to start with this. It's a brilliantly written, absorbing book with great characters; it's hard to put down once it gets going; and it's laugh-aloud funny in places. This is John M. Ford's World Fantasy Award–winning masterpiece, and it really is notably brilliant. It's a historical fantasy that plays games with history. I suppose lots of historical fantasies and alternate histories play games with history, but most of them are playing tic-tac-toe while *The Dragon Waiting* is playing three-dimensional Go.

It's a Richard III book, though it takes a while to figure that out. Indeed, it takes a while to figure it out at all, because the first part that introduces the three main characters seems like the beginning of three different books, set in three different worlds. The wizard Hywel Peredur lives in a post-Roman Wales, the boy Dimitrios Ducas lives in a Gaul reconquered by Byzantium, and the doctor Cynthia Ricci lives at the Renaissance court of Lorenzo the Magnificent. Yet this is all one world and the three of them meet up with Gregory von Bayern, a vampire

228

gun-maker, at an inn in an Alpine mountain pass, and go on together to work against Byzantium's designs for reconquering Britain, and suddenly we are into the reality of the Wars of the Roses, the plotting nobles, the princes in the tower, vampires, wizards, Henry Tudor with Byzantine backing, exploding guns, dragons, witches, ciphers, poisons, and intrigue.

The world is an alternate history where Julian the Apostate lived to ensure no one faith had priority over any other, and everyone is largely pagan. I don't think anyone else has written a feudal world without Christianity that I'm convinced by, never mind medieval Europe, so this in itself is a major achievement. Justinian and Theodora became vampires, and held on to and consolidated Belisarius's reconquest of half of Italy, going on to divide up France between themselves and the English crown. Now they're mopping up the rest of Italy.

Real-world Byzantium fell in 1453. It's hard to feel all that sorry the alternate world counterpart is trying to swallow up all of Europe fifty years after that, which makes them an interesting choice of bad guys. We never see them all that clearly, what we mostly see are the individuals manipulated by them, not Byzantium itself. Still, it makes a convincing menace.

I normally hate alternate histories where the turning point was hundreds of years before and yet there are characters with the same names and characters, but it doesn't bother me at all here. I think I don't mind it because Ford does it so perfectly, and not only that but he knows the history and geography so well that he never puts a foot wrong. There are very few books written by Americans and set in Britain (and only this one in Wales) where the geography works and the scale of the landscape feels right. (Similarly, I'd never dare set anything in the US.) Ford knows the real history well enough that it sits up and does tricks for him.

Similarly, if there's one thing that puts me off a book it's vampires. Yet *The Dragon Waiting* has a major vampire character and a plot and backstory that rely on vampires. It helps that they're not sexy, or attractive, it helps that they're much more like heroin addicts and that Gregory is using animal blood as methadone. Most of all, it helps that it doesn't have vampires because vampires are cool, but because vampires are necessary. At least it doesn't have any pirates. (But perhaps Ford could have made me like pirates, too. He made me almost like a *Star Trek* novel, after all.)

The characters are wonderful, all the way through. The book gives you time to get to know them and then uses them in precise ways, so you feel they're doing exactly what they would do. This is true even of minor characters. It also uses Arthurian motifs to underscore the story, without ever getting tangled up in them. Part of the satisfaction of re-reading a complex book like this is seeing the mechanism, knowing what's going to happen and seeing the inevitability of each action. It's surprisingly hard to do that with this—it's hard to hold on to. It's as if in twisting the tail of history Ford could somehow manage to twist his own tale and make it come out differently.

What a good book this is, what an enjoyable read, and how incredibly clever. I love it.

It's not likely to have a U.S. reprint soon, so I'd grab this attractive Gollancz "Ultimate Fantasies" edition while it's available.

66. A very long poem: Alan Garner's Red Shift

Alan Garner's *Red Shift* (1973) is a book I have practically memorised, which makes re-reading it weird—it's more like reading
poetry than prose, because my brain keeps filling in the whole
line from the first word. The reason I know it so well is because
I like it a great deal, and also because it's a very difficult book
(again like poetry) and one that I first read as a teenager and kept
coming back to and back to in an attempt to understand it.
Garner's previous books—*The Weirdstone of Brisingamen* (1960),
The Moon of Gomrath (1963), *The Owl Service* (1967), *Elidor*
(1965)—were children's books deeply rooted in place and
mythology. *Red Shift* is all that, but it definitely isn't a children's
book. It's much too challenging and elliptical. Almost the whole
book is dialogue, there's practically no description and very little
attribution of dialogue. It's set in the same places in three distinct
time periods—Tom and Jan in the contempory 1973, Thomas
and Madge in the Civil War, and Macey and the remnants of the
Ninth Legion at the borders of Roman Britain. They're linked
by location and by a paleolithic axe and by a vision they all share
of something that is blue and silver and very bad. You don't find
out what the blue and silver thing is until the end of the book.

231

The story can be seen as a version of *Tam Lin*. It's also a naturalistic story about a romance between young people with no money, and a story about some Roman soldiers trying to live on a hilltop, and a story about the kinds of betrayals you get in civil wars. It's a story about the history of Cheshire, and about the way history has deep roots and happens right where you are. It's about sex and love and longing and how hard it can be to hold on to connections between people. It's full of beautiful imagery and language. It jumps between times that are linked thematically. It really is a lot more like poetry than prose, it makes more sense if you read it with the protocols of poetry.

> "I'm not sure about the mean galactic velocity. We're with M31, M32 and M33 and a couple of dozen other galaxies. They're the nearest. What did you say?"
>
> "I love you."
>
> "Yes." He stopped walking. "That's all we can be sure of. We are, at this moment, somewhere between the M6 going to Birmingham and M33 going nowhere. Don't leave me."
>
> "Hush," said Jan. "It's all right."
>
> "It's not. How did we meet? How could we? Between the M6 and M33. Think of the odds. In all space and time. I'm scared."

If you like this, you will probably like the rest of it. Garner's most recent book, *Thursbitch,* is also written like this. I've recently read it, just once, and I think I liked it, I'm not sure yet. If *Red Shift* is *Tam Lin,* then it is a *Tam Lin* where Janet does not hold on to Thomas as he changes. If it's a thing like the motif in Guy Kay's *Ysabel* and *Fionavar* where the pattern repeats and maybe somebody will hold on sometime, then that makes the mention of "next time?" in the coded note even weirder. We also have three pregnant women, none of them pregnant by the men who love them, but it is the men who connect up through time, the men who see the vision of the train that parts Tom and Jan. It's perfectly possible that the girl on Mow Cop and Madge are Tom's ancestors, but Macey and Thomas Rowley are not. Yet Macey and Thomas are picking up Tom's anguish back through time as it's manifested in the blue-silver blur of the train. But the *Tam Lin* thing is actually reversed, it's Tom who doesn't hold on to Jan, he gives up the Bunty. Macey and Thomas do hold on to their women—Thomas seeing the lights on the cars on the motorway and thinking they are waves is one of the most impressive images in the book.

I understand the weirdness about Tom's reaction to Jan's previous relationship a lot better now than I did when I first read the book, where it was quite incomprehensible to me. I actually understand it better than I did even the last time I read it, because I have been reading Kathleen Norris in between. The whole obsession with female virginity still seems bizarre, but at least I see where it's coming from. It seems particularly bizarre because it's Tom that I identify with in *Red Shift,* and this, significant as it is for the story, is where I can't follow him. Oh well.

All three partnerships, in their different times, are across barriers. With Tom and Jan it's straight-up class, her parents are professionals, Tom's parents live in a caravan and he is struggling to win a scholarship to university. With Madge and Thomas it's that Thomas has fits, visions of Tom and the train. With Macey and the unnamed girl they're from entirely different cultures, and he's ridden by visions and the whole berserker thing.

The Romans talk like soldiers, in soldier slang and local dialect. Their names, Face, Magoo, Logan, Buzzard, Macey, are not Roman names. Yet they don't at all feel like modern people, even with all of that. The lack of distancing in the language and names makes them more different. The things they do—the slaughter and rape in Barthomley especially—are horrific. There's a wonderful line about Face, but it applies to all of them really: "He has lost Rome and is tribal, far from his tribe."

The Civil War episode contains a lot of backstory packed into very few words. Madge has been involved with two men, both called Thomas, Thomas Rowley and Thomas Venables. She is married to Rowley. Venables comes back and rescues them from the general slaughter of Barthomley. John Fowler the Rector's son has been fighting on the Parliament side. He's also tangled up with Madge and the Thomases. He has been a thorn in the village's side for a long time. Civil wars lead to people killing people they know, or sparing them, there aren't any strangers. There are three locations that link all the times. Most significant is Mow Cop, the hill with its quarries where the Romans retreat, where Thomas Venables comes from, where Madge and Thomas Rowley end up (with the stone axe) and where Tom and Jan visit in trying to find somewhere real. Barthomley village, where everyone gets slaughtered twice in the two historical periods, is a haven of peace and tranquility for Tom and Jan. And Rudheath is where Tom's parents live, and where the Romans begin and Thomas and Madge end up. Crewe, the city, is modern and unreal; although Jan and Tom spend time there it is constantly described in images of unreality, or being too real.

> "Each of these shops is full of one aspect of existence. Woolworths is a tool shed; Boots a bathroom; British Home Stores a wardrobe. And we walk through it all but we can't clean our teeth, or mend a fuse, or change our socks. You'd starve in this supermarket. It's all so real we're shadows."

They find their way to Barthomley by finding a path "older than Crewe" that cuts through and across the city. Crewe is, of course, for most British readers, famous as a railway junction. I have changed trains there thousands of times without ever venturing out of the station. And this aspect of it is emphasised in the novel, not only with meeting and parting at the station but in the tracks they cross following the path and in the views of Mow Cop Jan gets from the train. (It's actually visible only on the train from the North, not from the London train.)

The book is also seamed with graffiti—the inscriptions on the bells, the park benches, on the screen in Barthomley church ("Let there be no strife for we be brethren") and the actual ungrammatical graffiti carved in the house on Mow Cop: "I came back Mary" and "Pip loves Brian: not really now not any more." These, with Tom's constant quotations from Tom O'Bedlam in *King Lear,* serve to root the times and histories even deeper together.

Red Shift is a sad story of a love that doesn't work, though the deeper historical stories have happier endings. It says something for the way it's written that the beauty of the language and the landscape and the depth of resonance shine through sufficiently to make it comfortable reading. I love it. I'm not sure I entirely understand it, even now, but that doesn't matter.

67. Beautiful, poetic and experimental: Roger Zelazny's *Doorways in the Sand*

Roger Zelazny was a demented genius who could squeeze words until they sang. I first read *Doorways in the Sand* (1976) when I was thirteen years old. It blew my head off. I've read it a couple of times since then, but it isn't in my frequent rotation, like *Isle of the Dead* (1969) and *This Immortal* (1966). Like those books, it has a typical Zelazny first-person smart-ass protagonist, like them it has aliens and shiny SFnal ideas, but unlike them it is written in an experimental way, where almost every chapter starts in the middle and then goes back to get you up to speed just in time for a new chapter and a new reverse-cliffhanger lurch. I didn't like this when I was thirteen, though I thought it was clever, and I don't like it now. It seems like grandstanding, and it gets in the way of my enjoyment of the story. It isn't possible to read the book without spending a lot of time thinking, "Huh? How did that happen?" and waiting to find out. It makes it easy to identify with a protagonist who doesn't know what's going on either, but it's irritating. However, the Zelazny I really like is getting too familiar for me to read, so it's time to turn to the less favourite and therefore still readable.

236

The too-clever story shaping aside, there's a lot here to like. There's the way Zelazny invented this awesome system of education whereby you can take courses in whatever you like, and learn about absolutely everything without ever graduating and getting a degree. He explains it was invented by a Harvard professor called Eliot, in typical science fiction as-you-know-Bob explanation. I was astounded when I found out (too late) that it was real. Fred Cassidy has been a full-time student for thirteen years without graduating. He has a hobby of climbing on buildings, which he dignifies with the name acrophilia. He knows quite a lot about a vast range of subjects. By the terms of his uncle's will, Fred gets a comfortable monthly income until he graduates, so Fred has bent the rules and stayed in school. Meanwhile, we've discovered aliens and are part of an alien cultural exchange ring—the *Mona Lisa* and the Crown Jewels have left Earth in exchange for a very odd machine that reverses stereoisomers and the mysterious Star Stone. The Star Stone goes missing and lots of people and aliens seem to think Fred's got it. Fred thinks he hasn't.

Things get weird from there on, but Fred wisecracks his way unflappably through the plot from crisis to crisis, climbing on things from time to time for recreation or escape. It's a future without technology or social mores having changed much from the mid-seventies when this was written but apart from the way everyone (even the aliens) smokes cigarettes all the time, you almost don't notice. There's an alien that disguises itself as a wombat, and another that looks like a Venus flytrap, after all.

In some ways this is like a very simple adventure story. In other ways, it's like a story of humanity glimpsing the complexities of a galactic civilization. What it's really like is the stereoisomer of both of those stories, the inverse inside-out twisted version of them. The whole twisted-chapter thing is a

237

meditation on the stereoisomer theme. It really is very clever, and fortunately, very beautiful.

> Sunflash, some splash. Darkle. Stardance. Phaeton's solid gold cadillac crashed where there was no ear to hear, lay burning, flickered, went out. Like me. At least, when I woke again it was night and I was a wreck. Lying there, bound with rawhide straps, spread-eagle, sand and gravel for pillow as well as mattress, dust in my mouth, nose, ears and eyes, dined upon by vermin, thirsty, bruised, hungry and shaking, I reflected on the words of my one-time advisor Doctor Merimee: "You are a living example of the absurdity of things." Needless to say his speciality was the novel, French, mid-Twentieth century.

Since this is the beginning of a chapter, you have as much context as any reader for why Fred is tied up, and he doesn't get around to telling you for pages and pages. If this is going to drive you mad, don't read this book. If you can bear it, then you have the pretty words and the promise of aliens and a machine with a moebius conveyer belt running through it and the taste of bourbon and fries when you've been reversed by the machine. Nobody but nobody else could juxtapose all the things in those five little paragraphs and make it all work. Zelazny could certainly be very odd, and this is a minor work, and not where I'd recommend starting. (That would be with his short stories, presently being reissued in gorgeous editions by NESFA.) But it's short—I read it in about an hour and a half—and it's got the inimitable Zelazny voice which will keep singing in my mind when all the details and the irritation have sunk back into oblivion.

> There is a man. He is climbing in the dusky daysend air, climbing the high Tower of Cheslerei in a place called

238

Ardel beside a sea with a name he cannot quite pronounce as yet. The sea is as dark as the juice of grapes, bubbling a Chianti and chirascuro fermentation of the light of distant stars and the bent rays of Canis Vibesper, its own primary, now but slightly beneath the horizon, rousing another continent, pursued by the breezes that depart the inland fields to weave their courses among the interconnected balconies, towers, walls and walkways of the city, bearing the smells of the warm land towards its older, colder, companion.

Yup, that's definitely one of the ways science fiction can make you long to be there. Nobody ever did it better.

68. Waking the Dragon: George R. R. Martin's A Song of Ice and Fire

Re-reading these books right now is a mistake. Before I picked up *A Game of Thrones* again, I had only a calm interest in Jon Snow's true parentage, I'd forgotten who Jeyne Poole was, and best of all, I only mildly wanted *A Dance with Dragons*. I sagely nodded when I read that George R. R. Martin is not my bitch. I have every sympathy for this position. All the same, I know that by the time I get to the end of *A Feast for Crows* I'll be desperate, desperate, desperate, so desperate for my fix that I'll be barely able to control myself. I will be *A Dance with Dragons*-seeky, and is it out? Is it even finished? Like heck it is. And I know I'm not entitled to it but I waaaaaaaaaant it! If I were a sensible person, I'd have waited to re-read until it was ready and I could have had a new installment to go with the old. But now it's too late.

So what is it about these books that makes me talk about them in terms of a two-year-old snatching at sweets in a supermarket?

Firstly, they have a very high "I-want-to-read-it" quotient. This "IWantToReadItosity" is hard to explain, is utterly subjective and is entirely separate from whether a book is actually good. Who can say why Robert Heinlein and Georgette Heyer and Zenna Henderson have it for me and Herman Hesse and Aldous Huxley don't, despite the fact that Hesse and Huxley are major world writers? I'll happily acknowledge that *The Glass Bead Game* is a better book than *Job: A Comedy of Justice,* but nevertheless, *Job* has that IWantToReadItosity, and if you left me in a room with both books and nothing else, it would be *Job* I'd start first.

Now, even within genre this is something that varies a lot between people. The Wheel of Time books don't have it for me. I've read *The Eye of the World* and I didn't care enough to pick up the others. Ditto Harry Potter, where I've read the first three. These are books that have IWantToReadItosity for millions of people, but not for me. The Song of Ice and Fire books do, though, they grab me by the throat. This isn't to say they're gripping in the conventional sense—though they are—because IWantToReadItosity isn't necessarily to do with plot or characters or any of the ways we conventionally divide up literature. It's got to do with whether and how much you want to read it. You know the question, "Would you rather read your book or go out with your friends?" Books have IWantToReadItosity if you'd rather read them. There are books I enjoy that I can still happily put down to do something else. *A Game of Thrones* is eight hundred pages long, and I've read it six times, but even so, every time I put the bookmark in, I put it in reluctantly.

These books are often described as epic fantasy, but they're cleverer than that. Most epic fantasies are quests. This is a different kind of variation on a theme from Tolkien. In those terms, it's as if when Sauron started to rise again in Middle Earth, Gondor was in the middle of the Wars of the Roses. They're about human-scale dynastic squabbles on the edge of something wider and darker and inhumanly dangerous. The world is wonderful, with a convincing history leading to the present situation. It has good names (Winterfell, Greyjoy, Tyrion, Eddard), great characters who are very different from each other and are never cliches—and Martin isn't afraid to kill them, nobody is safe in this world because of being the author's darling. There are mysteries that you can trust will be resolved, everything fits together, everything feels real and solid and full of detail.

But the thing that really lifts them above the ordinary is the constant balance at the edge of the abyss, the army marching off south to win a kingdom when the real (supernatural) danger is north. There are human problems on a human scale, tragedy, betrayal, honour, injustice, and always the creeping reminder underneath of something . . . colder.

If you like history, and if you like fantasy, and if you like books where one page leads you on to the next and you can't believe it's that time already, you should definitely read these. Also, if you haven't read them you're lucky, because you have four eight-hundred-page volumes to go before you're reduced to a slavering hunk of waaaaaaaant.

69. Who reads cosy catastrophes?

Cosy catastrophes are science fiction novels in which some bizarre calamity occurs that wipes out a large percentage of the population, but the protagonists survive and even thrive in the new world that follows. They are related to but distinct from the disaster novel where some relatively realistic disaster wipes out a large percentage of the population and the protagonists also have a horrible time. The name was coined by Brian Aldiss in *Billion Year Spree: The True History of Science Fiction* (and used by John Clute in *The Encyclopedia of Science Fiction*) by analogy to the cosy mystery, in which people die violently but there's always tea and crumpets.

In 2001, I wrote a paper for a conference celebrating British science fiction in 2001. It was called "Who Survives the Cosy Catastrophe?" and it was later published in *Foundation*. In this paper I argued that the cosy catastrophe was overwhelmingly written by middle-class British people who had lived through the upheavals and new settlement during and after World War II, and who found the radical idea that the working classes were people hard to deal with, and wished they would all just go away. I also suggested that the ludicrous catastrophes that destroyed civilization—bees, in Keith Roberts's *The Furies* (1966), a desire to stay home in Susan Cooper's *Mandrake* (1964), a comet in John Christopher's *The Year of the Comet* (1955)—were obvious stand-ins for fear of the new atomic bomb that really could destroy civilization.

In the classic cosy catastrophe, the catastrophe doesn't take long and isn't lingered over, and the people who survive are always middle class, and have rarely lost anyone significant to them. The working classes are wiped out in a way that removes guilt. The survivors wander around an empty city, usually London, regretting the lost world of restaurants and symphony orchestras. There's an elegiac tone, so much that was so good has passed away. Nobody ever regrets football matches or carnivals. Then they begin to rebuild civilization along better, more scientific lines. Cosy catastrophes are very formulaic—unlike the vast majority of science fiction. You could quite easily write a program for generating one.

It's not surprising that science fiction readers like them. We tend to like weird things happening and people coping with odd situations, and we tend to be ready to buy into whatever axioms writers think are necessary to set up a scenario. The really unexpected thing is that these books were mainstream bestsellers in Britain in the fifties and early sixties. They sold like hotcakes. People couldn't get enough of them—and not just to people who wanted science fiction, they were bestsellers among people who wouldn't be seen dead with science fiction. (The Penguin editions of Wyndham from the sixties say "he decided to try a modified form of what is unhappily called 'science fiction.'") They despised the idea of science fiction but they loved Wyndham and John Christopher and the other imitators. It wasn't just *The Day of the Triffids* (1951), which in many ways set the template for the cosy catastrophe, they all sold like that. And this was the early fifties. These people definitely weren't reading them as a variety of science fiction. Then, although they continued to exist, and to be written, they became a specialty taste. I think a lot of the appeal for them now is for teenagers—I certainly loved them when I was a teenager, and some of them have been reprinted as YA. Teenagers do want all the grown-ups to go away—this literally happens in John Christopher's *Empty World* (1977).

I think that original huge popularity was because there were a lot of intelligent middle-class people in Britain, the kind of people who bought books, who had seen a decline in their standard of living as a result of the new settlement. It was much fairer for everyone, but they had been better off before. Nevil Shute complains in *Slide Rule* (1954) that his mother couldn't go to the South of France in the winters, even though it was good for her chest, and you've probably read things yourself where the characters are complaining they can't get the servants anymore. Asimov had a lovely answer to that one: If we'd lived in the days when it was easy to get servants, we would have *been* the servants. Shute's mother couldn't afford France but she and the people who waited on her in shops all had access to free health care and good free education to university level and beyond, and enough to live on if they lost their jobs. The social contract had been rewritten, and the richer really did suffer a little. I want to say "poor dears," but I really do feel for them. Britain used to be a country with sharp class differences—how you spoke and your parents' jobs affected your healthcare, your education, your employment opportunities. It had an empire it exploited to support its own standard of living. The situation of the thirties was horribly unfair and couldn't have been allowed to go on, and democracy defeated it, but it wasn't the fault of individuals. Britain was becoming a fairer society, with equal opportunities for everyone, and some people did suffer for it. They couldn't have their foreign holidays and servants and way of life, because their way of life exploited other people. They had never given the working classes the respect due to human beings, and now they had to, and it really was hard for them. You can't really blame them for wishing all those inconvenient people would . . . all be swallowed up by a volcano, or stung to death by triffids.

The people who went through this didn't just write, and read, cosy catastrophes. There were a host of science-fictional reactions to this social upheaval, from people who had lived through the end of their world. I'm going to be looking at some more of them soon.

70. Stalinism vs Champagne at the opera: Constantine Fitzgibbon's When the Kissing Had to Stop

When the Kissing Had to Stop was published in 1960, and republished in 1980, which is when I first read it. It's a book set in the near future of 1960, clearly intended as a warning "if this goes on" type of story, about a Britain taken over by a Soviet plot aided by a few troops and some gullible British people, much as Norway was taken over by Hitler in 1941 and Tibet by China in 1959. (Russia never in fact used that kind of tactics.) It's written in a particularly omniscient form of bestseller omni, it has a large but consistent cast of characters, and many of the chapters consist of such things as saying what they were all doing on Christmas Eve. The characters are very well done, there are Aldermaston marches (cynically funded by Russia for their own ends), there's a coup, and by the end all the characters except one are dead or in gulags. I think I've always read it through in one sitting, sometimes until very late at night, it's not a book where it's possible for me to sleep in the middle.

Re-reading this now, I've just realised that this was a very influential book. I'm not sure if it was influential on anyone else, indeed, though my copy quotes glowing reviews from the British mainstream press, I'm not sure if anyone else ever read it at all. But it was very influential on *me,* and particularly in the way I wrote about people going on with their ordinary lives while awful things happen in the Small Change books. Fitzgibbon does that brilliantly here, they're worrying about who loves who and whether to get a divorce and all the time the Russians are coming. He also keeps doing the contrasts between upper-class luxury and horror—from carol singing in a country house to carol singing in the gulag, from the Kremlin plotting to champagne at the opera.

This isn't a subtle book, and it isn't really science fiction—it was clearly published as a mainstream book. Fitzgibbon tries harder than most mainstream writers of Awful Warnings to do extrapolation. The Irish lord who works in an advertising agency and who is one of the more significant characters is working on a campaign for "fuelless" atomic cars. Otherwise, he has extended the trends of the late fifties forwards without actually coming up with any of the actual developments of the sixties. They're getting a Russian invasion and atomic cars, but they are listening to big band dance music and they have teddy boys. This isn't a problem. He tried, and it feels like a reasonable 1960 anyway.

It isn't a cosy catastrophe, but it does have some things in common with one. First, there's a catastrophe, though all the book leads up to it. Second, all but two of the characters are middle or upper class—and those two are very minor, a black American soldier and his Cockney girlfriend. All the others, including the defector who returns briefly from a gulag, are very definitely of the ruling classes. The omniscient narrator says that the working classes have been made just as comfortable and have a high standard of living—but we see lots of servants, and lots of riots and discontent. The main difference is that nobody survives—but a lot of the characters are quite unpleasant, in quite believable ways. The positive characters tend to die heroically, and as for the others, I'm delighted to see some of them get to the gulag. There's a strong flavour of "they got what they deserve" about this book, even more than "it *could* happen here." And there's a huge stress on the cosiness of luxury and alcohol and country houses and church on Sunday.

We spend most time with Patrick, Lord Clonard, who works in advertising, helps the CIA, and worries about his love for the actress Nora May. Nora isn't really a character, we see very little of her point of view. She's married with a son, but having an affair with Patrick. Her sister, the novelist Antonia May, drags Nora into the anti-Nuclear movement. Antonia is really obnoxious. She has a lovely body but an ugly face, she doesn't like real sex and she's pitifully in love with the politician Rupert Page-Gorman—my goodness, his name is enough. Page-Gorman is shown as cynically manipulating the people. He started as a Conservative MP and crossed the floor to Labour when he saw he could do better there. (Did you know Churchill started off as a Tory, crossed to Liberal, became an independent and then ended up back with the Tories?) The Russians, whose inner councils we see, are shown as just as cynical, barely paying lip service to their supposed ideals. The other politicians on both sides are shown as indecisive and narrow of vision—except for Braithwaite, who is genuine and stupid and totally conned by the Russians.

There's one very odd and interesting character, Felix Seligman. He's a financier. (Stop cringing.) Felix is an English Catholic of Jewish ancestry. He's portrayed as genuinely generous, hospitable, loyal, brave and patriotic. He's also the only character to survive out of the camps—he ends up as a notorious guerrilla leader in Wales. (He spent WWII in the Guards.) He's also surprisingly civilized to Nora, even though she doesn't love him and is having an affair with Patrick. He loves their son, and traditions, and he's the only person in the whole book who is entirely uncompromised. Yet though Fitzgibbon is bending over backwards to avoid anti-Semitism, he does give Felix an instinct (which he doesn't obey) that he inherited from his ancestors who used it to get out of Russia and then Germany in time. And he is a financier and he does get a large part of his money out of the country through loopholes—not that it does him or his son any good as things turn out.

Fitzgibbon himself had an interesting background. His father was of the impoverished Irish aristocracy, and his mother was an American heiress. He went to Exeter College Oxford in 1938, and joined the Irish Guards when WWII began in September 1939. When the US came into the war in December 1941 he transferred to the US Army. After the war Fitzgibbon divided his time between London and his Irish property, making a living with writing and journalism. I've read some of his history and biography, it's lively and makes no attempt at impartiality. I think his status as an Irishman in England gave him a particular angle in writing this book, a deep knowledge but a useful slight detachment. I think his class background and experience with living through the British resettlement of the forties led to this particular story, though I suspect the immediate impetus for it was the 1956 events of Suez, proving Britain's political impotence in the wider world, and Hungary, demonstrating Soviet ruthlessness.

I think this book is meant not just as a warning but as a reminder as well. The text states outright that Britain isn't Latvia or Tibet—he means his readers of the Cold War to consider what has happened to Latvia and Tibet, and as the Americans in the story abandon Britain to the USSR, he means the readers to consider that they have abandoned Eastern Europe to it. If you read Orwell's *Collected Essays, Journalism and Letters,* which I very much recommend, you can see Orwell in 1937 suggesting that people buy printing presses, because the day was coming when you wouldn't be able to, and it would be useful to have one for producing samizdat. (He doesn't call it that.) That day didn't come, in Britain, but it did in Eastern Europe, for the Czechs, the Hungarians, the Poles. *When the Kissing Had to Stop* is drawing a real parallel there, saying that Britain shouldn't be comfortable and complacent when the gulags were real and Communism was dominating half the world. The real Russians weren't much like Fitzgibbon's Russians, the real world didn't go his way, but the resolution in the UN in the book to protect the British way of life is modeled on the one brought before the UN in 1959 with reference to Tibet.

71. The future of the Commonwealth: Nevil Shute's In the Wet

I first read *In the Wet* (1953), along with most of Shute, in the seventies when I was a kid. Nevil Shute was, according to his fascinating autobiography *Slide Rule,* an oddly technically and scientifically minded man for a member of the British upper-middle classes in the twenties and thirties. He spent much of his life around flying machines (airships as well as planes) and when he came to write popular fiction, flying machines featured heavily in it. Some of his work is clearly science fiction, *On the Beach* (1957) is probably the best known, and the rest of it tends to be interested in science and engineering in just exactly the way in which SF is and mainstream fiction isn't. Shute flourished from the thirties to the seventies, he was a bestseller. He's always a comfort read for me, and I am especially fond of the work he produced at night during WWII, when he had no idea who was going to win, while working designing planes all day. His best work I think is *Requiem for a Wren* (1955) (aka *The Breaking Wave* in the US, in a particularly stupid example of "what were they thinking" retitling), a novel about getting over WWII, and *A Town Like Alice* (1950) (aka *Legacy* in the US, because how stupid can you get to replace a terrific title with a bland one), a novel about how civilization works. I'm delighted to see that all these books are in print from Random House UK—though they're also the kind of thing your library may well have, and that you can pick up secondhand easily because they were printed in vast quantities.

Shute has huge quantities of the elusive "IWantToReadItosity" that I talked about with reference to Martin's Song of Ice and Fire series. It doesn't matter how many times I've read his books, once I pick one up and read a paragraph I always want to read the whole thing again. Having said all this, it's only fair to say that viewed objectively, *In the Wet* is a very odd book, and clearly influenced by the British upheavals I talked about in the cosy catastrophe post.

This is not the kind of book where spoilers matter.

In the Wet begins with 80 pages (in the Canadian hardcover) of setup. A British Church of England parson explains, in first person, that he's spent much of his life in Australia, that he has malaria, and the circumstances in which he meets a drunken old man called Stevie, and then comes to be at Stevie's bedside during the wet season, as Stevie is dying. Stevie relates his life story—only he doesn't, the priest has malaria and is delirious, a nurse who was also present the whole time heard nothing. Also, the life Stevie tells is a life that takes place in the future—the book was published and this frame is set in 1953, the main part of the story takes place in 1983. It's Stevie's next life as David Anderson that we hear about.

This isn't a frame a science fiction writer would have found necessary or desirable, and it opens up questions about reincarnation that somewhat get in the way of the actual story. Having said that, H. Beam Piper wrote about reincarnation in an entirely SFnal (as opposed to fantastic) way, so it isn't inherently an illegitimate subject. Shute returns to the frame briefly in the middle,

253

as David Anderson's nightmare, and at the end, where the priest christens David as a baby and gets enough evidence from external sources to convince himself that what he has heard is true. It works surprisingly well, though it puts the happy ending in an odd place.

So, we have a story set in 1983. In the afterword to this Canadian edition (which I'm sure wasn't in my old British paperback) Shute says he intends this as speculation about the future of the British Commonwealth. That strikes me as an odd thing to want to do. The US is mentioned twice in the book, once geographically (they're flying over part of it) and once politically—an Australian is asked if he'd want Australia to leave the Commonwealth and join with the States, and reacts with horror. While Canada and other Commonwealth countries get more prominence, this is really a speculation about the future of the two countries Shute knew well—Britain and Australia. Now, the Commonwealth does still exist, and it is of course utterly different from the way Shute imagined it. The Royal Family still exists, as well, but is probably if anything even further from what Shute imagined.

The story of *In the Wet* concerns David Anderson, an Australian pilot who gets a job with the Queen's Flight at a time when Canada and Australia and the rest of the Commonwealth love the Queen and Britain doesn't. There's a constitutional crisis, Britain gets a Governer General, Australia gets the Queen, David Anderson falls in love and becomes engaged to a British girl. It's essentially a sweet love story against a science-fictional background, though there don't seem to have been many technological or social changes since the fifties—people still change for dinner, for instance.

Shute's future Britain is one in which housing prices have collapsed to nothing because of massive emigration, Britain has a shrinking population due to massive emigration, and the country has been socialist for thirty years. It has however remained a world leader in technological advances, despite everyone being pale and pasty and still living on badly managed rations. (He was so wrong about rations. WWII rationing produced the healthiest generation ever.) He simultaneously says that the working classes have had their standard of living raised so it's very high, and talks about how underfed and poor everyone is compared to Australia. This 1983 is an "if this went on" of the post-war settlement taken to great extremes—and also one in which Britain remained economically part of the Commonwealth and not part of Europe, despite geography, while having no immigration at all. Rosemary, the British heroine, has never seen a new house. Shute seems to think it's very important that the British population shrink until the island can feed itself. I don't know why importing food isn't the trivial matter it is in reality. And while I have myself emigrated, Britain has generally been a magnet for immigration.

There's an interesting point here that again demands comparison with Piper. (I wonder if Piper read Shute? Or Shute read Piper either?) Gumption is not in fact genetic. If all your people with gumption emigrate, you'll have just as many people with gumption in the next generation. The same goes with engineering skills. As long as you still have your school system working, it doesn't matter in the long term if you lose technically trained people. Shute's Britain, unlike Piper's Sword Worlds, manages to retain technology, indeed their ability to technologically innovate goes far beyond the real 1983. Japan doesn't seem to be significant in this world. We don't actually see any technology, except for the planes, but there are constant mentions in the abstract of British innovation and engineering. What we don't have, oddly, considering, is any aerospace—this is a 1983 where there hasn't been a moon landing and there are no rockets.

Australia, where Shute emigrated at about the time he was

writing this book, is thriving. The reason it's thriving is because it's had a lot of immigration from Britain (but not from elsewhere in Europe or Asia, unlike in reality) and also because it has thrown out the system of "one man, one vote" and replaced it with a system in which everyone has one vote, and then people get extras for being nifty. It's stated outright that this has produced a better kind of politician, handwave handwave, and this is why Australia has more food, a better climate and new housing developments. The votes are quite explicitly social engineering. Everyone gets one vote. Then you get another for higher education. (David, who has none, got that for becoming a flying officer, which is considered equivalent, and probably is.) There's one for working outside the country for two years—David got that in the war. (Oh yes, BTW, WWIII has happened, we don't know who participated but it wasn't nuclear and seems a lot like WWII in terms of theatres and scale.) Then there's a vote for raising two children to the age of fourteen without getting divorced—husband and wife both get it. There's one for being rich—if your personal income is above a certain high figure. There's one for church officials—any Christian churches. And the Seventh Vote is a special honour, like a knighthood, awarded in special cases to recognise excellence.

David would have three votes in this system, and so would I—do take a moment to calculate how many you'd have, and whether you think the world would be better if you had that much more input. (I think it's reasonable to consider the "wealth" vote at $60,000.) This is a direct response to the "Oh no, the working classes are people!" effect. A typical working-class person isn't going to get more than a maximum of two votes. It's also not as totally bizarre as it looks today—I mean it is, but it wasn't in the context in which Shute was writing. Until 1950, there were additional MPs for university graduates and in Ireland even now, Trinity College Dublin has its own Seanad member. This does mean that qualified people had an extra vote, as Trinity graduates do today. (The present Trinity Seanad member, David Norris, is so cool that it's hard to argue against.) So Shute's idea was an extension of this, and not something completely out of the air. He says that women voting and the secret ballot were first introduced in Australia and then spread to Britain. Of course, while Australia does have compulsory voting, they just have one vote each like other democracies.

All of this is interesting and weird background, but the thing that makes reading *In the Wet* painful now is David Anderson's unfortunate nickname: "Nigger." Shute may have been prejudiced against the working classes, but he really was vastly less racist than was average for his time. Indeed he was miles ahead of almost everybody on not being racist—for 1953. There's a thing that happens sometimes where people are way ahead of society on some issue like this, where because they're out there alone they've made up their own rules, which look much odder to us (who have advanced with society or been born since) than the default ordinary racism (and also sexism) of the time, which we're at least used to.

David Anderson is "a quadroon"; his mother was a "half-caste" Aborigine. David has a "built-in tan." Now in some ways, Shute deals with this excellently, even by today's standards. He has David say proudly that he's "an older Australian than any of them," his "grandmother's tribe ruled the Cape York Peninsula before Captain Cook was born or thought of." Shute's reason for making David a quarter Aboriginal is intended to demonstrate that people of colour are as good as anyone else, and also to give David a disadvantage that he's overcome—he was "born in a ditch in North Queensland" and he is entirely self-made. It's hard to think of another character of colour done this well in popular fiction at this time. I think David must have been quite a surprise to white readers in 1953. I have no idea how Aboriginal readers, or people of colour from other backgrounds, would have taken him, but it was a time when it was notable to have a non-white character visible at all. David is an entirely admirable character, and the book's hero and romantic hero, and the Queen's own pilot. Also, Shute doesn't make this easy by making it a world where colour prejudice has disappeared. David has had to deal with racism all his life. He explains his origins twice in the book, once when offered a job and again when he meets a girl. He says the reason he hasn't married is the colour problem. (That everyone immediately reassures him that he doesn't look all that dark is another indication that prejudice hasn't gone away.)

David's main way of dealing with prejudice is to get it right out into the open by using the nickname "Nigger," so as to have the issue of his mixed-race origins in people's faces. The text seldom or never refers to him that way, but his friends do. It wasn't a nice word in 1953, and Shute was clearly trying to show a world where things were better, and it might be a nickname like "Blondie" and the word has been reclaimed—though it does say that David used to fight people who used it in an unkind way. However it is surprisingly difficult for a modern reader (well, me anyway) to read sentences like "Good night, Nigger darling," without wincing. The word hasn't become neutral, hasn't been reclaimed and is so much more unacceptable now than then. As for actual racism, there are two bits of it. There's the one sentence where David gets to be a "magical negro"—David has an instinctive feeling that something is wrong aboard the plane: "He was one quarter Aboriginal, not wholly of a European stock, and in some directions his perceptions and sensibilities were stronger than in ordinary men, which possibly accounted for his excellence in flying and his safety record." It's only one sentence, but it's pretty bad. There's also the implication that Stevie's rebirth will be lower down the karmic chain, as

Stevie has been an alcoholic wastrel, and I'm not sure the Aboriginal blood isn't supposed to represent that.

But anyway, it's in print again, and there certainly isn't anything else like it.

72. Twists of the Godgame: John Fowles's The Magus

The Magus (1965, revised 1977) is one of those books that ought to be science fiction and is ultimately less satisfying than it could be because it isn't. Fowles himself admits in the introduction that it is a book with problems, and that the people who really like it are adolescents. He's right: I adored this book when I was a teenager. At the same time I was gulping down Heinlein and Piper and Le Guin and Brunner, I couldn't get enough of this. I think of this sometimes when people talk about writing simple books to appeal to young adults—the complexity of The Magus was part of what I loved about it. At the same time that I was failing to understand why Lord of Light (1967) was a classic I was writing lists in my notebook ("Best Books In The World, Ever!!!") that ranked The Magus second only to Tolkien, with The Dispossessed third, Triton fourth and The Moon Is a Harsh Mistress fifth. I like it rather less now for a variety of reasons.

> I was born in 1927, the only child of middle-class parents, both English, and themselves born in the grotesquely elongated shadow, which they never rose sufficiently above history to leave, of that monstrous

dwarf Queen Victoria. I was sent to public school, I wasted two years doing my National Service, I went to Oxford; and there I began to discover I was not the person I wanted to be.

The Magus is a coming-of-age story. A young Englishman, Nicholas, gets a job teaching on a Greek island in 1953. It's worth noting here that the book was written in 1965 and revised in 1977, which allows Fowles to have Nicholas make correct remarks about future trends. Once on the island, Nicholas encounters a Greek millionaire, Conchis, who tells him his life story and involves him in what is eventually called the "god-game," a set of masques, masks, and mysteries, in which nothing and nobody is what they seem, psychological games are played on Nicholas, scenes acted out with and about him, and he is led to question everything he has complacently accepted about himself and the world. What's brilliant about it is the masque, the whole thing is fascinating. Fowles's prose really is marvellous. The stories of Conchis's life are absorbing, and the constant hints of revelation of the purpose of the psychological wringer Nicholas is put through are intriguing. This is a story that twists and turns and tantalises but never quite makes satisfying sense, because the palette with which Fowles found himself equipped didn't lead him to the possibility of any really interesting answers.

When I read this as a teenager, I could identify wholeheartedly with any first-person protagonist—I didn't appreciate that both Bron (the protagonist of *Triton*) and Nicholas here were supposed to be unsympathetic. I did notice some weird gender-essentialism, but supposed it to be one of Nicholas's psychological problems. I'm reluctant to ascribe to authors the faults of characters, but I've since read enough of Fowles to find his women very odd. He seems to think that having a woman withdraw and encourage a man to chase her is the essentially feminine

261

thing—and framing that as women being better than men at seeing relationships doesn't actually help. He also sets up oppositions of England in relation to Europe which don't quite work in this filter.

The Magus is a really good example of the advantages and disadvantages of writing in first person. As Orwell said, we're inclined to believe anything an "I" tells us they did, no matter how improbable. It's easy to swallow improbabilities, it's easy to enter into sympathy. Unsympathetic first-person narrators are a nifty thing to do, but some people won't get it, and not just fifteen-year-olds. The story is filtered entirely and completely through them, you're inclined to believe them and you have to believe them, you have no other source of checking. It's perfectly possible to have a first-person narrator who isn't observant, or who isn't introspective, or who isn't intuitive or a good judge of character—but the norm is to make them all these things because it makes the writer's life so much easier to be able to have them notice things about the world, themselves, and other people. Fowles does some bravura first person in *The Collector*, and he really is an incredibly good writer. But here he wants to have it both ways—he wants Nicholas to be selfish and unempathic, and yet he wants to get away with Nicholas's guesses and intuitions to be more often right than wrong. You can see from that first paragraph I quoted that Nicholas is insightful, has a wider context, and yet we're simultaneously supposed to accept him as insular and ineffective. Fowles has him lurch from one to the other as it's convenient.

I'm going to talk about the end now, so stop reading if you don't want spoilers.

After having the benefit of being the focus of the godgame, having all that attention and all those people revolving around him, nothing could possibly ever be enough for Nicholas. Alison wasn't enough for him before and wouldn't be again. Fowles himself clearly didn't know how to end the story—it had a different ending in the original 1966 version. And by making the focus of the end Alison, it makes the godgame—and by extension life—all about love, about Lily rather than Conchis, it twists at just the wrong moment and sends it away from metaphysics into triviality and romance. Yes, love is important, yes, trusting people is important, yes, Alison is authentic, but can that be the point of the stories of Neuve Chapelle, Seidvarre, de Deukans and the Occupation? I have always been unsatisfied with this resolution. They are at the end floating in blank space, as Cherryh puts it, desperate for any input, any echo. I'm not sure sanity is reachable from there. I can't believe it is supposed to have been a healing. Nicholas's earlier image of himself taken to pieces and needing help with reassembly seems even more apposite at the end.

This is a long book and I always enjoy it as much as or more than I am frustrated by it. But as I was reading it this time, I found myself thinking about the hints Stephenson drops about Enoch Root in *Cryptonomicon* and The Baroque Cycle. I am absolutely sure that Stephenson knows the whole backstory and that it all makes sense and is satisfying and that I will one day either figure it out or have it revealed. In the exact same way, I'm increasingly sure Fowles doesn't know what he's doing, that the underlying reality that is never explained doesn't make sense. I think that what Ted Chiang's "Story of Your Life" does is what Fowles may have wanted to do. In Chiang's story, the protagonist learns an alien language and everything is transformed forever. Chiang manages to convey a sense of that, Fowles doesn't.

It's beautifully written. The characters are so real, I'd recognise them if I saw them at the bus stop. And there's nothing wrong with it that couldn't be fixed by having them go off in an alien spaceship at the end.

73. Playing the angles on a world: Steven Brust's Dragaera

Dragaera is a really cool world, and the publication of *Iorich* in January will be the seventeenth book set there. Seventeen is a pretty significant number for the Dragaerans, and for Brust, so even though I did a post on the Vlad books when *Jhegaala* came out, that was ages ago and it seems like a good time to do some re-reading. Brust tends to write books with seventeen chapters, or double-length books with thirty-four. The Dragaerans have seventeen Houses, and a cycle that gives each House power in turn—though all the books are set when the House of the Phoenix is due to give way to the House of the Dragon real soon now.

Dragaera looks like fantasy but there's no doubt in my mind that it's science fiction underneath, even though there are sorcerers doing magic, witches doing witchcraft, and the occasional person who can manipulate the forces of chaos with his bare mind. (This goes spectacularly wrong sometimes. The Great Sea of Chaos and the Lesser Sea of Chaos, the one where the capital used to be, are evidence for that.) What gives it the science-fictional underpinning is the detailed complicated backstory and the underlying axioms about how things work. You can argue about it, but there are aliens and genetic experiments. It's at least as much science fiction as *Lord of Light*. One of the things that makes Dragaera so real is that Brust has given us two different kinds of stories set there, which lets you triangulate on information in a way I really like. You get this with Cherryh too, but it's unusual. It may also be what's stopped Brust souring on the world and the series—there have been gaps between books, but he has kept them coming, seventeen books since 1983, as well as unrelated books. The series isn't finished, but it is continuing pretty reliably, and there's no sign that Brust's tired of it.

No spoilers at all.

There are the Vlad books (*Jhereg, Yendi, Teckla, Taltos, Phoenix, Athyra, Orca, Dragon, Issola, Dzur, Jhegaala, Iorich*), twelve of a projected nineteen. They tell the story of an Easterner (human) assassin who lives in the underworld of the Dragaeran (elf) Empire. Vlad's all wiseass first person. He has a flying lizard (jhereg) familiar, Loiosh, who's always making psionic wisecracks like, "Can I eat him now, boss?" and "Two dead teckla on your pillow!" Vlad knows a lot about witchcraft, a lot about cooking, quite a bit about how House Jhereg runs its criminal activities, and a lot about how to kill people individually without getting caught. He's less good on history, geography, the way the empire works, and personal relationships. He has some powerful friends, including Morrolan, who has the only floating castle in the world these days. (That disaster that destroyed the capital stopped sorcery from working for a while, so everybody's floating castles crashed. Talk about the bottom falling out of the housing market. . . .) The Vlad books aren't all entirely from Vlad's point of view, *Athyra*'s from the point of view of a Dragaeran boy he meets, and *Orca* alternates between Vlad and another very interesting other person. But mostly, we have Vlad telling the story of his life—and the question of who he's telling it to and why has some interesting answers.

Then there are the Paarfi romances. Paarfi is a Dragaeran, which means he expects to live for at least a couple of thousand years. He's writing historical romances set in his world, about real historical events and real people, much the way (and in the style) Dumas did in ours. The Paarfi romances (*The Phoenix Guards, Five Hundred Years After, The Paths of the Dead, The Lord of Castle Black,* and *Sethra Lavode*) are (mostly) set years before the Vlad books, and deal with events that are backstory or history to Vlad. But some of the people, being Dragaerans, are still alive, and Vlad knows them well, whereas Paarfi is working from historical accounts. Paarfi's good on getting titles and dates right, he understands how the Empire works, he's also great at making up dialogue and motives. If Vlad and Paarfi contradict each other, for instance about the origins of the Interregnum, you have to consider that Vlad knows some of the participants well, but Paarfi will have looked things up. Vlad is Morrolan's friend, and knows some things about him Paarfi doesn't know, but Paarfi's researches might have dug up some information about him that he never mentioned to Vlad, because Vlad didn't meet him until four hundred years after the events of Paarfi's books.

These books are all great fun, good adventures, you don't have to read them looking for background-world clues. All the same, one of the things I love about them is the way you can absolutely trust that Brust knows what he's doing, that his details add up, that he mentions a really good restaurant called Valabars a handful of times and finally takes you there in *Dzur*, that by the time you meet the Jenoine and the Serioli you have such a healthy curiosity about the hints dropped about them that you want to ring your friends and tell them there's a Serioli! And it never falls flat. Brust pulls off bravura tricks of storytelling, revelations, secrets, backstory, complexities, and it's never silly, never too much, never unbelievable. Although he's been writing these books since 1983 they are consistent in feel, almost never contradictory, and build up a solid world.

So, onwards to the individual volumes!

74. Jhereg feeds on
others' kills:
Steven Brust's Jhereg

One of the things we disagree about in our house is series reading order. (Families in movies always squabble about whose turn it is to take out the garbage or wash the dishes. It must be very boring to be them.) However, generally where publication order and internal chronological (IC) order are different Emmet likes reading a series in publication order and I like reading them in IC order. (We first met on rec.arts.sf.written disagreeing about reading order for Womack's Dryco books, so this is a long-standing difference of opinion.) I think I mentioned when I re-read the Miles books in publication order that I always normally read them in IC order. I used to do the same with the Vlad Taltos books until with the publication of *Dragon* Brust made that impossible. The reason I prefer it is that with reading in publication order you can see how a writer develops and how they develop their idea of where the series is going, but by IC order you can see how the characters develop when events happen to them in order. Pamela Dean once said that you should read Patrick O'Brian's Aubrey and Maturin books in order if you normally read chapters of a book in order. That's how I feel. Reading them out of IC order requires building a structure in my head to fit the characters and events into, with "how we got from here to there" arrows and bars as part of it. But since playing with structure and making you hold things in your head is one of Brust's things, here we go, publication order.

I have to say that *Jhereg* (1983) is a very satisfying introduction to the series and to the world. There are seventeen Houses of the Dragaeran Empire, and the series is intended to have a book for each House plus an introduction and a conclusion, making nineteen in all. In each book, there's a significant character belonging to the House in question, and also Vlad acts in the way characteristic for that House. So in *Jhereg* he is hired to kill someone and it runs into complications. *Jhereg* begins with a little about Vlad's early life and how he acquired a jhereg familiar—a poisonous flying lizard with human intelligence and psionic capability. It then plunges directly into the story, showing Vlad running his own area, happily married, with powerful friends, he accepts a contract for more money than he's ever had before, we learn a lot about the world.

The way the characters are introduced as friends, and the way they work as friends, is excellent. We're going to see in earlier-set books, these relationships beginning, we're going to see Vlad a lot less confident, and then in later-set books we'll see him develop a conscience. *Jhereg*'s a good introduction and also a good story. This was the first Vlad book I read—I'd previously read *Brokedown Palace* and *The Phoenix Guards,* which is a much less good introduction to the world. I can remember thinking with the overcast that perpetually covers the Empire and the way the Cycle works that now I got it.

If you haven't read these, *Jhereg* is a fine place to start.

Spoilers from here on, potentially for everything except *Iorich,* which I haven't read yet.

Chronologically, *Jhereg* comes about a year after *Yendi* and pretty much immediately before *Teckla*.

Thematically, Vlad spends the book trying to assassinate a member of the House of Jhereg, thus acting like a Jhereg and with the book revolving around a Jhereg. There's also the acquisition of Loiosh in the prologue and of Rocza at the end, providing plenty of jheregs.

The actual plot of *Jhereg* is extremely neat. Mellar has been plotting for several hundred years to destroy the Houses of the Jhereg, the Dragon and the Dzur. He's doing this because he's a mixture of all three and feels underappreciated by all of them. His death at Jhereg hands in Castle Black really would accomplish what he wants. The shape of the book is really the shape of Vlad working out what's going on. The pace of revelation is excellent, both for the Mellar plot, the world, and the revealed backstory about Vlad's soul and the beginning of the Empire. The information about that and the Interregnum directly contradicts Paarfi, and I'm going with Vlad's account direct from Aliera's mouth here. I also very much like the way everyone has to go around Morrolan's code of honour and the Jhereg code of honour—the idea that they'd recover from a war in ten thousand years, but if they lost their reputation they'd never recover.

Despite trying hard, I can't see any setup here for the unhappy marriage in *Teckla*. There's some in *Yendi,* but here I don't think it's Vlad being oblivious—I'm not seeing it either. Cawti would like to work, sure, but that's all. I remember when I first read it liking very much that there wasn't a romantic subplot—romances and divorces are common in fiction, people who are quietly happily married all through a book are notably rare. Oh well.

Neat little things: Vlad's vision, including Devera. We know what almost all these bits are now?

"There is a cry of 'charge' and five thousand Dragons come storming at the place the Eastern army is entrenched." (*Dragon*)

"Making love with Cawti that first time—the moment of entry even more than the moment of release. I wonder if she plans to kill me before we're finished and I don't really care." (*Yendi*)

"The Dzur hero, coming alone to Dzur Mountain, sees Sethra Lavode stand up before him, Iceflame in her hand." (*Dzur*)

"A small girlchild with big brown eyes looks at me, and smiles." (Devera getting everywhere as usual—possibly specifically from *Tiassa*?)

"The energy bolt, visible as a black wave, streaks towards me, and I swing Spellbreaker at it, wondering if it will work." (*Issola*)

"Aliera stands up before the shadow of Kieron the Conquerer, there in the midst of the Halls of Judgement, in the Paths of the Dead beyond Deathsgate Falls." (*Taltos*)

I've always wondered how much of the whole story he knew before he started it and how much he's making up as he goes along, and this implies "lots." It must take a lot of confidence to make a first novel the start of a nineteen-book series.

Other cool things: it sets up an insoluble problem and then finds a very satisfactory solution to it. Also, Brust is doing a thing where he has a wisecracking assassin professional criminal and you accept him as a good guy. He's setting that up for undermining later, but it's worth noting the way he takes genre conventions here (as with *Agyar*) and uses them to mess with your head.

75. *Yendi coils and strikes unseen: Steven Brust's Yendi*

Yendi (1984) was published a year after *Jhereg* but is set a year or so before it. If I hadn't read them bound in one (phenomenally ugly) volume I'd have assumed I'd picked them up in the wrong order. But indeed, Brust's plan in writing a series was to choose immediately to go back and fill in a volume of earlier events. That's risky, as the reader who reads in publication order knows how it's going to come out. Brust doesn't rely on suspense for tension, but rather on the interest of the twisty plot. You know Vlad's going to survive and win and get the girl—but there's a general expectation of that anyway in the kind of book this purports to be.

Vlad's voice, hard-boiled and cynical first person, has been compared to Zelazny, and also to classic American hard-boiled detective fiction, but Vlad isn't a detective, he's a criminal. Nevertheless, in both *Jhereg* and *Yendi* he solves mysteries. The plot in *Yendi* is complicated and twisty, as you might expect— yendi the animal are kind of heraldic poisonous snakes.

I think *Yendi* would be a perfectly reasonable place to start the series.

Spoilers for *Yendi* start here. Actually, a general spoiler policy on these posts. I haven't read *Iorich* yet, and neither have most other people. Please don't spoil it. When I read it, there'll be an *Iorich* review, and it will have a spoiler section. Until then, no spoilers in comments please. However, spoilers for any of the other Dragaera books are fine. I'm going on the general assumption that you've either read them all or don't care.

Vlad in *Yendi* is notably younger, brasher and less confident, but still himself. That's quite impressive. Not all writers can make that work. Apart from the fact it's set before *Jhereg* and has Vlad's meeting with Cawti, *Yendi* doesn't play games with time. We know Vlad's going to be married to Cawti the second we see her—even before we hear her name, because we were told about how they met. We know Vlad's going to win the Jhereg war and get an enlarged area. What keeps us reading is finding out how, which is itself a twisty Yendi thing to do.

As for Cawti, the whole "killing him first and then falling in love" is done very well. Here we do see setup and warning signs for the relationship and for the situation as of *Teckla*—most noticeably Vlad thinking of Cawti as a female version of himself, and Vlad leaping to conclusions about her and about himself. They fall in love awfully quickly and with really insufficient thought—but that's how people do. We see Noish-pa for the first time here, though he was mentioned in *Jhereg*. There couldn't be a nicer happy ending.

Everything is still upbeat and light, even with the hard-boiled tone. With the plot, re-reading, it's obvious that every time the Sorceress in Green is mentioned Vlad assumes she's an Athyra and Morrolan doesn't get the chance to correct him. She is in fact the Yendi of the title—and as well as her long plot, Vlad spends much of the book plotting and trying to figure out plots. The whole situation with Norathar is interesting—and it's also interesting that Brust doesn't really make much use of Norathar

273

in the series. She's been Cawti's partner, but she's very much kept in the background.

I like *Yendi*, it's sufficiently like *Jhereg* that it satisfies my "give me another cookie" craving and sufficiently different to be interesting.

76. A coachman's tale: Steven Brust's Brokedown Palace

Brokedown Palace (1986) was the first Brust I read. I'd heard him
well spoken of online, and I couldn't quite bring myself to pick up
the extremely ugly British edition of the first three Vlad books,
and this was in the library. It was an unusual place to start with
Dragaera, but not a terrible one. It's a very odd book, and it was
very odd of Brust to write it after *Yendi* and before *Teckla*. It's set in
the East, in Fenario, and you wouldn't know it was Dragaera at all
except that it clearly is. It's written like a fairy tale—and it is punc-
tuated with things written even more like fairy tales. It draws on
Brust's Hungarian background, and it's connected to the Grateful
Dead song "Brokedown Palace."

I really like this book and I thoroughly enjoyed reading it,
but it's so dreamlike and odd that I find it very difficult to talk
about coherently. It's like trying to pick up fragments of mist.
Brilliant book. Very weird.

The story is about a family of brothers who live in the kingdom
of Fenario, on the borders of Faerie. The eldest, Laszlo, is the king,
and he beats up the youngest, Miklos, because Miklos mentions
that the palace is falling down. Dying, Miklos slips into the River

that flows out of Faerie, and one of the great powers of the land. Then he meets a talking horse and after that it gets weird. The book is a fairy tale about brothers, death, life, renewal, magic, love and keeping norska. (Norska are rabbits. Rabbits like the rabbit in *Monty Python and the Holy Grail*. I instantly recognised that as a norska the first time I saw the film.)

This book is undoubtedly a fairy tale. It's also undoubtedly set in Dragaera which is easily seen as science-fictional. The orange overcast that covers the Empire is here as the "hand of Faerie" and in the same way the magic here is infinitely more magical. There's a lot less of it. In the Vlad books, people routinely make psionic communication and raise the dead. Here a bit of magical healing is very unusual. But what there is, isn't taken for granted, isn't routine, is magical, perhaps even magical realist—there's a taltos horse (which raises questions about why Vlad is called "taltos") that can talk, there's a tree that becomes a palace, and a river with an agenda. All the magic in the Vlad books can be categorised, repeated, relied on. Here, none of it can.

I find myself reading it now with double vision. Looked at one way Miklos goes into Faerie and labours for two years and comes back as a wizard. Looked at another he goes into the Empire, becomes a Teckla, gets a perfectly ordinary connection to the Orb and learns a little sorcery. There's the whole thing of killing Verra and stopping sorcery from working. It's a very weird book, and I suspect it contains some keys to the universe if only I could see them clearly. Certainly, standing here I never had any confusion about the overcast, that the Furnace is the sun and that you never see clear sky.

The book starts with the legend of Fenarr, which is seen from the Dragaeran side in *The Phoenix Guards*. This is clearly the same incident, the same set of events, seen through that doubled vision—from the Eastern side it's ringed about with fantasy, mist, legend, magic, from the Dragaeran side it's a clever bit of diplomacy. This may have something to do with the length of time an Easterner lives. Fenarr is a legend in Fenario, but "Lord Kav," with whom he arranged the peace, is still alive.

It doesn't say so in the book, but I have heard as extra-canonical information that Brigitta's baby (the one people will have to look out for) is Cawti. Interesting if true, and a bit mind-boggling.

77. Frightened teckla hides in grass: Steven Brust's Teckla

The first time I read *Teckla* (1987) I hated it. Hated it. I like it now, but it took quite a lot of time for me to come around to it.

Teckla is set in the same fun fantasy world of Dragaera as the first two books of the series, but unlike the romps that are *Jhereg* and *Yendi* it's a real downer. The animals the House of the Teckla are named after are mice, and the Teckla are the peasants and proletarians of the Empire. The book takes places chronologically immediately after *Jhereg* and it is about a proletarian uprising among the Teckla and Easterners (humans) of South Adrilankha. It's about ordinary people getting caught up with the Jhereg and the nasty side of assassins—it's no fun at all when it's killing ordinary men and women who are threatening the profits of organized crime. It's also about the messy end of a relationship. It's about passing and being proud or ashamed of what you are.

What I hated about it was that it was grim and depressing and realistic in a way that turned the first two volumes inside out. That's what I now appreciate about it. *Teckla* provides some necessary grounding, some chiaroscuro to the palette of Dragaera.

Spoilers.

Brust really uses his American-Hungarian heritage in these books. The Easterners, Fenarians, have Hungarian names and Hungarian culture, and he also uses Hungarian mythology and ideas about magic and witchcraft. But it's not only that, it's also the whole thing of being an immigrant in a wider culture, either getting trapped in a ghetto or getting out and despising those who don't. Vlad is a third-generation immigrant. His grandfather came from Fenario and lives in the ghetto, his father got out and aped the Dragaerans he lived among, and Vlad is uncomfortably caught between cultures. He knows he can't really be a Dragaeran, but he has a Jhereg title and there's the whole question of his soul that came up in *Jhereg*. He's uncomfortable with all this, and when Cawti gets involved with the revolutionary group he gets uncomfortable about that. There's a lot here that demonstrates understanding of what it is to live on the underside of a rich culture and the kind of things people do about that.

Vlad spends a lot of this book literally hiding, and being frightened and miserable. As *Yendi* was the beginning of his marriage with Cawti, this is the end. This is a closely observed example of one of the ways a couple can split up—Cawti is more interested in what she's doing in South Adrilankha than in her marriage, and Vlad can't won't and doesn't want to change. She has moved on and left him behind, and what he wants he can't have—if the Cawti of his imagination was ever real, she's gone.

The Teckla of the title is probably Paresh, who tells Vlad his life story at length. This is one of the most interesting bits of the book, how Paresh, a peasant, became a sorcerer and a revolutionary. Vlad isn't solving a mystery here, as in the first two books. He tries to deal with a problem, and finds some answers, but the conclusion is at most only a deep breath—the real conclusion is in *Phoenix*. (If there were any sense to the multiple volumes, *Teckla* and *Phoenix* would be bound together.)

None of Vlad's noble friends from the earlier books appear here. Morrolan tries to contact Vlad once, but we don't see any of them and they're barely mentioned. This is in keeping with the general Teckla tone of the book, and the general depressing tone too. It would be livened up with some of Morrolan and Aliera's sparkling dialogue. There's not much that sparkles here at all.

The peasants are unhappy, the urban poor are unhappy, they're getting organized—that's really unusual for a fantasy world. It could be described as socialist fantasy, and it's certainly informed by a Marxist worldview—which we learn in *Phoenix* is the view from the wrong world. That isn't how things work in Dragaera. (So clever he should watch out he doesn't cut himself.)

Teckla has a fascinating organizational structure. It's the usual seventeen chapters, but the book begins with a laundry list—a list of clothes sent to the laundry with instructions about cleaning and mending them, and each chapter is headed with a little bit of that list like "remove bloodstains from cuff," and in that chapter you see how the cuff got bloodstained, or how the cat hairs got onto the cloak, and so on. I've never seen anything even remotely like that done before or since.

78. How can you tell? Steven Brust's Taltos

Taltos (1988) is set before all the other books in the series, or at least all the books written so far. It's a great place to start, especially for people who like reading by internal chronology. It's also a very good book, one of the best. It's surprising that Brust preferred to circle back and tell this story instead of finishing the story he'd started in *Teckla,* but I'm sure he had his reasons. *Taltos* is the story of how the young Jhereg assassin Vlad Taltos grew up, met some of the friends and colleagues he relies on in the earlier written later-set books, and how they get him embroiled in larger events and have an adventure.

Spoilers, including a spoiler for *Orca.*

Taltos is the first of the Vlad books to have a weird structure. The book is ordered in seventeen chapters, as usual, but each chapter begins with an account of Vlad doing a spell that, if written chronologically, he does in the last chapter. Each chapter also contains a flashback to Vlad's childhood and youth—these are in chronological order in themselves, but not in terms of the overall story. There are two threads, Vlad growing up and Vlad's buttonman going to Dzur Mountain and the consequences of that. That's three threads with the spell. Fortunately this is all held together by Vlad's voice and by the interest of the events.

Reading in publication order, the reader is already aware that they succeed in rescuing Aliera—Aliera is a major character in the later-set books. However, seeing Vlad meeting Morrolan and Sethra and Aliera, and discovering something about the Paths of the Dead, is so inherently interesting that this doesn't matter at all. Also, if you read the books in chronological order, you get *Taltos* and then *Yendi* (well, you used to), which gives you two books in sequence in which a new Dragon Heir is discovered. This way, they're well separated.

Taltos is very much about Vlad as a human, and what it means to be an Easterner among Dragaerans. It's also strongly about Vlad doing witchcraft. If "taltos" has the meaning that "taltos horse" has in *Brokedown Palace,* then it definitely has something to do with innate magic. Vlad creates a spell to move an object.

It's clear to see how the object itself, the god's blood that Kiera gives Vlad, lets Morrolan escape. It's less clear why Kiera/Sethra gave it to Vlad with such vague instructions. Surely it would have been more useful for her to tell him to take it. I'm not sure what odd rules Sethra is playing by—I don't know if it's possible for us to understand. Maybe making Vlad work it out for himself is part of it. Similarly, seeing Vlad without Spellbreaker makes it clear how powerful sorcery is and how much Spellbreaker does for Vlad.

Taltos is one of my favourites of the series. I like Loiosh, I like the stuff about Noish-pa, I love the way people in the Paths of the Dead keep being surprised they're alive and Vlad keeps asking them how they can tell, I like the first meetings, especially with Lady Teldra and with Morrolan. I like the way Vlad doesn't understand why Verra is so pleased Aliera's soul has been found. (It must have been an awful shock for Verra when Aliera's body and the Orb showed up.)

282

79. Phoenix rise from ashes grey: Steven Brust's Phoenix

Maybe it's just me, but it seems like when things are going wrong—your wife is ready to leave you, all your notions about yourself and the world are getting turned around, everything you trusted is becoming questionable—there's nothing like having someone try to kill you to take your mind off your problems.

Phoenix (1990) completes the story begun in *Teckla* and starts a whole new phase of Vlad Taltos's life. It's the story of how Vlad Taltos the Jhereg assassin is sent on a mission by a god, and everything changes. It's written in the general form of a "how to assassinate" manual, and yet it's the furthest from that pattern of story of any of the books so far. I don't know if it would be a good introduction to the series—I suspect not, I suspect that it works best if you already know the characters. For the first time, we meet Zerika, the Empress. For the first time we get to see somewhere outside the Empire. It's a different kind of book. Did anyone start here? Did it work? I really can't tell.

This is the first one I have in a nice edition—the British

publishers gave up after *Taltos,* perhaps surprised that nobody bought books with such awful covers.

If you hate *Teckla,* you may hate *Phoenix* too, but I never did. Unlike *Teckla* it has many saving moments—"where I come from, we call this a drum." There's trouble between Vlad and Cawti, there's an Easterners and Teckla uprising, but that isn't the whole focus, the book doesn't get sunk into it.

The phoenix is a bird, mythical in our world but presumably real in Dragaera, though we're never shown one. It "sinks into decay" and "rises from ashes grey." Vlad seems to believe that nobody is born a Phoenix unless a phoenix is passing overhead when they're born, but in the Paarfi books we see ordinary members of the House of the Phoenix, they just almost all died in Adron's Disaster. The Cycle is in the House of the Phoenix and Zerika (the only living member of the House of the Phoenix, a reborn Phoenix rising from the ashes) is Phoenix Empress. It's hard to say what it's like to be a Phoenix apart from being Empress, what they'd be like in another House's reign. If it's true that as Alexx Kay has calculated the Cycle will turn in 61 years, perhaps Vlad will still be alive to see. In any case, Zerika is the Phoenix that the book mentions, and for Vlad to behave like a Phoenix means putting the good of the Empire above his own concerns. Vlad's constantly sacrificing himself for something or other in this book, and ends by betraying the Jhereg to the Empire and going into exile.

Brust must already have been gearing up to write *The Phoenix Guards* when he wrote *Phoenix.* There are a number of mentions of how things were before the Interregnum, which has never been mentioned before, and one mention of Paarfi himself, when Cawti is reading one of his romances. My favourite of these is when Vlad and Cawti have a choice of crossing the city by weary walking or nauseating teleporting and they wish that there were another option, like the carriages people used to have before they could casually teleport everywhere. The amulet Noish-pa makes Vlad against the nausea caused by teleporting, or "crossing fairyland" as he puts it, is one of my favourite moments—the nausea has been established and taken for granted and it turns out that there's been a way to fix it all the time.

I tend to think of these books as having progressing time and gap filling. In progressing time, *Phoenix* is the last of the books in which Vlad Taltos is an assassin based in Adrilankha with an organization and an office with a secretary (genuinely shocking betrayal by Melestav, after so long) and Kragar coming in unnoticed. Vlad's spent a lot of time away from the office in the books, but that's always been there behind him. There is a sense of death and rebirth about Phoenix, endings and new beginnings. Whatever Vlad is in the subsequent books, he's not that.

In chronological order it would be *Jhegaala* next, and I've never read them like that. (Next time!) In fact, onward to *The Phoenix Guards,* and thence *Athyra*.

80. I have been asking for nothing else for an hour: Steven Brust's The Phoenix Guards

The Phoenix Guards (1991) is a novel in the mode of *The Three Musketeers*. It's set in Brust's world of Dragaera, but almost a thousand years before the Vlad books. The Vlad books are hard-boiled wisecracking first person, the Paarfi books are long-winded romantic omniscient. *The Phoenix Guards* is delightful. Four young (barely a hundred years old) Dragaerans travel to Dragaera City on the accession of the Phoenix Emperor Tortalik with the intention of taking up positions in the newly formed Phoenix Guards. They are of different Houses but they're all young and enthusiastic, they love honour, adventure, dueling and sword-play. They share an immense zest for life. Khaavren is an honour-loving Tiassa, Tazendra is an impetuous Dzur, Aerich is a thoughtful Lyorn who likes crocheting, and Pel is a devious Yendi. They fight crime! And they have adventures! And the adventures are related by a historian who insists he is sticking to the facts, which does seem doubtful from time to time.

I think Paarfi's style, as well as being infectious—an infection that I am endeavouring to the best of my ability to resist for the purposes of this article—is something people either love or hate. I love it. Give me chapter titles like "In which the author resorts to a stratagem to reveal the results of a stratagem" or "In which our friends realise with great pleasure that the situation has become hopeless" and I am happy all day. If you like the style this is a lighthearted adventure about four high-spirited friends bantering and dueling their way into trouble and out of it again, and I recommend it highly. I read this before I read the Vlad books, and there are things about the world that were utterly opaque to me but I still thoroughly enjoyed it.

For those who pretend they have no objection to spoilers, and on the general assumption the reader has done themselves the honour of reading the books . . .

So, with Brust's having given us Vlad and alternated between novels in the main continuity and novels set earlier than *Jhereg*, and throwing everything into confusion with *Brokedown Palace*, I think it's reasonable to say that nobody could have expected this Dumas pastiche. It isn't a retelling of *The Three Musketeers* in Dragaera, it's more something inspired by the concept of *The Three Musketeers* and Sabatini mixing with a solid fantasy world to come up with something totally original. This was Brust's first book for Tor, though he continued to publish with Ace as well for a few more books.

As far as the world of Dragaera is concerned, it gives us another angle, and it tells us a lot about life before the Interregnum, when things Vlad takes for granted like revivification, psionic communication and teleportation were incredibly difficult. It's a very different world, and yet it's recognisably the same world, with the Houses, the Cycle, and glimpses of the science-fictional explanations underlying the fantastic surface. Of all the Khaavren romances, *The Phoenix Guards* has the least historical relevance. The battle of Pepperfields, and the peace that Khaavren ("Lord Kav") makes with the Easterners, is the same battle that we see in *Brokedown Palace,* from an utterly different perspective. (Reading these two first made me think this was a lot more significant than it turns out to be.) We meet Adron, five hundred years before his famous rebellion and disaster, and Aliera is born—announced by Devera.

I go through the Vlad books like cookies, gobbling them as fast as I can, grabbing another as soon as I finish the one in my hand. *Brokedown Palace* is like a baked Alaska, hot and cold at once, and very puzzling. *The Phoenix Guards* is like a warm croissant with melted chocolate and strawberries, you can't gulp it down like a cookie, you have to savour it, but it's an utterly delicious confection.

81. Athyra rules minds' interplay: Steven Brust's Athyra

Athyra is a complete departure from the rest of the Vlad Taltos series, in that it isn't in Vlad's voice. All the other Vlad books up to this point, whatever order they've been written in, have had Vlad's first-person wiseass voice to carry them along. Yendi starts: "Kragar says that life is like an onion, but he doesn't mean the same thing by it that I do." It goes on to do wonderful things with that simile, the Dragaeran Houses, life, and it connects through the whole book. You can't trust Vlad to know about things, or even necessarily to tell the truth—he's not so much unreliable as shifty, and he has his own agenda. But you can rely on his storytelling to carry you through anything. So when I picked up *Athyra* it was a shock to find myself in third person, and the point of view of a young Teckla boy. *Athyra* was the second book of this series, after *Teckla,* that I hated the first time I read it. It grew on me—indeed, it grew on me much more than *Teckla,* which is always difficult to read. *Athyra* is now one I really admire, and I like it for the change in perspective as much as anything.

Viewed away from the context and expectations of the rest

of the series, *Athyra* is an exceptional fantasy novel, and I almost wish I had read it first. Savn is a peasant boy of about ninety, of an expected lifespan of a couple of thousand years. The book gives us a good view of his life in his village. He's embedded in his life, his village, his friends, his apprenticeship to the doctor, the harvest, his parents and sister. The village makes sense. The way the magic fits into his worldview is different from anything we've seen in Dragaera and yet it's smooth and easy. Savn's a great character. He's curious and intelligent. Without the other books, the story of *Athyra* is "mysterious stranger comes to town and turns everything upside down." The other point of view is Rocza, and she's also done brilliantly—Loiosh with his wisecracking is a great foil for Vlad but even with "Two dead teckla on your pillow" and "Can I eat him now?" he's too human, he's been brought up with Vlad from an egg. Rocza is plausibly an intelligent animal.

Writing the lines from the Cycle as headings for these posts, I'm surprised to find I know some of them, and this was one. I have never consciously set out to learn them, but some of them are very memorable. Also, some Houses are very significant in the series. We've seen a lot of Athyra before *Athyra*. I had a lot of expectations about meeting some wizards. Well, we do, but not in the way I expected. The Athyra in *Athyra* is Loraan, who we thought had been killed in Taltos. Vlad acts like an Athyra very directly—he philosophises a great deal, and as he tells Savn, Athyra use people, and Vlad uses Savn. Vlad's been using people all along, but not quite like this.

> "There are two types of Athyra, some are mystics who attempt to explore the nature of the world by looking within themselves, and some are explorers, who look upon the world as a problem to be solved, and thus

reduce other people to either distractions or pieces of a puzzle and treat them accordingly."

Vlad does both of these things in this book. The first time I read it, I wondered if it wasn't out of character, and then I started wondering if Vlad showing typical characteristics of each of the Houses in each book wasn't all acting out of character, and what it means about character that he does. I think that's one of the benefits of seeing him from outside here, because one of the things about first-person voice is that it's very convincing, whatever it says. Vlad philosophising here sounds like Vlad talking about the simile of the onion, he isn't out of character at all, he just has a multi-faceted character. Maybe the Houses were a Jenoine experiment in dividing character, or maybe people think they ought to have the characteristics of their House and concentrate on that—which is why Kragar left but is still a Dragon.

I love the bits that wouldn't work as well if this were a standalone book, the bits where the reader is privileged to know what's going on with Vlad and the jhereg, and Vlad and the Jhereg, where Savn isn't. That's done beautifully. This is also the first time we see Vlad's missing finger and hear the first of his lies—or rather misdirections—concerning how it happened. At the end of *Phoenix* we see him heading off to a new life, and this is our first view of him in it—from outside, and considerably battered.

The thing I still hate about *Athyra* is the end. After spending a whole book with Savn and coming to really like him, it's unbearable to see his mind broken that way. If it wasn't for that, this would be one I'd look forward to reading.

Onwards to *Five Hundred Years After,* that'll cheer me up!

82. What, is there more?
Steven Brust's Five Hundred Years After

Five Hundred Years After is a direct sequel to *The Phoenix Guards* but the interesting thing about it is what a different kind of book it is. *The Phoenix Guards* is an unabashed romp, this is quite a serious novel—after all it is the story of something known to history as "Adron's Disaster." As *The Phoenix Guards* is very loosely based on *The Three Musketeers,* this is even more loosely based on the sequel, *Twenty Years After.* But while *The Phoenix Guards* is about equally rooted in Dumas and Dragaera, this is much more a work of Dragaeran historical fiction, and a kind of meta-commentary on the whole concept of historical fiction.

It is a commonplace for a historical novel to deal with an event with which the readers are familiar. Readers may not know the details of the French Revolution, or the Civil War, but when they pick up a novel about it they'll know at least that heads will be lost by, on the one hand aristocrats, and on the other King Charles. It's possible for the writer to use that knowledge to draw upon historical irony to underline the story. It's a very unusual thing for a fantasy novel to do, because the reader doesn't have that background—usually in genre fiction the writer has to feed the reader the context along with the story. Brust gets away with it here because we've been hearing about Adron's Disaster since *Jhereg,* and anyone who has read the books up to this point does know of the event in general outline. I have no idea what *Five Hundred Years After* would look like to someone who hadn't read the Vlad books. I wanted to read it as soon as I'd finished *The Phoenix Guards,* but Emmet (who, you may remember, vastly prefers reading in publication order) absolutely insisted that I had to have read at least *Jhereg* first. I think it would have been a very different experience, but what I wouldn't have had is the interesting experience of historical inevitability informing a fantasy novel.

All of the ingredients of *The Phoenix Guards* are here, but the tone is much less carefree. For much of the book Khaavren is lonely and alone, he is united with all his friends at once only at the end. There's a feeling of inevitable doom hanging over everything, until at last doom strikes.

> In a flash, in an instant, all were gone, as was the Palace and all the landmarks and buildings by which the city was known and for which it was loved, as well as those others, all but unknown yet landmarks in their own way—the Silver Exchange, the Nine Bridges Canal, Pamlar University, the nameless cabaret in the Underside where Lord Garland had conspired with his daughter, the equally nameless inn where, upon entering the Guard five hundred years before, Khaavren had killed a man named Frai. All of these were now gone forever, preserved only in the memories of those who had seen them, or in such works of art as happened to depict them—of all the buildings and artifacts by which the city was known, only the Orb itself was preserved.

The Phoenix Guards is a comedy and *Five Hundred Years After* is a tragedy—yet it's a tragedy told in comic mode. Paarfi remains as funny as ever, with his asides and manner of speech. The inimitable banter is as good as ever. Khaavren finds true love, and all the friends miraculously escape the calamity. Of all of this I'm least satisfied with the romance; it is (as Paarfi acknowledges) perfunctory—when all the other characterisation is so good, Daro remains a cypher. I also find the villains less interesting than in *The Phoenix Guards*.

Of course Paarfi contradicts some of what we thought we knew about Adron's Disaster, and gives us another angle on it entirely. That Aliera and the almost mythical Mario should be having a relationship is news, and the way the disaster came about isn't at all what Aliera told Vlad in *Jhereg*. Aliera wouldn't have talked to Paarfi—but he's undoubtedly right about all the checkable details.

Paarfi wrote this several years after the events of the Vlad novels as we have them, in the reign of Norathar. He was writing as early as the time of *Phoenix,* because Cawti reads one of his romances. He therefore lives after the Interregnum, at a time when sorcery is vastly more powerful, teleporting others or oneself is common, and telepathic communication is trivial. It's strange that he writes about Sethra's teleport as something astonishing and unheard of and as if he's expecting his readers to be astonished by it. David Goldfarb suggests in the *Phoenix Guards* thread:

> I have a strong suspicion that magic wasn't quite so difficult nor rare during this period as Paarfi portrays it. I think Paarfi doesn't like magic, and rewrites his histories to downplay it. That would explain a lot.

83. Orca circles,
hard and lean:
Steven Brust's Orca

Orca was the first Dragaera book I had to wait for—all the others up to this point were out when I started reading. This is one of the ones I loved straightaway. It's set in what I'm calling the main continuity, following on fairly directly from *Athyra*—by which I mean that I'd be very surprised if there were a book set between them. (I wouldn't faint from astonishment, because honestly, Brust has surprised me so many times in this series and made it work that I wouldn't put anything past him.) I was going to say that *Orca* would be a terrible place to start, and certainly it contains spoilers for everything up to this point, as well as many fascinating revelations and reversals, but I don't know, for some people it might be a great introduction to the series. These books are so smart and complicated and subtle, I'm really glad that they sell well. Whenever I feel irritated with the concept of genre fantasy I think of the success of the Vlad books as evidence that you can get away with doing something different and exciting with it.

Spoilers: I mean it!

Orca alternates first-person points of view between Vlad and

Kiera the Thief, who is revealed at the end to be Sethra Lavode in disguise. I'd never have guessed—even re-reading here, I don't notice the things that give her away to Vlad, and generally I don't see it in the other books. It doesn't feel wrong, but . . . very odd. It makes sense of some things. There is a lot of "I tele-ported home" or "to a place where I could . . . ," which with the context is clearly Dzur Mountain, but which you can't tell with-out. It's more of that Agyar-shadow-space expectation-shaping by misdirection. Kiera/Sethra's sections are narrated to Cawti—at least, mostly. She says she's leaving things out, and we don't know if she tells Cawti about her true identity. At the very end there's one mention of the child Vlad Norathar—a child Vlad doesn't know about, and with which she must have been pregnant at the end of *Phoenix*.

Vlad is on top form throughout *Orca,* wisecracking, convers-ing with Loiosh, and after *Athyra* I was very glad to have his voice back. Yet as his parts are related to Kiera/Sethra and not to mys-terious metal boxes or whatever, he's different. *Orca* are capitalists and sailors. He doesn't go on any ships, but he spends the whole book acting like an Orca, tangled up in business, trying to untangle the complicated business affairs of a dead Orca, Fyres, to sort out the property rights of a woman who is trying to cure Savn. The whole complicated property scam sounds remarkably like what happened to the U.S. mortgage market last year, which is impressive for a book published in 1996. It's interesting—the whole plot of *Orca* is very interesting, especially as the implica-tions widen and widen.

Savn's partial recovery is encouraging, but I do hope we see him again.

84. Haughty dragon yearns to slay: Steven Brust's Dragon

Dragon was the first Vlad book to come out from Tor. It was published in 1998, a year after Emmet and I had met Steve Brust when he was guest of honour at Convocation in Cambridge, and when I first read *Dragon* I did wonder whether he'd written it this way deliberately to stop it being possible for me to read the series in internal chronological order. *Dragon* is not in the ongoing chronology, but set way back between *Taltos* and *Yendi,* with a frame story set immediately after *Yendi.* In addition to that, it's told with the beginning of every chapter advancing one part of the story, while the rest of the chapter goes back in time. The book has three timelines within it—the post-*Yendi* interludes, the beginning-chapter advancing story, and the end-chapter advancing story. You'd think it would be as complicated as hell to read, but it isn't, it flows smoothly and clearly, but very very out of sequence. This flow works largely because it's carried by Vlad's voice at its most brash and bouncy, and partly because it's the story of a war. This is a different, but equally artificial, device from the cliffhanger-starter method Zelazny used in *Doorways in the Sand* but it gives me far less whiplash.

Like *Five Hundred Years After*, *Dragon* gives us a story we've heard alluded to before, the Battle of Barritt's Tomb. And again, Brust turns some of what we thought we knew inside out. The books do all stand alone, but I don't know if *Dragon* would work as an introductory volume. It isn't one I'd give someone to start out with, I think it probably works best for a reader already invested in Vlad and his story.

Spoilers. There are a large number of Dragons around, but then there always are. There's Morrolan and Aliera (and maybe Sethra), there's Sethra the Younger, there are all the Dragons in the army and most of all there's Fornia. I think there is always a characteristic member of the relevant House around, as well as Vlad acting like a member of the House. I've just realised that quite often it's an enemy—the Sorceress in Green in *Yendi*, Loraan in *Athyra*, Fyres in *Orca*, etc. The only real exceptions are *Phoenix* and *Teckla*. In any case, Vlad definitely acts like a Dragon here—he wants personal revenge on Fornia and he joins the army and goes into battle. He develops a sense of honour, and he has fun complaining about the food and the rain and the boredom and the indiscriminate slaughter. Also, he talks about talking to Sethra about tactics and strategy and logistics. I remain very impressed that Brust does Vlad at different ages and life stages so well. In *Orca* we have an older, wearier, warier Vlad, here he's young and ready for anything, quick to take offence, and not really frightened, yet Vlad does grow within the novel.

Vlad sees what was probably the picture that ended the Athyra reign and started the Phoenix one, as mentioned in *The Phoenix Guards*, but of course he has no idea of the historic context of what he's seeing, it's just a picture to him—unless it is just a different picture of a wounded dragon protecting her young, but I think that would be a twist too many. It's interesting to see him begin to run Morrolan's security. Meeting Daymar is interesting too—and especially meeting him through Kragar. (I wonder how they met?) It's nice to see a little bit more of Vlad and Cawti when they were happy, even if it is a very little bit. It's interesting to see how Aliera got Pathfinder and got rid of Kieron's sword. I loved Loiosh being the mascot and everyone feeding him, and I loved Vlad getting used to the awful food. The tricks Vlad plays, burning the biscuits and so on, are also neat. When I think of *Dragon* it's the little details that stand out, along with Vlad's long slow journey across a battlefield. This may be because the chronology of the book requires me to build a structure to hold it in my head to get the shape of the story, and after I've finished reading it, even if that was yesterday, it's work to hold on to that structure.

85. *Issola strikes from courtly bow: Steven Brust's Issola*

Issola would be the absolute worst place to start the Taltos series, because it is chock-full of revelation. The first time I read it I could feel my jaw dropping further and further as I read, stunned as things I'd wondered about and engaged in online speculation about were discussed and explained in detail and at length in a way I'd never suspected they would be. *Issola* contains more conventional fantasy plot and more revelation than all the other volumes up to this point put together. If this were an ordinary series, it would be a climactic book. As it is, it changes the shape of the possibilities of the series. In comments on my first post on these books, Carlos Skullsplitter asked, "Which will be most important to you at the end: the revelation, the conclusion, or the narration?" The answer to that would have been different before *Issola*, *Issola* changes everything. It's set in what I've been calling the main continuity, sometime not long after *Orca*.

Spoilers start here.

Issola are heronlike birds. We're told they sit full of grace and stillness and strike lightning fast when they see a fish, then return to stillness. The House of Issola are famous for their courtesy. *Issola* is framed as a manual on courtesy, and certainly Vlad is polite and considerate in it, and Lady Teldra tells him that he understands courtesy better than he thinks. The significant Issola is Lady Teldra herself, who we have seen previously only in Castle Black as Morrolan's greeter, saying and doing the right thing on all occasions.

The plot is relatively simple for a Vlad book: Morrolan and Aliera have disappeared, Sethra and Lady Teldra send Vlad to look for them, they've been captured by the mysterious Jenoine, Vlad rescues them, is captured, they rescue him, there's a big battle with the Jenoine in which Verra and other gods fight with our friends, Lady Teldra is killed and becomes part of Godslayer, a Great Weapon made of her soul, Spellbreaker and a powerful morganti dagger. I called this "conventional fantasy plot" as shorthand above. Of all the Vlad books, this is the most like a normal fantasy novel. All of the other books have plots that are moved by comprehensible individuals, and some kind of mystery that Vlad is trying to untangle. Here the mystery is the Jenoine, and what we find out about them from Sethra (who ought to know and has no reason to be lying) near the beginning is all we continue to know of their motivation.

There have been hints of the Jenoine before, but here Sethra sits Vlad down at great length and explains the Jenoine, the gods, and the way the world works. With what's said about "tiny lights" in *Dragon,* it seems quite clear that humans came to Dragaera from Earth, probably using some kind of Morgaine/ Witchworld gate-type science but perhaps in spaceships, met the native Serioli, got entangled with the non-native, powerful Jenoine, and were experimented on (genetically and otherwise) to make them psychic and to make Dragaerans out of them. Sometime after that point the gods (and being a god is a job and a skill set) revolted in some way involving the Great Sea of Chaos and Dzur Mountain, and since then have been trying, mostly successfully, to keep the Jenoine out of Dragaera. Oh, and we also learn a lot about Great Weapons, and that Adron is in some way conscious in the Lesser Sea.

I can never decide whether I like *Issola* or not. I find it unsettling—so much happens so fast, it leaves my head spinning. This sort of thing isn't often a problem for me when re-reading. It's one of the reasons I often enjoy re-reading more than reading something for the first time. But with *Issola,* I keep thinking next time I read it I'll be able to relax into it, and that never happens. This is a book with some lovely lines, and some beautiful set-pieces, but what I remember it for is the sensation of standing under a trapdoor and having a load of revelation dropped on my head.

86. What has gone before?

Dear Lords of Publication, Glorious Mountain Press of Adrilankha (or any appropriate representative on our world): I am writing to assert my complete and deep agreement with Sir Paarfi of Roundwood on the subject of synopses of previous volumes at the start of subsequent volumes, to whit, they are an abomination, irritating to the writer, unnecessary to the reader, and a complete waste of carbon and trace metals. Paarfi said those who agreed with him should have the honour to address you in these terms, and so I do. Generally, that's my position. I appreciate that summaries of the previous book are useful for people who aren't going to re-read previous volumes before reading the new volume, but I am going to re-read them, so they're of no use to me. I can also see that they'd be useful for people who randomly pick up sequels without knowing they're sequels and then read them. I never do that. Well, I never do it knowingly. I sometimes do it by accident, and if I find out before reading it (for instance by seeing a "what has gone before" summary) I save it until I have found the first volume. And similarly if I know I want a book and I find a later volume, I keep it. My in-pile has had the second and third Doris Egan Ivory books sitting on it for several years, ever since I found them shortly after enjoying *City of Diamond,* and being told that Jane Emerson and

Doris Egan were the same person. Sooner or later I'll find the first book, and read them in order. There are plenty of books. There's no hurry.

Synopses are so annoying—nobody could like them, could they? Could they?

Well, the rant against the practice that Steven Brust puts into Paarfi's voice at the start of *The Lord of Castle Black,* the second volume of *The Viscount of Adrilankha,* is so spirited and charming, and so well expressed everything I feel on this subject that I nearly change my mind and feel the existence of this one wonderful synopsis justifies the whole procedure. It begins with a rant against the practice as "futile and self-defeating," adds that "were any of the events of the previous volume such that they could have been omitted without severe damage to the narrative, we should have omitted them to begin with," then goes on to give a perfectly serviceable summary of the first volume, enlivened with comments like "several other persons of whom the reader who has failed to read the first volume of our work will bitterly miss the acquaintance," and then goes on to exhort the reader to write to Glorious Mountain Press expressing their agreement. In fairness to subsequent-volume synopses, I really have never liked them as a reader, but it's as a writer that I've come to loathe them. This is because anything sounds stupid when summarised. I don't know any writers who like doing them—though I suppose there may be some. But in my experience, being asked to do one leads most writers to mutter: "If I could have written this novel in a thousand words I'd have done that in the first place and saved myself a lot of work."

And so I most sincerely remain, dearest Lords of Publication of Glorious Mountain Press, your enthusiastic correspondent, Jo Walton.

87. The time about which I have the honor to write: Steven Brust's The Viscount of Adrilankha

The Viscount of Adrilankha is a three-volume novel consisting of *The Paths of the Dead* (2002), *The Lord of Castle Black* (2003), and *Sethra Lavode* (2004). I'm writing about them together because it feels to me that they are best considered as one work, divided into a beginning, a middle and an end for bookbinding purposes. All the Paarfi books are loosely connected by continuing characters and a developing world, but these three are really one story.

One of the things reading half a ton of Brust together does is make me realise how unquestioned the defaults of secondary-world fantasy are. Fantasy has a certain look and feel and style of conversation and tech level—and more than that, there's an expected mood, an expectation of the kind of serious it will be. There are exceptions, of course, but they are just that. There's no inherent reason why you can't have swashbuckling musketeer-style fantasy with dialogue that flashes like rapiers, but you need to justify it, as you don't need to justify a story of rivals for a medieval throne. As for the seriousness, there's certainly funny fantasy but a great deal of it consists of making fun of the concept, not much of it makes you laugh aloud at the humour inherent in the situation. With Brust's books, you laugh for the same reason a reader inside the world would laugh, even if you occasionally say "ah-ha!" with knowledge you bring from outside.

This three-volume novel is best enjoyed as a historical novel set within the fantasy world of Dragaera. It's historical accuracy is right up there with Dumas writing the nice and accurate history of France. Paarfi, the writer within the world, has a wonderful voice and a lovely way of putting things, he's slightly pompous, slightly dignified, he tries to be accurate but gets carried away in his own enthusiasm. He's a lovely person to spend time with as are his, and Brust's, characters. I understand that not everybody will get excited over chapter titles variously explaining whether the battle going on is the ninth or tenth battle of Dzur Mountain, but if that sort of thing delights you, then you should certainly read these books. I'd still suggest starting with *The Phoenix Guards* though I see no real reason why these don't stand alone.

Mild spoilers.

Historically, *The Viscount of Adrilankha* is the story of the end of the Interregnum and the re-establishment of the Empire. The three volumes divide neatly into "introducing all the characters and setting them in place," "Zerika returns with the Orb and wins a battle," and "re-establishing the Empire is more complicated than that." On an emotional level they concern the coming of age of Piro, the son of Khaavren, and Khaavren coming to terms with that. There's also a fair bit about the way Morrolan grows up, and the dealings of Sethra and the gods with the Jenoine. All of this works very well as story and history—and it has some splendid antagonists and excellent plotting.

While the overall plot is effective and affecting, what I like most about these books is the little incidentals—the way Morrolan builds his castle in the air, for instance, sorcery can get it up, and witchcraft can keep it up. I was also charmed by the explanation for the never-ending party. There's an ah-ha moment for those who have read *Teckla* when Aerich visits Tazendra's home and finds a Teckla living there. The chapter titles are adorable. The plots are cunning, but it's Illista ordering fish that sticks with me. I find Piro and his friends less appealing than Khaavren and his friends, but there's plenty of the older generation here—and Piro's dilemma with Ibronka answers something I've always wondered about, with regard to the Houses. Zerika's passage of the Paths of the Dead, and all the debates among the gods, have to be taken as speculative on Paarfi's part, not historical, but how interesting, after *Issola,* that a Jenoine nearly got in. I do wonder why the Interregnum had to be so long. Nothing would have stopped Sethra organizing this as soon as Zerika was old enough, and as Piro's about a hundred years old, why wait until Zerika was two hundred and fifty?

88. Dzur stalks and blends with night: Steven Brust's Dzur

Dzur is definitely my favourite Vlad book and one of my favourite of all books. It begins with a visit to Valabars, the famous Eastern restaurant in Adrilankha, which has been mentioned since *Jhereg* but never seen before. This visit to Valabars frames and shapes the book, each chapter begins with a description of a course. Here we have grown-up, mature Vlad, with Lady Teldra by his side, no longer an assassin but back in Adrilankha, solving a small-scale mystery. This book is set in the main continuity, it begins mere minutes after *Issola*. We get to see most, if not all, of the ongoing characters of the series. As well as Valabars, there's another thing that's been mentioned in various contexts and turns up for the first time here. Brust's on absolute top form in *Dzur*. It's a delicious book and I love it.

I think this might be a good place to start the series. It would certainly make you want to read the others to catch up, but I think it would work as an introduction. Besides, there's the meal in Valabars. Don't read this if you're hungry, or if you have no expectation of eating good food soon. Also, this might not be as much fun if you hate food. I don't identify with Vlad much, but he says at one point in *Dzur,* "I'm a fair cook, I'm a *superb* eater," and oh, me too.

I've had another thought about reading order, by the way. When the books are finished, it will be possible to read them in Cycle order, and that reading might have its own interest and benefits. I'll look forward to trying it.

I was so deeply absorbed in this book that when I read the description of Valabars mushroom and barley soup and the way Vlad can't make it exactly the same at home because there's something he's just not getting, I wanted to email him and suggest that he try just a tiny bit of nutmeg, going in when the mushrooms do. I didn't want to email Steve Brust to suggest this, though that would be a much more practical proposition, I wanted to email Vlad. Also, I'm allergic to peppers, so I found myself wishing that Brust had made up a Dragaeran name for "Eastern red pepper" so I could pretend it was some fantasy thing that wouldn't make me ill, instead of just thinking, "Well, you could just leave that out and it would be fine."

Vlad certainly behaves like a Dzur, stalking and striking and taking risks—not just being in Adrilankha at all, but rushing in to Verra's halls, and the confrontation at the end. Sethra says Dzur can tell the difference between strategy and tactics and Dragons can't, and we do see Vlad recognising the difference and changing plans as required. The member of House Dzur is Vlad's dinner companion Telnan, who's young and cheerful, has a great weapon and who will one day be called Zungaron Lavode. Oddly enough, House Dzur is one of the houses we've seen most of before their book. Not only is there Tazendra in the Paarfi books, but there's the Dragon/Dzur revenge in *Jhereg,* there are the Dzurlords who go charging up Dzur Mountain, there's Sethra, who seems to be a Dragon/Dzur hybrid though nobody would mention that, and there are a number of jokes about how many Dzurlords it takes to sharpen a sword. So I was if anything expecting more rushing in than there is—not that there's not plenty.

As for ongoing mysteries and revelations, Mario walking up to the table is priceless. Mario's been considered a legend, he makes his appearance in *Five Hundred Years After,* and now here he is, quietly walking up and having a conversation, doing an assassination, still alive, still Aliera's lover, still the best. The pacing on this one is brilliant. I could never write a series like this, because I couldn't wait for nineteen years and ten Vlad books to pull off something this cool, it would keep me awake nights with excitement.

The other thing is Vlad finding out about the existence of Vlad Norathar—we've known about him since *Orca* but Vlad hasn't. The book ends with the expectation of Vlad meeting his son and then going to Valabars again. I was just saying that this is grown-up Vlad, and it occurs to me that being a father, having a role as a father, would be the next thing for that. I don't see how he can manage it though, not if he can't be in Adrilankha.

The thing I like least is Verra messing with Vlad's memory. I don't mind unreliable narrators, but I hate characters not remembering things they used to remember, and I was afraid it was going there. However, what we seem to have is a great big excuse for a retcon of any events of *Taltos* that Brust wants to change. I'd rather have an excuse than have books contradict each other, and if they have to they have to—there's been surprisingly little of that. All I can think of is the sudden existence of wheeled transport in *Dragon* when the specific absence of it is mentioned in *Phoenix,* and the bit with Morrolan saying he was with Zerika at the top of the cliff, when according to Paarfi he was not in Piro's party. Anyway, the memory problems stopped being a problem with me after Vlad did his Dzur-like dash to confront Verra about them. Brust may be cheating with this, but he's cheating in style.

89. Jhegaala shifts as moments pass: Steven Brust's Jhegaala

Jhegaala is another one that I hated the first time I read it. As it only came out last year, I'd only read it once before this, so I haven't yet had time to get to like it. As I also hated *Teckla* and *Athyra* on first reading, I'm reasonably confident that I will. All the same, I picked it up with a certain amount of reluctance, and I didn't enjoy it all that much.

Jhegaala is definitely not where you want to start this series. It's out of the main continuity, set between *Phoenix* and *Athyra*. When I finished *Phoenix* I wanted to read it, because I never have read it there, where it belongs in internal chronology, and I swear next time I'm going to read them that way and see Vlad developing and having my events in order rather than doing all this complicated juggling. After *Phoenix*, *Jhegaala* might have more appeal. After *Dzur* it feels like stepping back. Vlad's less mature here, still smarting from *Teckla* and *Phoenix*, and we have to watch him go through the process of becoming more mature. I know it can't all be meetings with old friends and dinner at Valabars, and I would get bored if it were, you need shade as well as light, but even so, even appreciating that they can't be all "Vlad has a nice day," this book is a real downer.

Spoilers.

Jhegaala is an expansion of a couple of lines in two of the other books. Emotionally, it's an expansion of the bit in *Taltos* where Vlad mentions that the Easterner kids beat him up for being too Dragaeran and it didn't hurt as much as when the Dragaerans beat him up for being an Easterner, except that it hurt more inside. *Jhegaala* is Vlad discovering for real that Easterners are just as bad—good, bad, and mixed—as Dragaerans, it isn't that the ones he knows in South Adrilankha are immigrants damaged by the immigrant experience, they're like that in Fenario, too. And then, literally, it's an expansion of the bit in *Orca* when Loiosh suggests they go East and that it needn't be as bad as it was last time. This is the story of how bad it was, and it really was awful. It's also probably the true story of how Vlad lost his finger, though it's carefully not quite specific there.

Jhegaala seem to be some kind of insectoid thing that metamorphoses a lot. I don't remember anybody from House Jhegaala in any of the other books, and the only one we see here is in the chapter start-quotes from the rather odd mannerist murder comedy play *Six Parts Water*. There we are told that you need to find out what phase they are in. I suppose Vlad does metamorphose in this book and he also does a lot of waiting around and eating, and a lot of time when he might as well be in a cocoon, like the animal jhegaala in some phases, and he's certainly moody, so it does fit. Vlad comments that Jhegaala grow into and out of things in different phases, and this is certainly the book where he does some of that.

Good things: Vlad in the East, without any magic, without an organization or any friends. No, hang on, this was supposed to be good things. A little bit of Noish-pa. Some interesting information about Vlad's mother, which I'd have liked if it didn't go where it did. Some lovely Vlad and Loiosh banter: "There's nothing worse than a smartass who pretends not to understand hyperbole." The East, its reality, economics, and sky.

What is with the Overcast anyway? It's not something the Orb is doing—it was there during the Interregnum. Loiosh and Rocza hold their breath when they fly through it (*Athyra*, Rocza POV) but when they climb through it on the way up Dzur Mountain in *Paths of the Dead* it just gives a reddish cast to everything and they breathe normally. In *Phoenix,* Zerika talks about disasters the Orb prevents that weren't prevented during the Interregnum, and it struck me that they are natural disasters— mountains spewing fire and lava, people being blown away by strong winds, the ground shaking and cracking open. I assumed then if it was preventing volcanoes and hurricanes and earth-quakes it was causing the Overcast, but no. Also, what is it for? It hides the sun and the stars (no moon!) but while Vlad's blinking in the sunlight, Morrolan missed it when he went to the Empire after being raised in the East, so it can't harm Dragaerans, which was my first thought.

So, why don't I like this book? Too much torture, too much angst, too much helplessness, and a very complicated plot that relies on everyone being idiotic—very much the way that people are idiotic, but even so. I also can't help feeling that it doesn't entirely make sense—the whole thing with Vlad mentioning the Merss family being taken as a threat and then the way they're all killed doesn't entirely fit with the explanations at the end. I don't say "ah-ha!" I say "huh?" which no doubt means I'm missing something, but I missed it this time, too. On the subject of miss-ing something, the book has two layers of extra-narrative quotation. One layer, about the natural history of the jhegaala, fits perfectly and makes sense—it illuminates the stages the ani-mal goes through and these have some metaphorical relationship to what Vlad's going through, no problem. The other, the

313

quotations from the play, baffle me. They're mostly funny little bits of dialogue, but there's not enough there to deduce the whole play from the fragments, it seems to concern a Jhegaala but we don't know who, and they serve generally to cast shadows instead of illumination. As this is a book about shadows, I suppose that makes sense.

90. Quiet iorich won't forget: Steven Brust's Iorich

Iorich will be published in January, which probably means "any minute now." It's the latest Vlad book, the eighteenth Dragaera book (I miscounted before) and it's set in the ongoing continuity, a few years after *Dzur*.

I have an ARC. It's surprisingly odd to go from re-reading a long series of books—seventeen distinct volumes—to starting a new one. It's not that re-reading isn't pleasurable, but there's no sense of urgency to it. Even if I've forgotten the details, the general flow of the shape of the story will be in my mind, so that things will come back to me before I get to them, and I'll at least half-remember what's going on. Going on to a new one is entirely different. Suddenly, it is urgent. What is going on? Will characters I care about survive? Why is this happening? It's like, and yet unlike, the difference between reminiscence and experience. What it's actually like is when you're on a long familiar trip, and you're looking out of the window from time to time but mostly reading your book, and then the train takes a detour and you're suddenly way up in the mountains and you drop your book because you're suddenly riveted to the view out of the window. Only, you know, the other way around.

What can I say about *Iorich* without spoilers? Well, nothing at all, except that I enjoyed it a great deal. I happen to know that four people reading this have also read it, and I'm actually longing to have a spoiler-filled discussion about Devera and other matters, but I shall restrain myself until more of you have had a chance to have the book unroll itself before your eyes in the proper fashion.

House Iorich are concerned with justice and law, and so Vlad spends the book caught up in concerns of justice and law. There's an advocate of House Iorich who is the representative Iorich of the book. The animal iorich seem to be a kind of rhino dinosaur, judging from the silhouette on the representation of the Cycle. We don't see any, except in carvings, which is probably just as well. The book is mostly set in Adrilankha, and features all the characters you'd expect to see in Adrilankha four years after *Dzur*. They have some great interactions. There's also strong indication that there'll be another book between Dzur and this, because quite a lot seems to have happened to Vlad. Kragar mentions that he's looking older, which really struck me—I know Dragaerans don't age at the same rate, but having an Easterner friend must be really hard for them.

For some reason it suddenly struck me as I was thinking about the plot of *Iorich* that the Vlad books are remarkably self-contained. We were talking in the *Dzur* thread about who he's telling them to and why and when, and how he doesn't know if the reader knows about events of the other books. Vlad's life is continuous, but he's narrating episodes as stories, and either the episodes have the shape of stories or he's giving them that shape. The occasional comment about "skip it" or "that's another story" is part of that shaping, I think.

Most of the books cover about a week, as near as I can figure—*Jhegaala*'s longer, and so is *Dragon*, but generally they're intense minute-by-minute descriptions of about a week in Vlad's life, with gaps in between where his life doesn't fit story shape. Now they are all very self-contained. The volumes of this series definitely stand alone—I've been suggesting better or worse places to start, but really you could read any one of these books and want to read the others. They work in any order. Yet they're not episodic. I mean they are, but there's always a very strong feeling that each episode is part of an arc, part of a greater whole, that they are going somewhere. I think these break my definition of series and are a different kind.

Anyway, *Iorich*. You want it, you'll like it. But you knew that anyway.

91. Quakers in Space:
Molly Gloss's
The Dazzle of Day

The Dazzle of Day (1997) is an astonishing short novel about a generation starship.

There have been plenty of books set on generation starships by everyone from Heinlein to Wolfe, but the thing that makes this stand out is how astonishingly real the characters are, and how well fitted to their world. Gloss has an immense gift for getting inside people's heads. This story is about people both like and unlike us—they are culturally Quakers and they've been living on the ship for generations, which makes them very different, and yet they're unmistakably people. They're my favourite kind of characters, people I can understand and get inside their heads, and yet very different from the standard kinds of people you get in books. They're very much individuals, not types, and they're very much shaped by their culture and experiences.

The book opens with a piece of a memoir from a woman on Earth who's considering going on the ship, then the middle section consists of the rotating points of view of an extended family a hundred and seventy-five years later as the ship is approaching a planet, then it ends with a piece of memoir from a woman living on the new planet a hundred years after that. The way they live, the expectations they have of family and work and decision making are all very unusual, but they take them for granted and so I absorb them naturally as I'm reading. The characters, whose ancestors came from Japan, Costa Rica, and Norway, speak Esperanto, and Esperanto is used in the text for a few words for things we don't have, which gives it an unusual flavour. This is only the second time I've read this, as I completely missed it when it was published. I think of a second reading of a book as completing my read, a first reading is preliminary and reactions to a first reading are suspect. I loved this book just as much the second time. It's very well written and very absorbing. It isn't a cheerful story though—thematically it's about worlds and boundaries, and it's about those things very much on a human scale. This very much isn't a fantasy of political agency, one of the things it faces is the knowledge that change can be frightening, that responsibility can, but that the answer to that is not refusing to change or refusing to accept responsibility.

I sometimes read something and think "I'd have loved this when I was eleven." I'd have hated *The Dazzle of Day* when I was eleven, it's all about grown-ups, it has a lot of older women as significant characters, and while being on the generation starship is essential to everything, everything that's important is internal. But I love it now for those very things. If there's an opposite of a YA book, this is it.

92. Locked in our separate skulls: Raphael Carter's The Fortunate Fall

The Fortunate Fall (1996) is about the possibility of changing human nature. You wouldn't think that would be rare in science fiction, but it is, vanishingly rare. It's hard to address. What Carter does here is to give us a viewpoint from about a hundred years in the future, a viewpoint with an awareness of a quite detailed future history and personal history, of which we see only as much as we need, but which gives us the illusion of much more. Maya is a camera, with new-style implants in her head plugged in to converters for her old-style ones. She broadcasts telepresence direct to the Net, her thoughts, memories, sensations, imaginings, and gets feedback from her audience. At the start of the novel she's in Kazakhstan doing a series on a holocaust that took place fifty years before and has been almost forgotten, and she's nervous because she has to work with a last-minute screener who for all she knows could forget to filter out the fact that Maya needs a bathroom break. And thus we're painlessly introduced to everything that's going to be important: the world, the Net, the history that lies between them and us, Maya, and her new screener Keishi.

When I first read *The Fortunate Fall*, I felt that it justified cyberpunk, it was worth having had cyberpunk if we could come out the other side and have this book. Re-reading it now for what is probably only the fourth time in fourteen years, with quite a different perspective, it seems that this was, as well as a completion to cyberpunk, also the first science fiction novel of the twenty-first century. It has dated remarkably little. Parts of it, like the Guardian regime where the Americans ran the world and ran the Square Mile camps as franchises (McGenocide, the text jokes), seem regrettably more plausible now than they did when I first read it. By and large with near-future Earths, they fit precisely into pre- and post-9/11—by that classification *The Fortunate Fall* seems definitely post. It's also one of the first post-Vingean books to deal with the Singularity and find interesting answers to it. In 1996 I didn't know this was going to be an irritation much worse than cyberpunk, but if the curse of Singularities is the price I have to pay for *The Fortunate Fall*, I'll take that too.

This is an important book, certainly one of the most important books of the last twenty years. It's a book I tend to assume everyone interested in science fiction's potential will have read. And it's also about as good as books get. Nevertheless I know a lot of people haven't read it, so I'm going to discuss it as far as possible without spoilers.

It's a very intense book both emotionally and intellectually—in that way I'd compare it to *Stars in My Pocket Like Grains of Sand* and *Cyteen*. Like those books it is about what it means to love, and what it means to have your life path readjusted and hack your brain with technological mediation. They'd make a wonderful thematic trilogy of, "Look, this is what SF can do and the kind of questions it can ask!" *Cyteen* (1988) doesn't have a Net but the other two do, and how interestingly different they are! Carter's Net has the cameras transmitting what they see and feel, and everyone else consuming that, it's had a neuro-viral plague that transformed everyone who caught it to an Army that ended the Guardian regime, and it has no clear distinction between what's in the Net and what's in the brain, when one can be hacked by the other. It has Postcops, people who wake up running software named after Emily Post who go around doing law enforcement for the day before, resuming their normal lives the next day. It has Greyspace, where feral AIs have their own ecologies. It has Weavers, who are doing slow complicated fixes for things they don't want to see, like homosexuality and Christianity—a "nun" chip in your head for the first that stops you feeling any desire. They're working on subtler fixes, where people just lose their faith or desire. And this is just in the primitive Fusion cultures, because there is also Africa, where technology is incomprehensibly higher. It is part of the human condition to be imprisoned in separate skulls, but for Maya it is something to long for. Technology has made everything fundamentally different. If there's a small s "singularity," they are on the other side of one, they are forced both closer to each other and further away by the technology that links their brains, takes over their brains, edits their brains. Yet Carter writes about them as people we can know and care about. Their Net has changed not only what love means, but what it can mean, yet I have had conversations about Maya's dilemma at the end of the novel that are all about love—in passing through Carter's changed world, we come to re-examine our own axioms. (I think what Maya decides is just right. I will acknowledge that this is not the only valid point of view.)

It's also worth saying that Carter's prose is always astonishing, whether it's hilarious:

I menued the chip's colour to a grey that matched the fabric. I stepped back and checked the effect in the mirror. The transformation was amazing. Ten minutes ago I'd looked like a typically encrusted old-time Netcaster. Now I looked like a dangerous lunatic with no fashion sense. Stop me before I accessorize again.

Or philosophical:

"We are a machine made by God to write poetry to glorify his creatures. But we're a bad machine, built on an off day. While we were grinding out a few pathetic verses, we killed the creatures we were writing about; for every person writing poems there were a hundred, a thousand, out blowing away God's creation left right and center. Well, Maya Tatyanichna? You know what we have wrought. What is your judgement? Which is better? A tiger, or a poem about a tiger?"

The first paragraph of the book has been so extensively quoted I won't type it in again, even though I always turn back and read it again at the end.

The book is so mind-blowingly much itself that it isn't really like anything. But it was reading Thomas Disch's *Camp Concentration* that made me think of reading this now, because there are thematic similarities. The comparison Carter explicitly invites and the one I think is the most ultimately satisfying is with *Moby Dick*.

I wish it were in print.

93. Saving both worlds: Katherine Blake (Dorothy Heydt)'s The Interior Life

The Interior Life (1990) is really not like anything else. It was published by Baen in what seems to have been a fit of absentmindedness, as Baen are generally really good at branding, and you could go a long way without finding something less typically Baen than this. *The Interior Life* is a fantasy novel about an ordinary American housewife who begins to hear voices in her head from a fantasy world. She never goes to the fantasy world and nobody from the fantasy world ever comes to this world. The story passes seamlessly between Sue in this world joining the PTA and painting the kitchen to Lady Amalia in the fantasy world battling the forces of Darkness. The weird thing is that this works. The stories reinforce each other, they drag you along by ratcheting, you want to follow both halves of what is happening, and the mundane details of Sue's life are not only enhanced by the fantasy in her head but made fascinating by it.

I expect that if you did a survey, people wouldn't say that they valued masculine virtues above feminine virtues, and likewise they wouldn't say that the depressing is inherently better than the uplifting. Nevertheless, in written fiction this does seem to be people's unconscious bias. There are more downer books than heartwarming ones, and those heartwarming ones there are get scoffed at and diminished. Nobody calls *Nineteen Eighty-Four* a "guilty pleasure." Similarly there are a lot of books in which characters go to the library for tech support and very few where they go to the library for cookbooks. *The Interior Life* is grounded in the feminine virtues of nurturing and support, and it takes this seriously in a way that a lot of feminist SF and fantasy doesn't quite manage. From *Tehanu* to *Thendara House* there's a self-consciousness in the way we're told these things are important while being shown that they're not. Heydt avoids that entirely by writing about them with a heartfelt sincerity.

It's also a cheerful positive book—not just a book with a happy ending, but a resolutely upbeat book. It's a really enjoyable read. No wonder it sank without a trace.

The Demouria portion of the story would, on its own, be a fairly standard world-saving fantasy. The Sue portion alone wouldn't even be a story. It's odd that there are so few stories about people cleaning their house and joining the PTA and organizing dinner parties for their husband's work colleagues and helping their kids with their homework, even in mainstream fiction. There are stories about people who escape from that, and there are stories about people who do that effortlessly in the background of having adventures, and there are stories about people, men mostly, who suddenly have to do it and notice that it's hard work, but this is the only book I know that focuses on keeping house in this way. I like that it isn't about Sue abandoning Fred and her boring life but rather getting on top of her life and making it one that she likes. This could have been published as a mainstream novel of beating depression by having an active fantasy life—and yet, it's a fantasy novel too. If the fantasy helps save Sue, Sue also helps save Demouria. It's an odd combination, and yet it's very effective.

The narrative switches between worlds without missing a beat, sometimes several times in the same paragraph—by the time you're switching between the PTA tea party and the coronation you don't even notice that it's odd. Heydt has said that she intended to use different typefaces to represent the different viewpoints, but this didn't work out—fortunately it wasn't necessary, all the cues are there and it is never hard to follow.

The story is very firmly set in the late eighties: the forward-thinking PTA are considering building a computer lab for the school; computers are new and expensive and weird; CDs are just getting started, most people still listen to records. The medieval fantasy world has not dated in the same way.

I tend to get into the mood to pick this up when my kitchen has got out of control—and by the time I finish it, I generally have it back in control. As well as being a nice, if relatively standard, fantasy quest, it makes me feel good about housework. I read it in the first place because it was given to me by a friend because Heydt was a friend on Usenet. (She published this as Blake for odd reasons that don't matter, she later published other things under her own name.) I never saw a copy new, and I seldom see a copy around used—and when I do I grab it to give to someone. It's a pity that the Tiptree Award for works of gender relevance wasn't instituted until 1992, because this book would have been an interesting and thought-provoking nominee.

94. Yearning for the unattainable: James Tiptree Jr.'s short stories

I own a copy of the second (1979) edition of James Tiptree Jr.'s collection *Warm Worlds and Otherwise,* which contains an insightful and interesting introduction by Robert Silverberg. Silverberg's introduction, while generally terrific, is wrong about two things. He's famously wrong about her "ineluctable masculinity"—in this second edition he backs down as graciously and sincerely as anyone ever has. If you want a model of how to acknowledge your public mistakes with grace, you could do a lot worse. The other mistake he makes is in assuming that Tiptree will someday write a novel, and that novel will be even better than the short stories he's praising.

Tiptree did cobble together a couple of novels later in her career, and I quite like them, though they do not have the novel nature. Some people are natural short story writers, and I think this may have been a more inherent and significant thing about Tiptree than her gender. Tiptree wrote some of the best short stories the field has ever seen, stories that are unforgettable, the kind of story that gets under your skin and keeps coming back. There's a weird belief that short stories are somehow inferior to novels, are beginner's work, when in fact they are their own thing. Some writers excel at all lengths, others have natural lengths. Tiptree's natural length was the short story. She seldom extended even to novellas and novelettes. She built whole memorable universes and characters to inhabit them in remarkably few words, and that was part of her genius.

Warm Worlds and Otherwise is out of print, but her "best of" collection, *Her Smoke Rose Up Forever,* is still available, and I recommend it. Re-reading a short story collection I always find myself identifying themes and motifs. Tiptree wrote a lot about aliens and being alienated, but the strongest theme I can see is the yearning for the unattainable. All of these stories have characters yearning for what they cannot have, whether it's Timor and his lost paradise planet in "The Milk of Paradise," or P. Burke and her perfect robot body in "The Girl Who Was Plugged In," or the humans and their desire for alien sex in "And I Awoke and Found Me Here on the Cold Hill's Side," or the unbearable biological imperatives of the aliens in "Love Is the Plan the Plan Is Death." What unites Tiptree's stories is the skillful blending of SFnal concepts with this overpowering yearning for something forever out of reach.

I've read Julie Phillips's biography of Tiptree and while I thought it was in many ways brilliant, I couldn't help feeling that Phillips underestimated the value of Tiptree's work. Phillips is interested in how Alice Sheldon constructed the persona of James Tiptree Jr., and that is indeed interesting. Phillips is interested in the way that being Tiptree let Sheldon write, where before she hadn't been able to, and not just write but communicate with other writers. I'm much more interested in the way that science fiction let her write, in the way she could find a way to write about her experiences as someone alienated from the world and find that writing welcomed. Delany talks about how science fiction can transform a sentence like "she turned on her side" from the boring restlessness of a sleepless night to the activation of the cyborg. In the same way Sheldon's inchoate longing for something impossible to articulate was alchemised through Tiptree's science fiction writing.

Tiptree's stories really are brilliant—I loved them when I was a teenager, I love them now. She did things that hadn't been done before, she expanded the edges of possibility for the field. Phillips wasn't really interested in Tiptree's influence in our genre, and so far as she was she wanted to talk about the Tiptree Award and gender and so on, which is all really related to Sheldon personally, and not so much to Tiptree as a writer. Tiptree did write "The Women Men Don't See" and "Morality Meat," but gender and "female issues" were far from central to her concerns. I think one of the things being Tiptree gave her was permission to step away from this sort of thing, permission to write as "normal" (it was 1970) and unmarked, to be who she was, to be a person away from the confines of being a female. There's this thing that happens with acknowledging and sequestering women's stuff at the same time, and she escaped that.

Tiptree was constantly pushing the boundaries of science fiction. "The Girl Who Was Plugged In" (1973) prefigured cyberpunk—it's one of the three precursor stories, with John M. Ford's *Web of Angels* and John Brunner's *The Shockwave Rider.* "Love Is the Plan the Plan Is Death" made a space for Octavia Butler's later writing about aliens and sex and identity. "And I Awoke and Found Me Here on the Cold Hill's Side" did the same for Varley—for a lot of the writers who came into SF in the later seventies and the eighties Tiptree was part of their defining space, and the genre would have been very different without her. Science fiction is constantly a dialogue, and her voice was one of the strongest in the early seventies, when everything was changing. She wasn't a New Wave writer, and in many ways she was very traditional. "And I Have Come Upon This Place by

Lost Ways" could have been written by Murray Leinster, except for the end. She wrote what she wrote and expanded the possibilities for all of us. Science fiction would be very different without her.

95. SF reading protocols

Genres are usually defined by their tropes—mysteries have murders and clues, romances have two people finding each other, etc. Science fiction doesn't work well when you define it like that, because it's not about robots and rocketships. Samuel Delany suggested that rather than try to define science fiction it's more interesting to describe it, and when describing it, it's more interesting to draw a broad circle around what everyone agrees is SF than to quibble about the edge conditions. (Though arguing over the borders of science fiction and fantasy is a never-ending and fun exercise.) He then went on to say that one of the ways of approaching SF is to look at the way people read it—that those of us who read it have built up a set of skills for reading SF which let us enjoy it, where people who don't have this approach to reading are left confused.

If you're reading this, the odds are overwhelming that you have that SF-reading skill set.

(As I'm using it here, "science fiction" means "science fiction" and "SF" means "the broad genre of science fiction and fantasy.")

We've all probably had the experience of reading a great SF novel and lending it to a friend—a literate friend who adores A. S. Byatt and E. M. Forster. Sometimes our friend will turn their nose up at the cover, and we'll say no, really, this is good, you'll like it. Sometimes our friend does like it, but often we'll find our friend returning the book with a puzzled grimace, having tried to read it but "just not been able to get into it." That friend has approached science fiction without the necessary toolkit and has bounced off. It's not that they're stupid. It's not that they can't read sentences. It's just that part of the fun of science fiction happens in your head, and their head isn't having fun, it's finding it hard work to keep up.

This can happen in different ways. My ex-husband once lent a friend Joe Haldeman's *The Forever War*. The friend couldn't get past chapter 2, because there was a tachyon drive mentioned, and the friend couldn't figure out how that would work. All he wanted to talk about was the physics of tachyon drives, whereas we all know that the important thing about a tachyon drive is that it lets you go faster than light, and the important thing about the one in *The Forever War* is that the characters get relativistically out of sync with what's happening on Earth because of it. The physics don't matter—there are books about people doing physics and inventing things, and some of them are science fiction (*The Dispossessed* . . .) but *The Forever War* is about going away to fight aliens and coming back to find that home is alien, and the tachyon drive is absolutely essential to the story but the way it works—forget it, that's not important.

This tachyon drive guy, who has stuck in my mind for years and years, got hung up on that detail because he didn't know how to take in what was and what wasn't important. How do I know it wasn't important? The way it was signaled in the story. How did I learn how to recognise that? By reading half a ton of SF. How did I read half a ton of SF before I knew how to do it? I was twelve years old and used to a lot of stuff going over my head, I picked it up as I went along. That's how we all did it.

Why couldn't this guy do that? He could have, but it would have been work, not fun.

These days I much more often have this problem from the other end—the literary end. The best example of this I remember came from Making Light in a thread called Story for Beginners. A reviewer wanted to make the zombies in Kelly Link's "Zombie Contingency Plans" (in the collection *Magic for Beginners*) into metaphors. They're not. They're actual zombies. They may also be metaphors, but their metaphorical function is secondary to the fact that they're actual zombies that want to eat your brains. Science fiction may be literalization of metaphor, it may be open to metaphorical, symbolic and even allegorical readings, but what's real within the story is real within the story, or there's no there there. I had this problem with one of the translators of my novel *Tooth and Claw*—he kept emailing me asking what things represented. I had to keep saying no, the characters really were dragons, and if they represented anything, that was secondary to the reality of their dragon nature. He kept on and on, and I kept being polite but in the end I bit his head off—metaphorically, of course.

When I read literary fiction, I take the story as real on the surface first, and worry about metaphors and representation later, if at all. It's possible that I may not be getting as much as I can from literary fiction by this method, in the same way that the people who want the zombies and dragons to be metaphorical aren't getting as much as they could. But it's interesting that it's precisely those SF books that best lend themselves to metaphorical readings that gain credibility with academia—it's Dick who has a Library of America edition, not Sturgeon or Heinlein. It's Kelly Link who's getting that mainstream review, not Elizabeth Bear.

And then there are people like my aunt. She's one of the canonical people I lent SF to and she tried but could never get into it. When I was first published she worked her way through *The King's Peace,* and eventually managed to see past the metaphorical. "It's just like Greek myths or the Bible!" she said brightly. That was all the context she had. I fell over laughing, but this really was her first step to acquiring the reading habits we take for granted.

I once got into an argument on a Trollope mailing list with people who like footnotes. (I hate all footnotes not written by the author.) The people I was arguing with maintained that they needed footnotes to understand the story, because Trollope wrote expecting his readers to know what a hansom cab was and to understand his jokes about decimalization. I argued that they'd either figure it out from context or they didn't need to. After a while I realised—and said—that I was reading Trollope as SF, assuming that the text was building the world in my head. They quite sensibly pointed out that SF does it on purpose, but I don't think any of us enjoyed Trollope any more or any less, except that I continue to seek out Victorian novels in editions without footnotes.

Having a world unfold in one's head is the fundamental SF experience. It's a lot of what I read for. Delany has a long passage about how your brain expands while reading the sentence "The red sun is high, the blue low"—how it fills in doubled purple shadows on the planet of a binary star. I think it goes beyond that, beyond the physical into the delight of reading about people who come from other societies and have different expectations.

Because SF can't take the world for granted, it's had to develop techniques for doing it. There's the simple infodump, which Neal Stephenson has raised to an art form in its own right. There are lots of forms of what I call incluing, scattering pieces of information seamlessly through the text to add up to a big picture. The reader has to remember them and connect them together. This is one of the things some people complain about as "too much hard work" and which I think is a high form of fun. SF is like a mystery where the world and the history of the world is what's mysterious, and putting that all together in your mind is as interesting as the characters and the plot, if not more interesting. We talk about worldbuilding as something the writer does, but it's also something the reader does, building the world from the clues. When you read that the clocks were striking thirteen, you think at first that something is terribly wrong before you work out that this is a world with twenty-four-hour time—and something terribly wrong. Orwell economically sends a double signal with that.

Because there's a lot of information to get across and you don't want to stop the story more than you can help, we have techniques for doing it. We have signals for what you can take for granted, we have signals for what's important. We're used to seeing people's names and placenames and product-names as information. We know what needs to be explained and what doesn't. In exactly the same way as Trollope didn't explain that a hansom cab was a horse-drawn vehicle for hire on the streets of London that would take you about the city but not out into the countryside, and Byatt doesn't explain that the Northern Line is an underground railroad running north–south through London and dug in the early twentieth century, SF characters casually hail pedicabs and ornithopters and tip when they get out.

People have been writing science fiction for more than a century, and we've had more than eighty years of people writing science fiction and knowing what they were doing. The techniques of writing and reading it have developed in that time. Old things sometimes look very clunky, as if they're inventing the wheel—because they are. Modern SF assumes. It doesn't say "The red sun is high, the blue low *because it was a binary system*." So there's a double problem. People who read SF sometimes write

SF that doesn't have enough surface to skitter over. Someone who doesn't have the skill set can't learn the skill set by reading it. And conversely, people who don't read SF and write it write horribly old-fashioned clunky re-inventing-the-wheel stuff, because they don't know what needs explanation. They explain both too much and not enough, and end up with something that's just teeth-grindingly annoying for an SF reader to read.

There are however plenty of things out there, and still being written, that are good starter-sets for acquiring the SF reading skill set. Harry Potter has been one for a lot of people.

96. Incredibly readable: Robert A. Heinlein's The Door into Summer

The Door into Summer (1957) is one of the most readable books in the world. Whatever that elusive "I Want to Read It" thing is, this book oozes it. Is it because Dan, the first-person engineer narrator, keeps up such a cheery rattle, it just carries you along? Is it because the future is such a sunny one, though wrong in every detail? Is it the joy of watching Heinlein's worldbuilding and neat time travel dovetailing? I think it's the combination of all of these things and the sheer force of storytelling. Heinlein's prose isn't beautiful like Le Guin's, but it's always crisp and descriptive and somehow confidential. He draws you inside the world—it's as if he lifts a corner and invites you and you're thrilled to slip through.

The Door into Summer is short, but it isn't a juvenile; it was written for the adult market and has an adult protagonist, and that makes it unusual. When Heinlein was at his peak, he mostly wrote short stories for adults and novels for kids. There's only really this, and *Double Star* (which gets my vote for his best novel) and *The Moon Is a Harsh Mistress* before you get to his late-period novels. This was written in 1957 and it's set in 1970 and

2000. You'll notice that those dates when it's set were in the future when the book was written and they're in the past now. 1970 was in the past even when I first read the book in 1978. As predictions go, I'd say this scores a straight zero. None of the things predicted happened, with two exceptions—LA getting rid of smog, and the word "kink" developing a dirty meaning. The failed predictions show up more than usual because it's such a near future, and Earth, and because our narrator, Daniel Boone Davis, is an engineer and a designer of robots. There's a lot of talk about robot design and it's all charmingly wrong. But what the book is about is time travel, with neat paradox resolution. It also features a creepy love story that didn't seem so creepy to me when I was a teenager.

But none of this matters, none of this is why you want to read this book if you haven't or read it again if you have—you want to read it because it's got a wonderful voice and because reading it is an immensely satisfying experience. It starts like this:

> One winter shortly before the Six Weeks War, my tom-cat, Petronius the Arbiter, and I lived in an old farmhouse in Connecticut. I doubt if it is there any longer, as it was near the edge of the blast area of the Manhattan near-miss, and those old frame buildings burn like tissue paper. Even if it is still standing it wouldn't be a desirable rental because of the fall-out, but we liked it then, Pete and I. The lack of plumbing made the rent low and what had been the dining-room had a good north light for my drafting board. The drawback was that the place had eleven doors to the outside.

If that doesn't make you want to read the next paragraph, go and find something else to read.

From here on, the general assumption you've read the book

or don't mind mild spoilers, but I'll try to avoid the kind of spoilers that make things less fun.

Dan's thirty years old in 1970, and he's a robot designer who has been swindled out of control of his robot-designing company by his ex–best friend and his ex-fiancée, so he goes on a bender and decides to take the "long sleep," *When the Sleeper Wakes* kind of hibernation for thirty years, taking his cat with him. (Dan has read that book, and not just when the insurance companies started giving out free copies.) Then he sobers up and decides it's running away and he won't do it, only to be forced into it by the same evil ex-fiancée. When he wakes in 2000 he's indigent—the insurance company went bust—but gets by and learns to like the place. Then he discovers there is time travel, and goes back to 1970 to sort out the unfinished business he had there, rescue his cat and then head back to the future.

This is a future that never happened. It's also very cheerful, despite the limited nuclear war sometime in the sixties which the US won. But it's not the future Heinlein usually wrote about—it isn't the future of the juveniles with colonized planets and a dystopic Earth, nor the Howard Families future with over-crowding and longevity, nor is it in the *Past Through Tomorrow* "Future History." There's mention of shuttles to the moon, but this book isn't gung ho space colonies, this is Earth, and an Earth, and a US, doing very well for itself. Progress is real. Things are getting better. And the robots Dan invents are household robots aimed at making daily life better. I do think this is appealing, and I do think it's more unusual in 2010 than it was in 1957. This is a very bouncy future.

But we have had that time now, and it does get everything wrong. There wasn't any Six Weeks War and limited nuclear exchange. Denver never became capital of the US. And on the smaller things—this is Dan, back in 1970 complaining about the things he's got used to in 2000 that haven't been invented yet:

I wish that those precious esthetes who sneer at progress and prattle about the superior virtues of the past could have been with me—dishes that let food get chilled, shirts that had to be laundered, bathroom mirrors that steamed up when you needed them, runny noses, dirt underfoot and dirt in your lungs.

Yes, well, 2010 and where's my . . . but they are still going to the public library to look things up on paper and using typewriters and cloth diapers. Cloth diapers put on a baby by a robot worked by vaccuum tubes and transistors is an image that sums up the kind of ways SF gets things wrong even better than a flying car.

The robots are precisely and specifically wrong. All the things Heinlein assumes will be easy turn out to be almost impossible, and all the things he thinks will be impossible turn out to be easy. Computer memory—not a problem. Robots that could wash dishes or change a baby? Oh dear. We sort of have robots that wash dishes—what else are dishwashers?—but they're not doing it standing over the sink, and putting the dishes away in the cupboard is impossible. The drafting robot would have been lovely in 1957, now I can't help thinking that I have better drafting programs included for free in my operating system just in case I happen to need one. There's enough detail about Dan designing robots and seeing things where a robot would help to be notably and charmingly wrong. Transistors! Tubes! Heinlein sometimes managed to handwave computers in a way that let you fill in your concept (*Citizen of the Galaxy*) but there's just way too much detail here. You can roll your eyes at it, but it doesn't stop the story working. It makes it almost like steampunk, yay clunky 1950s robots. (And it isn't totally wrong. The original Hired Girl is basically a Roomba.) Anyway, wouldn't it be nice to have the family robot that does all the household cleaning and stuff and costs the same as a car?

Far more of an obstacle to enjoying the book is the creepy romance. When I was a teenager I entirely missed the fact that it was creepy. Dan's ex–best friend Miles has a stepdaughter called Ricky, who is eleven in 1970. Dan's been her pseudo-uncle for years, since she was a small child. While back in 1970, Dan at thirty-one—so he's twenty years older than she is—visits her at camp. He has privileged information, some of which he hasn't shared with the reader. He tells this eleven-year-old girl that when she's twenty-one she should put herself into cold sleep until 2000, whereupon he will only be ten years older than her (having cold slept again himself) and he'll marry her. When I was fourteen I was fine with this, and it took me a long time to actually think about it. Imagine an eleven-year-old girl and a thirty-year-old uncle she has a crush on. Now imagine living through the next ten years as that girl growing up, never seeing him, knowing he's waiting for you to be twenty-one, knowing you're then going to marry him after a twenty-year sleep. Imagine being twenty-one and lying down to cold sleep and giving them the instruction to wake you only if he shows up. It's not beyond what people do, but it's creepy and twisted and I can't believe I ever thought it was sort of romantic or that Heinlein in 1957 bought into this "made for each other" stuff so much as to be comfortable with writing this. It was a different world. And it's a very small part of a fast-moving book. And we see it from Dan's self-centred point of view, so imagining how Tiptree might have written Ricky growing up is always an option. But it's still sick.

This is a short, fast and deeply enjoyable read. If I read it for the first time now, I think I'd still get caught up in the readabil-ity. I might have been more squicked by the romance if I didn't already know it was coming. It's hard to detach nostalgia for previous reads from present enjoyment, but I really didn't want to put it down.

97. Nasty, but brilliant: John Barnes's Kaleidoscope Century

Kaleidoscope Century (1995) is one of the most unpleasant books I've ever read, I can hardly believe I've read it again. All the same it's a major work and very nearly a masterpiece. A man lives through the twenty-first century. Every fifteen years he gets ten years younger and forgets almost everything about the preceding fifteen years. He doesn't know what he's done, who he's been, both his memories and the notes on his computer are fragmentary and contradictory. He wakes up this one time on Mars, with few possessions, but dragging an awful lot of baggage of the other kind. He isn't a nice person, and he has done terrible things, for which he is intermittently and weirdly repentant. He thinks through what he can remember and dredge together of the century, then he goes looking for his old partner-in-crime. And then it gets weird.

This is the most unsuitable book for children in the history of the universe. I think it's quite appropriate that there be books for grown-ups, and that this be one of them. It's odd only in that it's the sequel to *Orbital Resonance,* which is pretty much a YA.

It seems as if Barnes sat down in 1990 when writing *Orbital*

Resonance and worked out in detail everything that happened from that day onwards for a hundred years, and then didn't change anything in the future history even when time changed it. This means that when he wrote *Kaleidoscope Century* in 1995 it was already alternate history—never mind Heinlein's 1957 giving us an out-of-date 1970 and 2000. This is weird, and while I don't think it hurts *Kaleidoscope Century* much—there are possible reasons for it—it is a real problem for me once the series gets to *The Sky So Big and Black*. The details sound like real science-fictional future history, but they are uniformly unpleasant—and far more unpleasant than anything that has actually happened in the 19 years since. This is a really detailed and well-thought-out future, with a good understanding of the way changing tech changes possibilities, but it seems to have been thought out by someone who always looks on the black side and doesn't have any faith in humanity. Having said that, horrible as Barnes's century is, even when made deliberately worse by the characters, it can't hold a candle to the twentieth century for real horror.

Barnes is always immensely readable. That's a problem here, actually. Joshua Ali Quare is an unreliable narrator, he's also a horrible person. There's more rape and murder in this book than in everything else on the bookcase put together—and it's rape and murder seen from the point of view of someone for whom they're fun. Yet most of the time Quare is written to be kind of endearing, just getting along, but getting along includes a lot of making the world a worse place in big and small ways. He starts riots. He assassinates people. He rapes—or as he puts it "serbs"—women and girls. He's a mercenary. And at other times he rescues a little street girl and brings her up as his daughter, works quietly as a rigger on a space elevator, or as a prospector on Mars. He justifies himself to himself and to his best friend and to the reader. He's too much of a monster, or not enough of one. You spend a lot of time in his head when reading the book, and his head is a nasty place to be.

Now actual spoilers: The plot doesn't quite work. Closed timelike curve me whatever handwaves you like, if you're dead you stop going through. And I'm not sure the book needs it anyway, it would have been perfectly good with the 15 years and losing memory thing without the endless repetition. And if they have ships that can do that, can skip bits of it, then it doesn't make emotional sense, and really in the end emotional sense is all you can hope for.

But despite making no sense, rape, murder, and a very unpleasant future, it's still an excellently written and vastly ambitious book, with a scope both science-fictional and literary. That's what ultimately makes it a good book, though I do not like it. It has such a vast reach that it doesn't actually matter that it exceeds its grasp, or that it seems to be Hell rather than Heaven that it's reaching for.

98. Growing up in a space dystopia: John Barnes's *Orbital Resonance*

Orbital Resonance (1991) is one of my favourite John Barnes novels, and I re-read it to take the taste of *Kaleidoscope Century* out of my brain. This didn't work quite as well as I'd hoped. On the one hand, *Orbital Resonance* could be a Heinlein juvenile—it's about kids growing up on a captured asteroid looping between Earth and Mars, about teenagers finding out they've been manipulated and taking control of their own destiny. On the other hand this really stood out:

> "Maybe you're right and people can't live like this for
> very long. But the best evidence—with so much lost and
> so many people dead—is that they can't live the old way
> at all. Individualism is dead because it didn't work."

Barnes doesn't seem to have much faith in human nature, and he seems very fond of those cold equations that say the characters have to do the hard thing for everyone's good. Of course, the writer makes up those equations for themselves. . . . I think there's a general tendency in SF to make those human equations very cold and the choices very extreme. Here it's "We had to do horrible things to our children so humanity would survive!" How can you possibly blame them for that! What kind of a softie are you, anyway? I think this does tend to get valorized, and I don't think it's a good thing.

However, *Orbital Resonance* is a brilliant and very readable book. It's from the point of view of a fourteen-year-old girl called Melpomene Murray, writing about the events of the year before, when she was thirteen. Barnes does the teenage girl point of view absolutely flawlessly without an instant of any kind of problem. Melpomene lives on the *Flying Dutchman,* cycling between Earth and Mars with off-Earth industry and cargo. She lives with her parents and her brother and she goes to a very interesting school. She takes her life for granted, but the book is in the form of a school project intended to explain life in space to people on Earth, and as the book goes on you discover that very human, very real Melpomene lives in a highly designed society, and one designed to produce consensus, cooperation, and good corporate employees—and she likes it that way. *Orbital Resonance* is as much a dystopia as anything you can find, but because Melpomene is our point-of-view character, and because she likes it, it's easy to miss that and mistake it for a bouncy growing-up-in-space novel with a happy ending.

This is the same universe as *Kaleidoscope Century.* Earth has been ravaged by the mutAIDS plague, which killed George Bush Sr. in the middle of his second term. Then there was a horrific war that was waged against biosystems, and now Earth is scrambling just to survive—these space habitats are an essential part of the survival of the human race. They had to make these kids be like that! They had no choice! And anyway, Melpomene doesn't mind that she's been manipulated, once she works it out, she's having fun.

But those people born on the ship are really different from

the ones that came from Earth. The worst thing they can call someone is "unco" which stands for "uncooperative." But we see them having fun. They race around the outside of the asteroid. They have parties. They have best friends and boyfriends and eat pizza and express their emotions freely. But when a boy from Earth comes along and can't move well in the gravity and thinks there are rules you follow only when other people are watching, everything goes the way you expect—for about three pages and then it completely turns that inside out. That's why I love this book.

Their school really does sound like fun. One of the things that really works is Melpomene's matter-of-fact attitude to working singly, in pairs, in teams, in pyramids. Two of her school friends are paired in math and the overall result pushes one of them down one place but brings the other up five, so they're delighted and hug each other. And their gym sounds wonderful—not only do they play games in complex gravity but the games have comprehensible rules and sound as if they'd be fun too. One of the climaxes of the book comes during a game of aerocrosse, where you have multiple teams and multiple mobile goals in microgravity, and double crossing is part of the game—but double crossing within the rules.

I generally don't like future slang, but I'll make an exception here. Barnes has a good ear, and doesn't overuse it. He also knows that slang tends to produce words for "very" ("lim" here) and "good" and "bad" ("koapy" and "bokky") and he limits it. I will admit that Sasha is still saying "pos-def" for strong affirmatives (positively-definitely) years after reading the book. It feels like language and it doesn't jar. I also adore the names—these are kids born twenty years after the book was written, and they have names that mark them as a generation, long Greek names (Theophilus), weird nifty names (Randy is Randomly Distributed Schwartz) and the occasional recognisable name like

Tom or Miriam for leaven. So many people get this wrong, and Barnes does it pitch-perfectly.

Melpomene is writing the story of the events of one week, a year before. This is what I call "first-person reflective," meaning that the first-person point-of-view character knows how things will come out and can comment on her actions from a later perspective. Barnes makes very good use of this to show us how it does come out before we know how it gets there. This is a very good book to read if you're interested in how to write characters and how to make stories interesting. The pacing of revelation—the way it tells us what it tells us about what happens after that week in particular—couldn't be better.

This may be Barnes's best book. (Or that may be *A Million Open Doors*.) It's a book almost everyone who likes SF will enjoy, and if it gives you a lot to think about as well, then that's all to the good.

99. The joy of an unfinished series

A long time ago I wrote a post on series that go downhill, and whether it's worth starting a series when everyone tells you that it isn't worth carrying on. Just now, Kluelos commented on that old post asking about unfinished series, saying:

> If you're one of us forlorn David Gerrold fans, you know the agony of waiting forever for sequels, so that's the opposite point, I guess. Is it better to endure a long wait, maybe never see the next book (I will never speak to James Clavell again, because he died before writing "Hag"), than to have the next book even if it is worse than disappointing? I dunno.

Well, if you come face-to-face with James Clavell in the afterlife, my advice is to tell him first how much you like his books, before asking if he's had time up there to finish *Hag Struan*.

I have an immediate answer to the question too, it's definitely better to endure a long wait and have a quality sequel, or no sequel, than have a bad sequel. A bad sequel can spoil the books that came before. A good sequel after a long wait enhances the previous books. No sequel, whether because the author died or lost interest in the series isn't ideal, but it doesn't spoil anything. "We'll always have Paris." Besides, there's something about an unfinished series that people like. I've been thinking about this recently. When you have a finished series, it's like a whole book. It's longer, but it's the same emotional experience, it's complete, over. An unfinished series on the other hand is much more likely to provoke conversation, because you're wondering what will happen, and whether the clues you have spotted are clues or red herrings. People complained that *The Gathering Storm* wasn't the one final volume to complete the *Wheel of Time,* but they're clearly loving talking about it. And I've noticed a lot less conversation about Harry Potter recently, now that everyone knows as much as there is to know. The final volume of a series closes everything down. With luck, it closes it down in a satisfying way. But even the best end will convey a strong sense of everything being over. An ongoing series remains perpetually open.

One series I read where the author died without finishing it was Patrick O'Brian's Aubrey-Maturin series. I started reading it while he was still writing them, but I read the last book after he had died. It did colour my reading of *Blue on the Mizzen,* but one of the things I kept thinking was that O'Brian was rather fond of killing off his characters, and nobody could kill them now. I have a term for this, "forever bailing" from *Four Quartets.* There will be no more books, but the characters will always go on traveling hopefully.

Some people find it off-putting to discover that a book is part of a long series. Other people are delighted—if they like it, there's so much more to discover. I've heard people say they're not going to start A Song of Ice and Fire until it's finished, but I think they're missing half the fun. My post on *Who Killed Jon*

Arryn won't be worth the pixels it's written in when everything's all down in black and white. If you read the books now, you get to speculate about where the series is going.

Anyway, reading unfinished series gives you something to look forward to. The first book I ever waited for was *Silver on the Tree,* the last of Susan Cooper's Dark Is Rising books. There were other books I'd read that had sequels I couldn't find—indeed, that was a normal condition for me. (I waited twenty years for Sylvia Engdahl's *Beyond the Tomorrow Mountains.* This is my record, so far.) But *Silver on the Tree* was the first book that hadn't been published yet when I started to want it, and that had a publication date that I waited for. The second, a few months later, was *The Courts of Chaos.* I'd gone from the normal chaotic state of turning up in a bookshop and being thrilled with whatever had come in since the last time, to a state of constant and specific anticipation of what was forthcoming. I was thirteen.

Right now, like everyone else on the planet, I'm waiting for *A Dance with Dragons.* I'm also waiting for *Tiassa,* the Vlad Taltos book that Steven Brust is writing even now. And I'm waiting desperately for *The City in the Crags* or whatever it ends up being called, the next *Steerswoman* book. (Rosemary Kirstein said at Boskone that she was working on books five and six together, so maybe they'll come out quite close together too.) I'm waiting for *Deceiver,* the new Atevi book, and this one, excitingly, is actually finished and coming out on May 4. And there's Bujold's new Vorkosigan book *Cryoburn,* which I know is finished, but which doesn't seem to have a release date that I can find. There's Connie Willis's *All Clear,* the sequel to (or as we say where I come from "the other half of") *Blackout.* That's coming in October. And there's Patrick Rothfuss's *The Wise Man's Fear,* due sometime early next year.

I travel hopefully, and there's always something to look forward to.

100. Fantasy and the need to remake our origin stories

Left to themselves, people remake their origin stories every few generations to suit present circumstances. Once our stories were set down in a way that made it hard to revisit them for different purposes, some of us turned to telling different kinds of stories, some to faking new origin stories, and then a whole generation to outright fantasies of origin—Tolkien, Lovecraft, Peake, Eddison, Dunsany, Mirrlees, Anderson, etc. Since then, fantasy has been retelling and reinventing their stories for our own changing purposes, because that's what people do, what people need to do. If they don't do it, they tend to go a bit mad. Patrick Nielsen Hayden and I put this theory together over dinner at Boskone, and yes, there was alcohol involved.

Graham Robb's *The Discovery of France: A Historical Geography from the Revolution to the First World War* (2007) is a book about the innumerable tiny subcultures of pre-modern France, and how wildly diverse they were until surprisingly recently. He discusses the way many of these little cultures changed their origin stories every few generations, without really being aware of it:

History in the usual sense had very little to do with it. In the Tarn, "the Romans" were widely confused with "the English", and in parts of the Auvergne, people talked about "le bon Csar", not realizing that "good old Caesar" had tortured and massacred their Gallic ancestors. Other groups—the people of Sens, the marsh dwellers of Poitou and the royal house of Savoy—went further and traced their roots to Gallic tribes who had never surrendered to the Romans.

Even if this was oral tradition, the tradition was unlikely to be very old. Local tales rarely date back more than two or three generations. Town and village legends had a rough, home-made quality, quite different from the rich, erudite heritage that was later bestowed on provincial France. Most historical information supplied by modern tourist offices would be unrecognizable to natives of the eighteenth and nineteenth centuries. After a four-year expedition to Brittany, a folklorist returned to Paris in 1881 to report—no doubt to the disappointment of Romantic lovers of the misty Armorican peninsula—that not a single Breton peasant had ever heard of bards or Druids.

In 1760, James McPherson faked a long epic poem in pseudo-Celtic style. *Ossian* became very popular. It was much more appealing in the eighteenth century than actual Celtic poetry, because it was so much more to their taste. This seems to me related to the way it's often easier for the work of someone in a majority group writing about a minority group to appeal to the majority, than it is for work directly coming out of the minority group. People enjoy just the right amount of strangeness, and authenticity is often too strange. *Ossian's Ride* provided a bridge for eighteenth-century readers towards Celtic originals—though

353

today it seems such a clear fake it's hard to believe anyone could have believed it real. As well as McPherson in Scotland there was also Iolo Morgannwg, the Welsh antiquarian and forger, who has irrevocably muddled the entire field of scholarship. Through the nineteenth century (and even more recently) there were people in Wales busily faking not only documents but whole archaeological sites.

Were they doing this because they needed to rewrite their origin stories, but with their origin stories written down and already too fixed to alter?

Our myths, our legends, aren't necessarily true, but they are truly necessary. They have to do with the way we interpret the world and our place in it. Origin stories, and perhaps fairy tales too, can be the story you need them to be, if you can change them.

A while ago I was involved in a discussion of Arthurian retellings, where I jokingly said that nobody updates them to the present. Nobody tells the story of General Douglas MacArthur as Arthur. Nobody says that when Cromwell left Ireland he'd killed everyone except for seven pregnant women hiding in a cave.

There are other kinds of origin stories. The stories we tell about how Paleolithic people lived are one. In the fifties, Paleolithic people lived in nuclear families with a hunting father bringing back food to a mother who cooked and looked after the children. In the sixties, they lived in larger more communal groups, with frequent festivals with art and music and sex. In the seventies, the women's contribution via gathering started to be noticed. In the eighties, we heard about the alpha male with a harem driving out the other males. In the nineties, we heard how the other more geeky males came back while the alpha was off hunting and impregnated the females. In the last decade we started to hear what an advantage it was to the cavepeople to have gay uncles. It's not that any of these stories are true or untrue, it's the way we tell them. I think the same can be said for the stories of the origin of the universe. It's not about the evidence, it's about interpreting the evidence to make a useful story.

With the invention of the printing press and widespread literacy, it becomes harder to revise origin stories, or any stories. Once canonical versions exist, retellings are a different thing. Several things happened—one was the advent of something quite new, mimetic fiction. This caught on in a huge way in the nineteenth century, people were for the first time reading stories about relatively realistic characters set in what was supposed to be the real world, with no fantastic elements at all. There were the fakers. Later came the new mythologies.

Tolkien said:

> I had a mind to make a body of more or less connected legend, ranging from the large and cosmogonic, to the level of romantic fairy-story—the larger founded on the lesser in contact with the earth, the lesser drawing splendour from the vast backcloths—which I could dedicate quite simply to: to England; to my country. (Letter to Milton Waldman 1951, *The Letters of J.R.R. Tolkien,* ed. Carpenter, 1981, p. 144)

It has always seemed strange that after centuries where people wrote very little original fantasy there should suddenly be this explosion of it at about the same time. First, in the late nineteenth and early twentieth century, came new children's fantasy—no longer retellings and revisions of old fairy tales, which now had canonical versions, but new stories. *Alice in Wonderland. The Jungle Book. Five Children and It. Peter Pan.* There hadn't been a separate children's literature, and what there had been was mostly morality tales. Then, a generation later, came the fantasists writing for adults—Lovecraft and Tolkien and Peake don't have much in common, but they lived at the same time and they reacted to their time with a new mythology. Dunsany's a little earlier, but a lot of what he wrote, and certainly where he started, with Pergana, also looks like a new mythology. Eddison too, and Mirlees—none of these people were influenced by each other (well, Tolkien had read Dunsany) and they were writing very different things, yet they all feel as if they were trying to achieve the same goal, trying to tell an origin story.

Fantasy, post-Tolkien, has been largely involved with retelling Tolkien, or revolting against Tolkien. That isn't all it's been doing, but that's one of the things that's been central. I think one of the things that caused the huge popularity of first Tolkien and then genre fantasy is that it provided a new origin story that people needed and liked.

Horror hasn't got stuck with this kind of problem. Horror has kept revising the stories into the present and relevant—there's no canon that stops it being reinvented to be useful. Those sparkly vampires are a sign of health, not sickness.

MARCH 26, 2010

101. The mind, the heart, sex, class, feminism, true love, intrigue, not your everyday ho-hum detective story: Dorothy Sayers's Gaudy Night

It's always the books I like the most that I feel I haven't done justice to when I write about them.

Gaudy Night was published in 1936. It's still in print, and more than that, it's still relevant. It's not science fiction or fantasy by any stretch, its genre is cosy detective story. It's about a series of incidents in a women's college in Oxford in which someone is trying to provoke a scandal. But what it's really about is the difficult balance between love and work and whether it is possible for a woman to lead a life of the mind wholeheartedly, and whether it's possible for her to do this and have love and a family. Sayers examines this seriously and with examples. You might think that the issues might be dated. Some of the attitudes are, but on the whole the fulcrum point of "having it all," marrying as an equal and not as a helpmeet, is still an interesting question.

Gaudy Night is one of Sayers's series of novels about Lord Peter Wimsey, and it's a courageous book because all the

357

previous books have been clever mystery puzzles rather like crossword puzzles, but this is a real novel about psychologically real people. The series starts out as shallow fun, gets better and deeper and develops continuing characters and events, and then, with *Gaudy Night,* becomes as good as books get. If you like classic cosy detective stories with timetables and letters of confession, I recommend starting at the beginning and coming at *Gaudy Night* with the full backstory. If you don't especially care for them, I recommend reading *Gaudy Night* alone— everything that's relevant is there, and you might be surprised how good it is.

I was thoroughly spoiled for *Gaudy Night* by Connie Willis's *To Say Nothing of the Dog.* I expect Willis thought that a book more than fifty years old would have been read by everyone who wanted to read it, but in fact new people come along all the time. Willis didn't spoil the mystery plot but the emotional plot—and I do think I might have appreciated it more without that. If you haven't read it, do consider that re-reading is forever but you can only read something for the first time once, and that after this paragraph I am going to have no hesitation about spoiling everything. (You could go and read it and come back. I'll still be here next week.)

George Orwell wrote a review of *Gaudy Night* in which he comprehensively did not get it, so comprehensively that it astonishes me. Orwell was a perceptive person, but he wrote about *Gaudy Night* as if it is just another episode in the detecting career of Lord Peter. I don't know if this was a blind spot of his, or a common reaction among men in 1936, or if possibly he didn't have time to read it and "reviewed" it on a quick skim. I don't know which of these is least discreditable. In any case, it is salutary to consider that one intelligent male reader, and one whole magazine, saw it as nothing more than a clever detective potboiler with an exotic setting, and one in which the detective finally gets the girl. The thing that makes me think that Orwell might not have actually read *Gaudy Night,* while having perhaps read some of the earlier ones, is that he swipes in passing at the way Sayers uses Lord Peter's title but doesn't enter into the actual class issues of the book at all.

There's no murder in *Gaudy Night.* The situation is that a women's college in Oxford, the fictional Shrewsbury College, is being plagued by poison pen letters and mean practical jokes, and Harriet Vane is asked to help capture the culprit, who could be anyone among the senior members or servants of the college. The atmosphere is all of academic women distrusting each other. The actual culprit turns out to be one of the servants, Annie, who has a grudge against one of the dons specifically and all of them generally for, in her eyes, taking jobs that should belong to men. Her husband was an academic who married beneath him, and after his suicide Annie has been reduced to scrubbing floors for a living. The first time I read this I had barely noticed the existence of Annie and was astonished at the revelation—as a servant she seems part of the wallpaper. So in one way Sayers was noticing class and making someone invisible visible, and in another she was reinforcing class prejudices by making the culprit an outsider and uneducated. You'd think Orwell would have found something to say about that, even if he was blind to the wider feminist implications. Annie is motivated by a desire to humiliate Miss de Vine, who revealed Annie's husband's plagiarism and made it impossible for him to continue as an academic which led to his suicide and Annie's subsequent poverty. From that she wants to humiliate all female academics. Annie sees her life ruined by Miss de Vine's adherence to academic truth—that in fact it was ruined by her husband's lack of such adherence is beyond her. She's part of a set of women we see mirroring each other. This is a book about women—culprit, victims and the primary detective are women. Annie's closest

359

mirror is Mrs. Goodwin, also a widow with a child away at school, who has trained as a secretary. We also see two old students, one whose marriage has ruined her mind, and one who has made a team with her husband and works with him. Then there's the young don Miss Chilperic, who is engaged to be married, and will therefore leave the college. It was actually illegal for married women to teach in Britain before WWII. Sayers doesn't say this because she assumes her readers will be utterly aware of it and can't imagine things being any different, but if ever there was anything that should be footnoted for a modern audience, this is it.

The other academics might as well be nuns, they are devoted not just to scholarship but to virginity as well. This is said explicitly—and really in 1936 those were the choices. Marriage meant giving up the work, and not marrying, for women, meant maintaining virginity. This leads me to Harriet. Harriet lived with a man in Bloomsbury without marrying him, somebody else murdered him, and she was tried for the murder and acquitted because of Lord Peter. (*Strong Poison*.) Because of the notoriety of the trial, Harriet's sexual status is known to everyone—and some people consider her utterly immoral because she had sex without marriage. This attitude—that people would care—is completely dated, gone like the dodo, and I have to work at understanding it. Harriet, in her thirties and unmarried, would be presumed to be a virgin were it not that her cohabitation had been gossip in the newspapers after her lover's death. Now the fact that she has had sexual experience is public knowledge, and affects people's behaviour towards her.

The book's attitude towards work, scholarship and creative work, is almost religious. I said "nuns" just now, and that applies here too—it is as if the nun's religious sacrifice of sexuality and family and personal love, on the altar of God's worship, is replaced by an expectation of that on the altar of scholarship.

This is very weird because of the inclusion of sex. Even if you leave that out, these days nobody expects that level of dedication. These days people frame work entirely in terms of money and not at all in terms of vocation. Annie, of course, sees it financially, it's all about (a man) earning a living to support a family. Work can be either, or any mixture. And of course, coming back to sex, there is the conversation with Miss de Vine in which she says that marriage can be a job for some women, that you can dedicate yourself to a partner the way you would to a fine passage of prose. We do not see any men doing this for their wives in the novel, the best we see is men not expecting their wives to do this for them.

The emotional heart of the book is Harriet's re-examination of her life and her work. For five years (and two novels) she has been refusing Lord Peter's proposals of marriage. Now she begins to consider them, and at last comes to see that they could have a marriage that would be a partnership, not a job. Before that she has to regain her self-respect, to have a place to stand and go on from. Harriet's conclusion is by no means assured, and the emotional trajectory of the book is extremely well done. The arguments for a marriage of equals, as opposed to the social expectation, have never been done better—we even see the disadvantage from the man's point of view: "someone who would try to manage me." Manipulation was the woman's trick, when the man had all the power, but having all the power and being manipulated wasn't much fun either.

There used to be a question of "what are women good for" and *Gaudy Night* would seem to give the answer that they are good for any number of things, Mrs. Goodwin and Phoebe Tucker as well as Miss Lydgate or Miss Hillyard—and that they are bad for them too, Annie and Miss Hillyard and Miss de Vine's lack of compassion. Harriet's choice is her own, and the best thing about it is that it pleases her. (Incidentally, who did

Sayers imagine was the audience for this erudite detective story, that could read Latin subjunctives and know all about Religio Medici? It's about Oxford dons, did she think they were the audience too? Or did she think, quite rightly, that the audience could look things up or let them go over their heads?)

102. Three short Hainish novels: Ursula K. Le Guin's Rocannon's World, Planet of Exile and City of Illusions

Rocannon's World and *Planet of Exile* were published in 1966, and *City of Illusions* in 1967. They're all available in one volume as *Worlds of Exile and Illusion* and I wish I owned it because the cover on my ratty old copy of *City of Illusions* was getting me some odd looks on the metro.

These books are all early works, all very short, and all set in the same universe—this is also the universe of *The Dispossessed*, *The Left Hand of Darkness*, *Four Ways to Forgiveness* and some other stories. Even when I was younger and had a passion for re-reading things in internal chronological order, I realised that reading the Hainish books this way wasn't very productive. What all the books have in common is some past history and some technology, there isn't an evolving arc of events the way there is, for instance, in Cherryh's Alliance-Union universe. Later books contradict earlier ones, late stories have people from planets that were contacted centuries apart working together and so on. The chronology between books written decades apart is best left unexamined. These three books, however, go together very well.

Rocannon's World is a story of an anthropologist stranded on a primitive planet. *Planet of Exile* is about a human colony abandoned on an alien planet. *City of Illusions* is about an alien lost on a far-future Earth. They are all about isolation and culture, and the different things people can choose to do when cut off from their own culture and immersed in another. They're all about exile and identity and coping with being cut off. It's possible to see them all as dry runs for *The Left Hand of Darkness*.

Planet of Exile is far and away my favourite of these three, I read it all the time and know it well. I hadn't read either of the other two for ages. I found them coming back to me as I read them. It's a fundamentally different experience of re-reading.

Rocannon's World begins with the short story "Semley's Necklace," a story that is science fiction and fantasy at the same time. Semley is a beautiful princess questing for a necklace made by and stolen by the dwarves. She goes into their underground kingdom, they take her to a strange place, she returns with the necklace to find that many years have passed, the baby she left is a grown woman, and the husband she hoped to please is dead. At the same time, she's an alien, the dwarves are another race of aliens, the strange place is on another planet and she lost the years by traveling at light speed. The story gains its power because we can see all this simultaneously as true. It's amazing and resonant.

The rest of the novel can't maintain this double level at the same pitch. We do see Rocannon both as an alien anthropologist and as an Odin figure, but it feels more forced. It's also hard to like Rocannon, he's too typical of the SF anthropologist hero, well equipped and resourceful, but too questioning of himself and the world to get away with that. I get the feeling that the story was pushing in the "what these people need is a honky" direction, in which Rocannon becomes a better alien than the aliens while saving their world and his, but Le Guin already right at the beginning of her career was pushing uphill against the weight of story.

One notably neat thing here is the overt notice of the colonialism of the human colonisers, collecting taxes from the aliens and raising their tech level without trying to understand them. This isn't the way we see the League of Worlds behaving later, but that Rocannon sees something wrong in it and stops it while he does his survey is something. Talking about not the way we see it later, there are more outright aliens here on Fomalhaut II than in all the rest of Hainish space put together. I seem to remember a mention later that the aliens are actually all genetically engineered humans like the rest of the Hainish variants, but they really don't feel like it.

The reason I like *Planet of Exile* so much is because it gives us the human and the alien points of view, and they're both given dignity and neither of them is privileged. Like *Rocannon's World* it has flashes of mythic resonance, unlike *Rocannon's World* they are myths in their own context and not in ours. It's also the Greenland colony in space—and in all of SF, which has done so many colonial worlds, I can't think of another example of this. Space colonies in SF are always America, except for *Planet of Exile,* which is the Vikings in Greenland, waiting for another ship to come from home and slowly losing their tech. The other reason I like it is because I love the long year. The planet has a sixty-year-long year, with children born in cohorts in spring and autumn. I love the society of nomads who build a winter city and the Alterrans clinging to the remnants of their civilization. I like the love story. It's a stark simple story, beautifully told, barely long enough to be a novel in 1966, hardly a couple of hours' read. I'd be quite happy if *Planet of Exile* were a modern novel and four hundred pages long, because while this is the story, the essence, the important bit, I'd love to know more.

The adaptation of the humans to the alien norm so that they might be able to interbreed may not be biologically realistic, but it's done very well, and I don't care anyway. It doesn't have the problem Butler thought she had with *Survivor* on intermarriage, because for one thing it took hundreds of years, and for another at the time Le Guin was writing that's what they thought did happen to the Greenland colony. Also, while it's potentially a happy ending for Rolery, it isn't unambiguously positive. Le Guin does have some of the humans horrified at the thought of assimilation—"Jacob Agat's grandchildren will be banging two rocks together."

I had forgotten, before this re-read of *City of Illusions,* that Falk, the lost alien wandering about on Earth generations after the conquest by the Shing, came from the planet of Exile and was a descendant of Jacob and Rolery. I'd also forgotten that it was called Werel, as that name isn't used there, and therefore horrified to realise that this is also one of the planets in *Four Ways to Forgiveness.* I don't want it to be! Banging rocks together would have been better.*

City of Illusions is the story of a man questing for himself and his context. Falk is left mindless, without memory, and alone in the forest because the Shing don't like outright killing people. He comes to a peaceful human settlement where he is cared for and becomes a person, a different person from who he was before. He travels west across what we recognise as a far-future America to come to the alien city of Es Toch and get back his memory and lose his self. Most of the book is about his journey, and is like the journey in *Rocannon's World,* one picaresque encounter after another. When he gets his mind back it becomes a much more

---

* Good news, it isn't. Le Guin herself forgot, and reused the name, she has a note on her Web page saying that the planets are not the same. Phew, what a relief!

interesting book, because then he has a dilemma rather than a quest. But it also becomes odd, because when Falk becomes Romarran he isn't the character you've been following across the continent for ages, he's someone different with Falk at the back of his head. I didn't like *City of Illusions* as a teenager—and yet I kept reading it, because I liked the rest of Le Guin so much, I kept thinking there was something I wasn't getting. Either I'm still not old enough for it, or it's mistimed somehow.

With the Shing, with their mindlying and hypocritical reverence for the outward forms of life, we have another take on colonialism. In *Rocannon's World* we have a coloniser noticing some problems with the system. In *Planet of Exile* we have the Greenland colony paradigm. Here we have Earth colonised and ruled for its own good and by arbitrary and alien moral standards and not liking it at all. We also potentially have a colony coming back to free the mother world. These three books are the books of the Enemy. In *Rocannon's World,* the League is preparing for the Enemy to arrive, and Rocannon thinks that the preparation itself is shaping the League badly. He also wonders whether the FTL bombers and ansible communications might be as useless as the swords of Hallan against the Enemy when they come. The enemy he faces and defeats are human rebels. But the League is being formed as a League of defence against this nameless, faceless, powerful and inevitable Enemy. In *Planet of Exile* the Enemy may or may not be the reason why communication has been cut off. The few humans have no idea what is happening in the wider universe. In *City of Illusions* the Enemy Shing have taken Earth, and possibly the rest of the universe, but we don't know about that. Romarran/Falk plans to get home before they know where his planet is and organise a force to free Earth.

In the later books set in this universe, we don't hear much about the Enemy. *The Dispossessed* is set much earlier, when very few worlds have been contacted and the ansible that allows them to be a League is only just being invented. (In a nifty connection, which must have been done backwards, in these books we hear every so often about Cetian mathematics, so much more advanced than Earth mathematics.) *The Left Hand of Darkness* and most of the other stories are set much later, when the Age of the Enemy is history, and history we don't hear anything about. I suspect Le Guin thought better of the Enemy and the Cold War mind-set they engender, or perhaps when she thought more about interstellar war she just didn't want to go there.

These are very early books—are they worth reading? They're not where I'd suggest starting with Le Guin—*The Left Hand of Darkness* and *The Dispossessed* and *A Wizard of Earthsea* are deservedly classics, up there with the best the field has ever produced. But if you already like Le Guin, then yes. She's always worth reading. I love *Planet of Exile* and always have, and the other two are travelogues across alien landscapes lit with flashes of brilliance.

103. On reflection, not very dangerous: Harlan Ellison's *The Last Dangerous Visions*

I suppose everyone knows the history of this volume. Harlan Ellison edited two brilliant anthologies, *Dangerous Visions* (1967) and *Again, Dangerous Visions* (1972). *The Last Dangerous Visions* was announced, and came out over budget and ten years late, and only then because Roger Elwood got on board to help Ellison with the heavy lifting. I'm not going to touch the question of whether Elwood's name should have appeared in the same size print as Ellison's on the cover—though it's a question that can still get fans buzzing whenever there's a new edition.

The important thing is the stories.

The first time I read the book I was disappointed. I don't think this was avoidable. After all the buildup and all the controversy, after the amazing success of the earlier books, I was expecting something that no book could possibly have fulfilled. "Visionary" proclaimed the cover, and even more provocatively, "We have seen the future!" Well, it wasn't visionary and they certainly hadn't seen the future. But we don't condemn science fiction for not being prediction—and it's just as well.

The best thing here is Ian Watson's "Universe on the Turn,"

a darkly funny satire of a future Britain that has become a surveillance state where everyone is obsessed with watching a
"reality" TV show about ordinary inane people trapped in a
house together. Calling the show "Big Brother" is perhaps a little unsubtle, but the parallels between the claustrophobia of the
show and the highly surveilled everyday lives is done with a
light touch that recalls the author's "The Very Slow Time
Machine" and *Whores of Babylon*.

Also brilliant, if implausible, is Bruce Sterling's "Living
Inside." This reminds me of his "We See Things Differently"
with its Islamic terrorists—but this time they steal planes and
crash them into the World Trade Center, bringing down both
towers. Don't ask whether that could even happen—within
days of the event people are questioning whether it was an
inside government job. Sterling makes you think you're getting
one kind of story and then gives you another—the attack
becomes the excuse for wars and loss of civil liberties across the
world. Chilling and memorable, much like *Distraction*.

Sterling's president is kind of an absent figurehead, but in
Sheckley's "Primordial Follies" the U.S. presidency has become
a dynasty of morons. I laughed, I always laugh at Sheckley's tall
tales, no matter how thin he stretches them. *The Monsters and
Other Science Fiction Tales* collects some of his best.

Jerry Pournelle is here with a story called "Free Enterprise"
in which NASA pretty much abandons space to robots, the shuttle fleet is allowed to decay, and prizes are offered for the first
private companies to meet various space goals. This has the usual
Pournelle style and flair, but this is a very familiar subject for
him—not dangerous, not visionary, not to mention so very
much not what happened. I like him better in more upbeat
romantic works like *Exile and Glory*.

I was impressed with Doris Piserchia's "The Residents of
Kingston," in which an ice storm in Canada paralyses the

country and one small city in particular. Nothing happens, and that's what's good about it. No looting, no riots, and the lights come back on because everyone works together. There aren't enough stories of cooperation and human kindness. This is a "Man against Nature" story in which man, though actually most of the characters are women, wins. We could do with more engineer heroes like Louise, out in the cold getting the power back, and domestic ones like Peggy making soup for the neighbours. I don't know that it's dangerous, it's certainly an unusual kind of vision.

James Gunn's "Among the Beautiful Bright Children" is a solid science fiction story about technology—"cell phones" and the "Internet" changing the way people communicate, and even meet. The "children" of the Internet age chat online and even fall in love through the medium of text as it whizzes around the world, living more and more of their lives through the computer. Now this is visionary, and maybe even dangerous. (Gunn has a new collection out, *Human Voices*.)

Other highlights include Cordwainer Smith, Octavia Butler (I like the way China's becoming capitalist without liberalising, interesting), Michael Bishop, Mack Reynolds (with a utopian story of the fall of the Soviet Union in which it all just collapses like a house of cards in 1989) and Clifford Simak.

Lowlights—well "Emerging Nation," Bester's story of a black president trying to force through a health care bill while the nation is engaged in a war in the Middle East that's just a carbon copy of Vietnam. (Did they really think it could take so long for the US to become a first-world country?) Michael Coney's story ("Susy Is Something Special") of the complete economic collapse of Iceland and a worldwide depression—this isn't visionary, this is just 1929 all over again. And I just couldn't buy Algis Budrys's "Living Alone in the Jungle"—all about a stolen election, way too much detail about the U.S. system and "hanging chads" and the Supreme Court—who cares about this stuff?

On the whole this is a good collection. It's not as good as the first one, but probably up there with the second. It's unfortunate that the delays and the hype made it into something that no book could live up to. It's also funny looking at all these stories by such different writers, all written at about the same time— they made such weird predictions about the future, while missing all the real developments that were about to happen. These futures, except maybe Gunn's, are so tame compared to what really happened. And were people paying attention? The first of the experiments that gave us cold fusion and put the solar system in our grasp had already been done by 1982, guys! And what's with so many people wishing away the Cold War? And why are these visions—with the honourable exception of Piserchia's—so very bleak? Oh well. Definitely worth reading. I'm glad Elwood helped Ellison get it out—for a while there I was thinking the universe was conspiring to suppress it for some mysterious reason.

April Fool! Yes, this is another April Fool jape. The truth is that Ellison never produced the much-hyped third volume. All authors and story titles are actually ones sold to Ellison for the volume. Elwood was a very prolific anthologist.

104. Why do I re-read things I don't like?

P-L asked an interesting question:

> You seem to re-read quite a few books that you don't actually like. (At least, I think this is not the first one you've mentioned. . . .) Can I ask why? There are so many, many books out there; it seems like it would be easier to find something new that you do like.

There are several reasons why I might re-read a book I don't like. The main reason is that I'm an hopeful kind of person. The second I think is habit. I started to read when I was very young, and I constantly encountered books that were too old for me. I was constantly being told that things were too old for me, and sometimes they were and sometimes they weren't, but I early became familiar with the idea of getting more out of something on a re-read. In any case, if I didn't enjoy something I'd plough my way through without even necessarily understanding it. I'd finish it with a sigh of relief.

The supply of books at home was finite. There were quite a few books, but some of them were forbidden and I had to go to the trouble of stealing them, and then reading and replacing them unnoticed. The books I was allowed I read and re-read. I so deeply internalised this state of things that P-L's "so many many books out there" still doesn't feel normal—it feels delightful, it feels like putting one over on the universe. The existence of all those unread books feels like a violation of the Second Law of Thermodynamics, like magic. It never quite feels like something I can rely on.

But since the supply of books at home was finite, eventually I'd have re-read all the books I liked too often to read them again, and at regular intervals I'd try the ones I hadn't liked to see if I'd grown into them in the interval. Sometimes, I would have. *Lorna Doone* and *Ivanhoe* were both books that I didn't get and then I did. So was *David Copperfield*. But even the earlier times I read them, I got something out of them. I didn't like them, no, but there were images that stayed with me, flashes, moments. I'd remember that moment and think that I was older and the whole book might be like that now. Maybe, I thought in the back of my mind, I'm old enough now. Maybe this time I will like it.

Or, I might decide that I hadn't been fair to a book other people like a lot. This is the case with *Lord of Light*. A lot of people think it's a wonderful book. It was Potlatch's Book of Honor this year. I have friends who think it's one of the best books ever. I'm always inclined to give a book the benefit of the doubt and think it might have been me. And *Lord of Light* certainly has those flashes. If I can remember the flashes, I'm prepared to give something another go.

My usual reason now for re-reading something I don't like, or I like less, is because it's part of a series and I'm re-reading all of it. I tend to read every word in order, not skip about the way I hear some people do, and if it's the kind of series where everything counts, I don't like to skip bits there either. This is how I read *Teckla* and *Athyra* frequently enough to have them grow on me. Sometimes I do normally skip a volume I don't like but I'll re-read it for completion when I'm planning to write about it. This is the case with *Cetaganda*.

But all the time here I have been talking about books I don't like or don't get, books I almost like and feel I ought to like and might like if the world or the book or I were older, or just a little different. If I really hate a book, I'm never going to re-read it, and this was the case even when I was a little kid. Nothing would induce me to re-read *The Sparrow* or *Xenocide* or *Grunts*. Or, for that matter, *A Laodician*.

105. Yakking about who's civilised and who's not: H. Beam Piper's Space Viking

Space Viking (1963) starts out looking like a story of vengeance among the neobarbarian remnants of a collapsed Galactic Empire, and then becomes a meditation on the benefits of civilisation and how that is distinct from technology. It contains a fundamentally flawed assumption about the way society works, but it's a fast fun read. It isn't my favourite Piper, but I'm fond of it and re-read it fairly often.

One of the things Piper's very good at is taking a historical situation and translating it to space. Here, as you'd expect, it's the centuries after the fall of Rome, spread out across the stars. The obvious comparison is Asimov's *Foundation*—and what a very different kind of book this is. *Foundation* is all about the centuries and society seen in stop-motion over time. *Space Viking* is one moment (about a decade) as time goes on heedless. *Foundation* is detached from time, seeing it from outside. *Space Viking* is immersed in it.

Another thing Piper is good at is having the one competent man (and it is always a man) who changes the world. Lucas Trask leaves his homeworld of Gram prepared to risk everything to seek revenge on the lunatic who killed his bride at their wedding. On the way to revenge, almost by accident, he builds a star-spanning trade empire, becomes king of his own planet, and realises that he's become absorbed in building civilisation and finds revenge an irritating distraction from that. Trask's adventures completely change the history of six planets, and possibly more.

In a neat bit of worldbuilding, the Swordworlds, where the Space Vikings come from, are named after famous swords—the first one was Excalibur. The ex-Empire planets are named after gods of ancient pantheons. This means the reader can immediately and easily tell them apart without a scorecard—if a planet's Baldur, you know it's an old Empire planet, if it's Durendal it's a swordworld. All of the science-fictional details make sense and fit together, the contragravity, the nuclear weapons, the wars on planets and in space. Time is given in multiples of hours, which is very authentic but which I find slightly irritating as it means constant mental arithmetic.

The thing Piper gets wrong, and which you have to bite your lip and ignore in order to enjoy the book, is the idea that when you take people out of a society the old society can never recover. If this were true, there would be no Einstein, no Tolkien, no Beatles, because the boldest and best people had already abandoned Europe for America and once that had happened no more intelligent people could ever emerge. It's true that if all the educated people leave a planet it will temporarily collapse, but if some leave and the schools are still there, which is what we see, in a generation it won't matter, because genes don't work that way. If you lose a thousand trained engineers out of a population of a billion, which is what Piper says, there'll barely be a wobble. And the whole eugenics angle is even more distasteful.

One of the things Piper's interested in here is showing how civilised planets collapse, and how barbarous planets become civilised.

There are two examples of the first, Gram and Marduk. Gram is feudal and is decivilising from the top down, as the leaders squabble and cheat the populace—timarchy decaying into oligarchy. Marduk suffers a classic democracy-collapses-into-tyranny modeled on the rise of Mussolini. Now, this is all in Plato (what do they teach them in these schools?) and it's all very pat—too pat. When you can choose your examples from anywhere you like it starts to look like dice loading. Any writer's doing this with any choices, but it works better if it doesn't look like special pleading. If it wasn't for the whole eugenics thing putting me on edge, I'd probably have let this Platonic cycle thing slide past without thinking too much about it.

In any case, the story begins with a madman committing murder and ends with the same madman dead, and everything else, the rise and fall of civilisations and Trask's journey back to being able to love, is what happens along the way. Like most Piper, this is a great book for teenagers. I gobbled it up uncritically when I was fourteen, and it did me no harm at all. My copy, with a horrible generic spaceship cover, was bought new for 85p.

106. Feast or famine?

In my post on re-reading books I dislike, I mentioned that I grew up with a finite supply of books that I'd re-read, and several people responded that on the contrary they grew up with an infinite supply of books they felt they could never get through.

P-L says:

> I have my own neuroses about reading as a result. Because life is finite and literature is, for all intents and purposes, infinite, choosing a book feels to me like a zero-sum game. Because I decided on a whim to read *The Magus* this week, the whole queue was pushed one step farther back, and as a result there is one more book (or two short ones) that I'll never get a chance to read.

And Individ-ewe-al:

> I basically don't reread, because when I was a kid I was always overwhelmed by how many new things there were out there, rather than afraid of running out of books. Nowadays I occasionally reread my absolute favourite books.

And Atrus:

> I lived pretty close to not one but three public libraries,
> so the concept of a limited amount of available books
> was—and is—completely alien to me. Like p-l, my
> problem at most was one of too much choice and not
> enough direction.

This is all very alien to me. Even though the world is full of
books, I don't want to read most of them. Even if you only count
fiction, there's a lot written in genres I don't like, or written by
authors I don't enjoy. Also I read fast, and I read all the time. I
don't find libraries infinite—I mean I adore libraries, but I can
read my way through everything I want to read in a couple of
months. When I was twelve I read all the science fiction in
Aberdare library in one summer: all of it, Anderson to Zelazny,
in alphabetical order. These days it wouldn't take as long, because
I'd already have read most of it. And I've read everything by my
favourite writers too, and they don't write fast enough to keep
me going. It never feels like a zero-sum game to me, it always
feels as if there isn't enough to read, and even if there is, as if
tomorrow there might not be. I'll admit I have a whole bookcase
of unread books, and when I moved to Canada I had four boxes
of them, labelled: "Misc Readpile," "More Misc Readpile,"
"The Further Adventures of Misc Readpile" and "Misc Readpile
Goes West." One or two of the books from those boxes may still
be on my unread shelves.

Even when I have plenty of books, and access to libraries,
that doesn't mean that I'll be able to put my hand on the kind of
thing I want to read this minute. Re-reading always gives me
that. There's a pleasure in reading something new, certainly, but
there's also pleasure in revisiting old friends. I think I've said
before that I consider the first re-read of a book the completion

of the reading experience, I don't really know how I feel about a book until I come back to it. I feel that something worth reading only once is pretty much a waste of time.

My ideal relationship with a book is that I will read it and love it and re-read it regularly forever. Sometimes I will know ahead of time that I'll love it, other times it'll be a surprise. Some books that lie around for years waiting for me to get to them later became favourites. More often I'll pick up something because it looks interesting and then immediately read all of that new-to-me author's backlist as fast as I can find it. I don't do this only with fiction, there are biographers and historians whose complete works I have gulped down this way.

I think the real issue is psychological. The people I quoted at the beginning of the post feel as if reading is finite and they shouldn't waste any time. I feel the complete opposite, that reading is infinite. Of course, some of this depends on reading speed—I read fast, and I read a lot. It's a rare week I don't get through at least a book every day, and some weeks a great deal more. If I'm stuck in bed it's not unusual for me to read half a dozen books in a day. I know I'm not going to live forever, I know there are more books than I can ever read. But I know that in my head, the same way I know the speed of light is a limit. In my heart I know reading is forever and FTL is just around the corner.

On the re-reading panel at Anticipation, I said a couple of things that Kate Nepveu described as "making lemonade out of very sour lemons." The first was that I have some unread books that are the last book, or the last book I got hold of, by favourite authors who are dead. They're never going to write anymore, and when I've read that book I've read everything. I'm saving these books for when I get diagnosed with a terminal illness. That way, when life does become inescapably finite, I'll have new books by favourite authors to look forward to. The other thing is, that should I not be diagnosed with a terminal illness but instead get Alzheimers, I'll forget writing my own books and be able to read them as if for the first time, as if someone else had written them. And that will be fun too!

107. Bellona, Destroyer of Cities, Jay Scheib's play of Samuel Delany's Dhalgren

When I posted on my LiveJournal that there was a play version of *Dhalgren,* one of my friends thought it was an April Fool. *Dhalgren*'s more than 800 pages long, a cult classic, it really doesn't seem like something that could be adapted for a stage version. Since it had been, I felt I had to go—indeed, since it was there and I could, that it would be irresponsible not to. So I went to New York on the train, and last Saturday evening ten of us went to an avant-garde theatre called The Kitchen to see *Bellona, Destroyer of Cities.*

The first thing is that it was *Dhalgren.* It felt like *Dhalgren.* What it felt like was quite familiar to me—it was just like when you go to see a Shakespeare play where they've cut some scenes, set it in a different period, switched the gender of some characters and conflated others. You want to argue with their choices, but that argument doesn't stop it being a legitimate version of the play. And that's just how this was. There were things I liked and things I didn't like, things that worked, odd choices, things that got left out or underplayed that I'd have kept, but it was inarguably *Dhalgren,* and that's really quite an achievement.

The set was the skeleton of buildings, with some walls present, so you could partly see in. Things happening that you couldn't see could sometimes be seen on a big screen, so your attention was constantly divided. I often don't like this kind of technique, but it worked really well for this material. A couple of other effective theatrical things were a character in a spacesuit being carried by two other characters as if weightless and floating, and Eddy flinging himself around and slamming himself to the floor. Most of the sex happens in flashes in the back room and is incomprehensible and multiplex, just like in the book. I loved the way we kept seeing the original *Dhalgren* cover, first on the floor behind a sex scene on the screen, and then as the cover of the poetry book.

When you reverse genders, you learn an awful lot about gender expectations. Charm, which the Kid has, is an expected quality in women, less so in men. So making her a woman made her much more conventional. The same goes for sexual receptivity—the Kid doesn't initiate but falls into what sex comes along. I think she's a less interesting character as female. You also lose a lot of the queer stuff, especially as they chose to leave out the threesome and the whole dynamic of that. The thing I didn't immediately notice is that the same goes for violence. In the book, Kid is beaten up, but later is violent himself, in the Scorpion runs, and mugging a guy. Here we see the beating, but not any of the performative violence. This changes the balance. I know why they did it. There's a way in which the plot of *Dhalgren* wraps—not just the Joycean beginning with "to wound the autumnal city" and ending with "I have come" but the parallel scenes and dialogue with the people leaving/arriving as Kid arrives/leaves. Those people are women when Kid is a man, and so it must have seemed like a great idea to have a female Kid and another iteration. But Delany had already been reversing expectations. Taking a largely passive gentle poet and making him female plays into stereotypes and expectations, not against them, and they could have done with more awareness of that.

Most of the play is very close to the book, but with very different pacing. Much of the dialogue is straight off the page. Characters are conflated, huge chunks are left out, but I could always see why they'd done it—and with all that, it's really surprisingly true to the original. *Dhalgren*'s a book with a lot in it, and because of its Moebius spiral structure it's hard to say what's essential. I have no idea how comprehensible the play would have been without the novel breathing down its shoulder. But they gave us the ruined city, the spiral, the whole thing with the poetry, the elevator shaft, George and June, and the vexed question of shots and the riot.

What we didn't have was science fiction. All the things that make *Dhalgren* take place in the vague future—the holograms, the orchids, the chain with prisms and mirrors and lenses—were left out. Instead of science fiction's promise of answers just out of sight, the play gave us magic realism, or maybe magic surrealism. I'd been wondering how they were going to do the holograms, which are very important to the novel, and had thought of several ways that would work. I was sorry but not distressed—what bothered me was replacing the orchid with a gun. Mind you, it bothers me when they replace swords with guns in Shakespeare plays, and for the same reason—it's a different distance of violence. Delany deliberately gives the Scorpions claws, not guns, there's a scene in the book where they explicitly repudiate a gun. It's strange that they got some of the hardest stuff so right and then did this. Oh well.

The actors were all very good and the doubling was clear and effective. The run is over, or I'd recommend it. Perhaps it will be revived. It was *Dhalgren,* and I'm very glad I saw it.

108. Not much changes on the street, only the faces: George Alec Effinger's When Gravity Fails

When Gravity Fails was published in 1987 and its future has dated astonishingly well. Indeed, it seems much more plausible as the future of 2010 than it did when I first read it in 1988—though it doesn't seem as if it will take as long as 2172 to get there. The Soviet Union has disintegrated at some point in the past into numerous splinter successor states. The United States has done the same, and so has the European Union, mostly splintering down beyond the country level—but Germany has reunited. The Islamic world looks on with hungry eyes. Meanwhile, everyone has a mobile phone, direct neural interfacing using modular personalities ("moddys") and add-ons ("daddies") is common, and gender reassignment (male to female or female to male) is optional, effective, and easy, but expensive. Marid Audran, son of a Fellahin mother and a French father, is just trying to make a living as a private investigator in an unnamed North African city somewhere east of Algiers, when his life gets complicated by a series of murders. It has barely dated at all.

I originally picked it up back in 1988 because the notion of a noir detective in an Islamic future intrigued me, and I bought it because the first paragraph just totally hooked me.

> Chiriga's nightclub was right in the middle of the Budayeen, eight blocks from the Eastern gate, eight blocks from the cemetery. It was handy to have the graveyard so close-at-hand. The Budayeen was a dangerous place and everyone knew it. That's why there was a wall around three sides. Travelers were warned away from the Budayeen, but they came anyway. They'd heard about it all their lives and they were damned if they were going home without seeing it for themselves. Most of them came in the Eastern gate and started up the Street curiously; they'd begin to get a little edgy after two or three blocks, and they'd find a place to sit and have a drink or eat a pill or two. After that they'd hurry back the way they'd come, and count themselves lucky to get back to the hotel. A few weren't so lucky and stayed behind in the cemetery. Like I said, it was a very conveniently located cemetery and saved trouble all around.

Effinger's writing on the word and sentence level is just beautiful, the voice is perfect, and remains so all the way through, and the way he wraps the theme around there is what he does in the whole book. This was a book that couldn't have happened without cyberpunk, but that itself isn't cyberpunk. There are no hackers here, and almost no computers—though it feels reasonable for the Budayeen that there wouldn't be. Holoporn, yes, drugs to get you up or down, prostitutes of all genders and some in between, personality modules of anything from salesmen to serial killers via sex kittens, but no computers. The Street is what comes from cyberpunk, and perhaps the neural wiring, a little.

But what Effinger does with it, making it a North African street that really feels like something out of the future of another culture, is entirely his own. Effinger said the Budayeen was based on the French Quarter of New Orleans, where he lived, as much as it was based on anywhere, but it has the feel of a real place, grimy and edgy and rundown and full of the wrong sort of bars.

The detective story is just the plot that keeps everything moving. The real story is about Marid Audran's orbit through the Budayeen and himself. He solves the mystery, both mysteries, but that's not the most important thing. The book's title, which sounds so solidly science-fictional, is from Dylan: "when gravity fails and negativity won't pull you through." This is the story of what happens to you when that happens to you. Effinger could really write and he doesn't pull his punches—this can be disturbing, and it's all first person and very close at hand. It's also very clever and darkly funny.

There are two sequels, *A Fire in the Sun* and *The Exile Kiss*. They're just as brilliantly written, but I seldom re-read them. There are two reasons for that. The first is that *When Gravity Fails* stands alone pretty well, there's room for more, certainly, but it finishes a trajectory. The three books taken together set up a new trajectory that aches for a fourth volume, which will never be completed due to the US's lack of a decent health care system and Effinger's consequent early death in 2002. The other reason is that the second and third book get very bleak, and I don't always have the fortitude for that.

109. History inside out:
Howard Waldrop's
Them Bones

Howard Waldrop is known for his imaginative and quirky short stories, *Them Bones* (1984) is his only solo novel. It's also original and quirky and weird, and I love it to bits and always have. There's an overall frame story about people in the dying post-nuclear horror of 2002 trying to go back in time to change the past that led to their future, but the real story is in three strands. There's the story of Yazoo, the advance scout who winds up in an alternate world, and there's the story of Bonnie and her group of soldiers who end up in the thirteenth century, and there's the story of Bessie and the archaeologists in 1929 who find something quite impossible when excavating a Mound Builder mound. These three strands alternate and interweave, so by the end of the book the reader knows everything without necessarily having been told everything. What makes this book so great is Waldrop's knowledge of history and masterful interweaving of stories to make them more than the sum of their parts.

This is a book I tend to remember as lighter than it is. Actually it's full of whistling past the graveyard—all the worlds in it are ending. The future world is hardly sketched in, it's assumed to be the default world the reader knows—in 1984 we were still regularly waking up from nightmares of nuclear destruction. Its future can go with Varley's "Air Raid" which also uses time travel to try to save humanity.

The worlds of the past are seen in much greater detail, particularly the Mound Builder culture in the alternate world in which Yazoo finds a home. Waldrop makes the details of daily life in that world seem very real. It also does a lot with our assumptions about pre-Columbian America and timelessness—this is an alternate history that's part of a complex changing dynamic culture that has traditions and innovations. It too is ending, with the introduction of plagues and wars—though why they have come now and not thirty years before when the traders first visited isn't clear. There's a lovely passage where the Greek-speaking Islamic traders give Yazoo an update on history on their side of the Atlantic—no Alexander, Carthage beat Rome, no Christianity, science has continued to advance slowly but surely. Waldrop's well aware that his average reader will be far better historically educated about this kind of thing than about the American cultures Yazoo has found and he's teasing us with this. It's the Mound Builder culture we see in detail and that really comes to life here.

The world of 1929 archaeology is also seen in fascinating detail—shellacking the anomalous horse bones—Bessie the female archaeologist and her male colleagues are working against time as the rains come to flood their site and wash away all their evidence. The story of the excavation interlocks with Bonnie's diary and the duty rosters of the camp—we're hearing what happened to the Americans in the past both from their own notes and from Bessie's excavations. What we don't know is whether this 1929 is part of our world, or part of the world they came from, or whether these are the same. It reads like our 1929, and there's nothing to indicate that their 2002 wasn't supposed to be our 2002, but they could both be slightly different worlds. Certainly time travel doesn't work the way they think it does—they were aiming for the 1940s. Maybe the future is easy to change, and maybe your own past is impossible to reach. The set of quotations used to start the book and as chapter headings strongly suggest the latter. Bonnie and her soldiers are lightly sketched, seen more in shadow than in substance, though the throwaway bit about the Book of Mormon is amazing.

A normal book about modern Americans thrown into the past would be like S. M. Stirling's *Island in the Sea of Time* or Eric Flint's *1632,* and comparing those to *Them Bones* really highlights some things. Firstly, those are books about success, about Americans winning, whereas this very much is about people setting off to change the past and finding themselves swallowed up in it. Secondly, they're books about modern Americans interacting with Europeans in the past, while this really isn't. There is an Aztec interlude in ISOT, but it's an interlude to the main plot. In *Them Bones,* the Arab traders are an interlude in the important interactions with the Americans of the past.

Them Bones was published as one of Terry Carr's Ace Science Fiction specials, and it starts with a heartening little introduction which says how science fiction is in the doldrums and needs originality and shaking up. It's always cheering to read things like that from thirty years ago and note that the genre is still here.

110. I'd love this book if I didn't loathe the protagonist: Harry Turtledove and Judith Tarr's Household Gods

Harry Turtledove and Judith Tarr's *Household Gods* is a well-written book that always annoys the heck out of me. I thought about it after finishing *Them Bones* and wondering what other stories have time travel that doesn't achieve anything.

Nicole Gunther-Perrin is a lawyer in Los Angeles, and she's the most irritating person you could ever spend a whole book with. Usually when fans call people "mundanes" in a sneering way it makes me recoil, but in Nicole we have a character who truly is mundane, or even a caricature of a mundane. She has no curiosity, no education (about anything other than her specialty, law), no idea how anything works, and poor social skills. Worst of all she's so self-centered, you can hardly escape her gravity well.

She needs to be like that for the plot to work—divorced with two little kids, passed over for promotion, she prays to the Roman gods Liber and Libera, about whom she knows essentially nothing beyond their names, for them to send her back to their time. They kindly do, sending her back to the body of an ancestress, Umma, in Carnuntum on the borders of the Roman Empire in the time of Marcus Aurelius. There, instead of behaving like any other protagonist of this kind of novel, she freaks out at the lice, disease, death, invasions, and sexism, and longs to be back in California. In some ways, yes, it's refreshing to have a time travel book where the protagonist doesn't know everything about history and technology and invent ninety-eight things and save the day, but did it have to be the one where the protagonist is a girl?

The good thing about this book is the background. Nicole finds herself in the body of Umma, a widowed tavern keeper in Roman Carnuntum. She's given the ability to speak Latin, but nothing else. She has to cope with Umma's life and responsibilities and problems. Carnuntum feels real in every detail, the baths, the tavern, the lives and relationships and attitudes of the other characters. As a story about how people lived at the edge of the Roman Empire, it's brilliant. That's why I kept reading it the first time and why I have re-read it since. (The rest of it is so good that I tend to forget between times just how annoying Nicole is.) T. Calidius Severus the dyer, his son Caius, Julia the slave who is afraid to be freed, Umma's children, her brother, her neighbours, even Marcus Aurelius—they're all wonderfully real, and especially nice to spend time with because they're not Nicole.

The problem with it is that ignorant selfish Nicole constantly gets in the way with her ridiculous attitudes. She sees a legionary soldier and thinks, "Didn't Rome have a Vietnam to teach them about the horrors of war?" She has no idea that while in her own time there's a glass ceiling, in the time she's come to women are legally chattels of men. Her father was an alcoholic, so she's horrified to see people drinking wine. I'd like the book more if I didn't feel that the entire novel is setup for her to be as ignorant and annoying as possible and then Learn A Lesson. This is a personal fulfillment story, and indeed she learns a lesson and is personally fulfilled, but I still want to kick her. Some of the lessons she learns—about the army protecting the town, about wine being safer than water, about science and technology making the world safer and more equal—are obvious. Some others, such as the bit about the benefits of smacking children, are odder, by which I mean that I don't agree.

Mild spoilers ahead. Though mostly they're the kind of spoiler I got for Card's Alvin Maker books when I discovered from external sources that William Henry Harrison was elected president and then died. . . .

The accounts of the pestilence and the invasion and the famine are vivid and individual. This is the kind of writing that's very difficult to do well, and Tarr and Turtledove carry it off perfectly—these are the kind of close-up personal views of history happening that make it seem real. The same goes for the encounter with Marcus Aurelius, with his famous personal integrity. This is the kind of encounter with a "celebrity" that often weights a story in the wrong way, but here it's excellent.

Now a couple of specific spoilers, but still fairly mild ones:

The thing about Nicole that I think best sums her up is that at the end of the book, when she is back in California, she goes into a bookshop to check whether she can really read Latin or whether the whole thing was a hallucination. She finds she can really read Latin. Then she *goes out of the bookshop again*! There she is, with the ability to look up the actual history and find out what happened next to people she saw what was for her literally yesterday, a bookshop where Marcus Aurelius' *Meditations* is very likely available, and she just walks out. This is typical of her whole attitude, even after the authors have piled calamities on her so that she has learned to thank people, and realize how nice hot showers, and doctors, and regular meals can be.

I remember a friend of mine complaining about Thomas

Covenant: "Any of us would give our right arms to be in the Land, and he goes about moaning and he won't even believe that it's real." That's my exact problem with Nicole—she's had this marvellous opportunity and there she is so passive and ignorant that I want to kick her out of the way and do it myself and prove that women can be Martin Padway and not all Nicole Gunther-Perrin. (Also, I have had head lice. They're not that bad.)

We never learn what happened to Umma—she wasn't in Nicole's body, so where was she? Is she going to wake up the next morning in the lumpy bed with no memories of the last six months? Or what? I'd really have liked a hint. Also, I'd have liked a companion volume of "Umma spends six months in Nicole's life" because I bet she would have coped just fine, though she might not have wanted to go home again.

The world really is excellent. The history is accurate, and the daily life is as accurate as possible. If you can put up with Nicole, it's terrific.

111. Screwball-comedy time travel: John Kessel's Corrupting Dr. Nice

Corrupting Dr. Nice is about time travel and con games, it's fast paced and funny, the chapter titles all come from classic screwball comedies, and it contains a cute dinosaur called Wilma. If you don't want to read it already, you probably won't care that it also has one of the best courtroom scenes ever, the trial of the apostle Simon for terrorism.

Corrupting Dr. Nice is the kind of book that's either your kind of book or it isn't. I bought it because the British edition had a very striking cover. It shows a red car whizzing past a row of Roman legionaries with rifles standing by a city gate, plus an Ursula K. Le Guin quote—the combination got me. It doesn't matter that this moment doesn't occur in the book, it accurately represents the story, as does Le Guin's comment "brilliantly intelligent, light-handed and warm hearted."

There are a lot of different ways of doing time travel stories. What Kessel does here is to take the idea of a very large but finite number of universes (137 splitting off every second) which he calls "moment universes." Time travel to different moment universes, whether settled and exploited from the future or "unburned" and never visited before, is easy but controlled—you usually move from one stage to another, stay in tourist hotels, and visit the sights.

This is in one sense a satire on tourism and exploitation of the third world, but along with that come the deeper implications of what it means to exploit different versions of the past. In the second half of the book we see what it's doing to the future—it's very hard for the ordinary people of the future to get a job when famous people from the past are available. The past might be full of locals begging for bacteriophages and televisions, but the future isn't a nice place to live either—people are selling off organs to survive. This is a comedy, and it is full of comedic set-pieces, but it's a better comedy for being set against a dark background.

Dr. Owen Vannice ("Dr. Nice") is the son of very rich parents, a klutz, and a palaeontologist who spends most of his time in the Cretaceous. He has a trusty bodyguard and sidekick, Bill, who happens to be an AI inside his head who can take over his body from time to time.

Genevieve Faison and her father, August, are con artists. Owen steals a baby apatosaur and illegally takes it forward through time. He meets Gen and August in the tourist hotel in first-century Jerusalem. They decide to scam him and things get complicated from there on, with the story involving true love, revenge, disguise, and of course the baby dinosaur.

With this setup, Kessel is potentially facing the "Riverworld problem"—if you can have anyone from any time in history, all mixed together, then what do you do with them? What he does works very well—he sticks to his protagonists from the future, Owen and Gen, and to Simon the apostle, who when we first meet him is working in the kennels of the hotel.

We see Jesus, Lincoln, Mozart, Freud, Jung, etc. in passing, enough to pull off the joke and create the illusion of a world full

397

of people that people in the near future would think are worth the trouble of "rescuing" from their own contexts, but we don't see enough of them to get bogged down. Feynman being recruited as the drummer for Mozart's band is a good one-line joke, that's all it needs and all it gets. Same with Jesus' talk show—Kessel mentions it, we don't need to see it. This is a believably complex future world, with time travel and with protesters against time travel, with neo-Victorians, with downloadable personalities and implantable AIs, and with James Dean working as a receptionist because he got fat at forty. You sail through it so quickly that it all glitters past.

On the human emotional level, I am seldom convinced that characters in romantic comedies who have deceived and tricked each other will be redeemed by love and remain together happily, and this is no exception. It isn't a problem, especially as the Simon strand ends so well, but I think Kessel was right to stop where he did and not a moment later.

I picked this up now because I was thinking about time travel. *Them Bones* and *Household Gods* both have time travel that doesn't work very well. *Corrupting Dr. Nice* has time travel that's well understood and works really well and can bring people and objects from the past, and is still not helping. This is in the Paratime tradition though it doesn't have alternate universes until time travelers have started to mess them up.

112. Academic Time Travel: Connie Willis's To Say Nothing of the Dog

Like *Corrupting Dr. Nice*, *To Say Nothing of the Dog* is a comedy about time travel. But while Kessel's model was the screwball comedy movie, Willis's was Jerome K. Jerome's gentle Victorian novel *Three Men in a Boat*. Like Willis, I was alerted to the existence of *Three Men in a Boat* by the mention of it in *Have Space Suit, Will Travel*, unlike her I've never been able to get through it. If I hadn't already been sure I liked Willis, I wouldn't have picked this up the first time. Fortunately, I was sure, and even more fortunately this is enjoyable even if Jerome makes you want to tear out your hair.

To Say Nothing of the Dog takes place in Willis's "Firewatch" universe, along with her earlier *Doomsday Book* and more recent *Blackout* (and much anticipated *All Clear*). In this universe, there's time travel but it's for academic research purposes only. It's useful to historians who want to know what really happened, and experience the past, but otherwise useless because time protects itself and you can't bring anything through the "net" that will have any effect. The thought of time tourists hasn't occurred in this universe, or rather it has been firmly squelched—and just as well, considering the problems historians manage to create all on their own.

Despite having time travel and time travel's ability to give you more time, Willis's historians seem to be like my family and live in a perpetual whirlwind of ongoing crisis where there's never enough time for proper preparation.

To Say Nothing of the Dog is a gently funny book about some time travelers based at Oxford in the twenty-first century dashing about Victorian England trying to fix a glitch in time, while at home Coventry Cathedral is being rebuilt on Merton's playing fields. Like all of Willis's writing, it has an intense level of "I Want To Read It," that thing where you don't want to put the book down. With this book she succeeds in a number of difficult things—she makes a gentle comedy genuinely funny, she has time travel and paradox without things seeming pointless, and she almost successfully sets a book in a real country not her own.

There aren't going to be any spoilers in this review, but I should warn you that the book itself contains spoilers for Dorothy Sayers's *Gaudy Night*.

To Say Nothing of the Dog is charming. It's funny and gentle and it has Victorian England and severely time-lagged time travelers from the near future freaking out over Victorian England, it's full of jumble sales and beautiful cathedrals and kittens. This is a complicated funny story about resolving a time paradox, and at the end when all is revealed everything fits together like oiled clockwork. But what makes it worth reading is that it is about history and time and the way they relate to each other. If it's possible to have a huge effect on the past by doing some tiny thing, it stands to reason that we have a huge effect on the future every time we do anything.

The evocation of Victorian Britain is quite successful, the only place it falls down is the way they go to Coventry, from

Oxford, just like that. I'm sure Willis had a Bradshaw railway timetable open before her and every train she mentions exists, but British people, whether in the nineteenth century or for that matter now, know in their bones that a hundred miles is a long way, and do not just take off lightly on an expedition of that nature, even with spirit guidance. That's the only thing that rings really false, which is pretty good going for an American. There is the issue of the lack of mobile phones in the future, which is caused by Willis having written *Doomsday Book* before cell phones took off, and which I think is one of those forgivable problems, like the astonishing computers in old SF that have big spools of tape that can hold 10,000 words each!

I read this the first time because it's Willis, and really I'm just going to buy whatever she writes because she's that good. I re-read it now as part of my continued contemplation of useless time travel. Willis's continuum protects itself: actual changes and paradoxes may be built into it but the real purpose of time travel seems to be to help people to learn lessons about themselves. There are no alternate universes, no "moment universes" and while there's often a threat of a change that will change everything, time itself is resilient. It's possible (from *Blackout*) that she's doing something more than this with time and the drops, if so, I'll be interested to discover what it is.★

★ No, she wasn't, unfortunately.

113. The Society of Time: John Brunner's Times Without Number

John Brunner's *Times Without Number* (1969) is a surprisingly short book, and the ideas are the best part of it. It's 233 pages and if it had been written today it would be at least twice as long. It wouldn't be any better for it. This is minor Brunner but I've always been fond of it, and it seemed to fit with all these other things I've been reading recently about useless time travel.

The Society of Time is an organization founded to take control of Time Travel. They're kind of time-traveling Jesuits—which isn't surprising, as they live in a world where the Spanish Armada conquered England, with the Spanish thereafter getting kicked out of Spain by a second Muslim conquest, and where their allies the Mohawks are the dominant people in North America. Don Miguel Navarro is an obedient servant of the emperor of Spain, a licentiate of the Society of Time, and a good Catholic. He goes into time to observe, without changing anything even by speaking to anybody, because any little change could be disastrous. Of course, things don't go as planned.

The thing about time travel here is that time can be changed, it has no elasticity or protective mechanisms, and nor are there multiple universes. Time travel works and isn't useless—you can go back to the past and mine resources that are under your enemy's control in the present, and bring them back to the future. But woe betide if you change anything—if you're doing the mine thing, better go for seams not yet worked. You can also change your own personal timeline—if there's a disaster you can avert it if you can find a place to change things before it happened—at the cost of having memories of something that never happened and no memory of the "real" past. And there are alternate worlds, made by careful experimenting and then putting everything back exactly the way it was, and for purposes of study only, as there can be only one world at a time.

Brunner introduces these ideas one at a time, and always through the devout and honest Don Miguel, who isn't always all that quick on the uptake. This starts off seeming like a simple story of an alternate world, and gets more complex as it goes. The end, when you reach it, is simultaneously surprising and obvious.

It's worth noting that here, as in *Corrupting Dr. Nice,* but unlike *To Say Nothing of the Dog,* the life of Jesus is of central interest—but it has been placed off-limits except to popes, for fear of changing anything.

At one point Don Miguel muses that time travel is inherently unlikely, because once you have it there's a temptation to make changes, and changes will eventually inevitably lead to a future in which time travel is not invented, like a snake swallowing its own tail. This is a view of the futility of time travel that I hadn't considered.

114. Five Short Stories with Useless Time Travel

I want to consider a selection of short stories on the theme of useless time travel. In SF, often a lot of the best work has always been at short lengths. I'm going to talk about Poul Anderson's "The Man Who Came Early" (1956), Alfred Bester's "The Men Who Murdered Mohammed" (1958), R. A. Lafferty's "Thus We Frustrate Charlemagne" (1967), Robert Silverberg's "House of Bones" (1988) and Robert Reed's "Veritas" (2002).

All five of these are excellent stories, all of them are thought provoking, and they're all in dialogue with the novels I've been discussing. Most of them have been much collected and anthologized and are easy to get hold of, but the only copy of "Veritas" I have is in an old *Asimov's*.

What I mean by useless time travel is time travel that doesn't change anything—either where somebody goes back in time and stays there without making any difference, or time travel that changes itself out of existence, or time travel that is in some other way futile. I don't just mean changing time. In books like Butler's *Kindred* where the protagonist saves the lives of her ancestors but doesn't otherwise affect the world, time travel still serves a useful purpose.

"The Man Who Came Early" is notable for being from the

point of view of the locals who meet the stranded time traveler and are not impressed by him. Anderson is taking the *Lest Darkness Fall* model and saying no to it, showing a man from the future failing to make any headway among the Norsemen. His protagonist is even less successful than Tarr and Turtledove's Nicole, who at least makes it home.

In "The Men Who Murdered Mohammed" it is the nature of time itself that confounds time travelers—history is personal, in Bester's memorable metaphor it's like a strand of spaghetti for everyone, and when you change history you become like the spaghetti sauce, detached from the world. So you can go back in time and change it, and it doesn't change it for anyone except yourself. Very clever, very funny, and quite chilling when you think about it. Typical Bester.

"Thus We Frustrate Charlemagne" is typical Lafferty in that it's very weird, very clever, and impossible to forget. It's the traditional three wishes fairy tale told with time travel and making changes, with the twist that after the changes have been made the time travelers are unaware of any changes, though the reader can see them plainly. The time travel isn't useless, but it appears to be, and ultimately everything returns to the way it was.

"House of Bones" is about a time traveler stranded among cavemen and Neanderthals, learning a lesson about what it means to be human. He doesn't change history and he doesn't go home, and so it's all useless in that sense, but it's a surprisingly heartening story nevertheless, and I'd list it among Silverberg's very best. Silverberg has written plenty of other things about time travel, but it's usually useful.

"Veritas" is set in a world that has easy time travel to "moment universes" as in *Corrupting Dr. Nice*. Once you've gone into a universe, you can't get back to your starting point. The story concerns some young men who go back to conquer Rome, and end up with a mission to spread Romanitas over as many worlds as possible. It's futile, or perhaps quixotic, because there are an infinite number of worlds, and they can never revisit any of them to see what happens.

115. Time Control:
Isaac Asimov's The End of Eternity

Asimov published *The End of Eternity* in 1955, and so it's short—my 1975 Panther edition is 155 pages, and cost 35p or $1.25 Canadian, and features a typical British paperback SF Chris Foss generic spaceship cover that has absolutely nothing to do with the book. It's a fast read, I got through it in a couple of hours, and still an interesting one. Asimov was incapable of being boring. I hadn't read it in a long time, and I only remembered the skeleton of the plot and one telling detail.

Time travel was invented in the twenty-third century, and Eternity was founded a few centuries later. Eternity stands outside Time, observing and messing about with it, to make the one and only reality the best of all possible worlds. Eternals are drafted from Time—they are people whose absence from history makes no difference. They're all men, because you seldom find women in that position. (This is firmly stated, and it's necessary for plot reasons, but I raise my eyebrows at it every time.) Time travel works only between centuries in which Eternity exists, you can't go back further than that. So what we have here, astonishingly, is a time travel book that is all about the future with nothing about history at all.

The Eternals live outside Time, though time passes for them

the same way it does for everyone. Paradoxes and the issue of meeting yourself can happen only within Time. The Eternals are incredibly smug and self-satisfied and busy making "Minimum Necessary Change" to keep everything nice. They change the one and only reality to promote lowest common denominator happiness. They take the technology they want and then change reality so that it doesn't exist in Time because it would be too disruptive.

Andrew Harlan is a Technician who identifies and makes those changes. His hobby is "Primitive" history, the history of the period before the invention of time travel, history that always stays the same. He thinks of himself as a monk in the service of Eternity. Then he falls in love with a young lady from the 575th century, gets caught up with a loop in continuity his bosses are arranging—and then everything goes wrong. The book is called *The End of Eternity*, so you may think you don't need a spoiler warning, but actually you do. Spoilers follow.

This is the ultimate book about the futility of time travel. Brunner suggests that time travel that changes reality will tend to wipe itself out by changing reality so it isn't invented. Asimov specifically says that it's a terrible idea because with the power to change things, however benevolent you are, you'll change things in a cautious way, to make things safer. Space flight dies out every time because of the changes they make.

In swapping Eternity for Infinity, time travel is expressly rejected in favour of space travel. One change is made—and not one that would be made today to bring about a brighter future! They give the people of the primitive era of 1932 a hint about atomics, which of course will lead to mankind going to the stars at the earliest possible opportunity. It's hardly possible to read this in 2010 with the same optimism as readers did in 1955, or even as I did in 1975, even given the recent discovery of lots more extra-solar planets.

The End of Eternity, with its all-male fraternity of paternalistic meddlers, seems almost painfully sexist, and Noys, the beautiful love interest from the decadent 575th century, seems like a bit of plot mechanism more than a character. However, when all is revealed—on what is practically the last page—it turns out that Noys is from the far future and has been manipulating everything else to get what she wanted, a future of humanity in the stars. I don't know if this is enough to redeem her as a character or the whole setup to that point. Asimov could write good female characters when he wanted to (Arkady from *Second Foundation*) so let's be generous and give him the benefit of the doubt here.

The one detail from the book that had stuck in my mind was the time traveler stranded in 1932 putting an ad in a magazine he knew would survive saying "All the Talk Of the Market" in front of a drawing of a mushroom cloud, to attract the attention of his friends in the future who were trying to rescue him. ATOM and the cloud would mean nothing in 1932 and everything in Eternity, or even in 1955. I don't know why this kind of thing has stayed with me forever when I had forgotten all the other details of the plot.

My other thought was what a Cold War book it is, without being one of those that has Soviets in the twenty-sixth century or anything like that. The controlled planned centuries of Eternity are explicitly contrasted with the free chaotic future expanding among the stars in a way that seems shaped by the rhetoric of Free World vs. Communist world. And I don't think there's much more to be said on useless time travel after this, where Harlan and Noys choose for humanity to give up hundreds of thousands of years of safe future on Earth for the possibility of freedom among the stars.

116. Texan Ghost Fantasy: Sean Stewart's Perfect Circle

Perfect Circle (2004) (U.K. title *Firecracker*) is one of Sean Stewart's best books. It's about Will, an ordinary working-class man living in Houston. He comes from a large and complex family and he sees ghosts. He sees them in black and white. They're often, but not always, people he knows. They can see him too, and sometimes communicate with him. He can't exorcise them or anything like that, he can just see them, and at night he can't tell them from living people, which is why he doesn't drive. Not driving can be a problem in Houston. He's a normal American everyman, which means he's a divorced father trying to have a relationship with his daughter, who is just becoming a teenager with distinct opinions about him and the whole ghost thing. She wants to go to Six Flags. He doesn't have any money. Then he gets a call from a cousin with a ghost problem, and then things get complicated.

Stewart has been writing excellent fantasy for years, but it doesn't fall into marketing-category-shaped boxes, so though he is a terrific writer he never seems to make it big. I don't understand it—you'd think he'd be a bestseller. Maybe he always gets the wrong covers—he certainly does seem to have been very unfortunate there. And *Perfect Circle* lost out on a World Fantasy

410

Award to *Jonathan Strange & Mr Norrell*; most years I expect it would have won. The book was published by Small Beer, a small press run by Kelly Link and Gavin Grant, themselves fantasy writers. Small Beer are definitely my favourite small press, and one to watch. They've done some terrific short story collections by some of the best writers in the field (Theodora Goss, Holly Black, Joan Aiken, Link herself) and they also publish a lot of wonderful but slightly quirky novels that might not quite meet mainstream tastes at the big publishers. They recently published Greer Gilman's Tiptree Award–winning *Cloud and Ashes,* for instance.

Perfect Circle is one of those books that's hard to talk about. The voice, Will's voice, is first person, confidential, and desperate. The whole situation feels completely real, including the thing with the ghosts. There's an uncle who was vapourised in a refinery accident, all but his boots, and Will sees him wandering around in black and white and barefoot. The ghost of a cousin (Will has a lot of cousins) helps her family get compensation for an industrial accident. There's a family reunion, there's a scene in a shooting range where Will admits that the problem with being kind of left wing is that you don't get to exercise your usual American constitutional right to make guns go boom, there's a vengeful ghost, and after all of that there's even a hopeful ending. I like it a lot. It's a book I don't start reading late at night, but it doesn't go over into being too scary for me.

If you like books set in the US in the present day, and if you like a little supernatural in among your natural, you should on no account miss this one.

117. The language of stones: Terri Windling's The Wood Wife

Terri Windling's *The Wood Wife* (1996) is a rural fantasy, rather than an urban one. It's the story of a forty-year-old woman rediscovering herself as a person and a poet when she comes to the mountains outside Tucson and encounters the local inhabitants, human and otherwise, and begins to unravel their secrets. There's a romance in it, but it doesn't fit with the kind of thing usually considered as paranormal romance either.

It is a great book though, one of my favourite American fantasies. It doesn't make it all up like Terry Bisson's *Talking Man*, it walks the more difficult balance of using both European mythology and the mythology of the people who were there when the settlers came. Windling makes it work, and in the process writes an engrossing novel that I can't put down even when I know what's going to happen. This is one of those books that hits a sweet spot for me where I just love everything it's doing—it's the sort of book I'm almost afraid to re-read in case it's changed. The good news is, it hasn't.

I called it an American fantasy, but what I mean is that it's a regional American fantasy. I think the reason there isn't one

412

"American fantasy" is because America is so big. So there are regional fantasies like this and like *Perfect Circle,* and there are road trip fantasies like *Talking Man* and *American Gods*, and they have the sense of specific places in America but not the whole country because the whole country isn't mythologically one thing. I might be wrong—it isn't my country. But that's how it feels.

In any case, *The Wood Wife* is doing one place and time, and the sense of the Rincon hills and Tucson and Arizona comes through strongly. Maggie Black has been a wanderer, growing up in Kentucky, educated in England, living in New York and California and Amsterdam. She's forty years old when she comes to the mountains of Arizona as an outsider who has inherited a house and a mystery from a dead poet. It's so refreshing to have a middle-aged woman heroine, one who's already successful in her career when the book starts, who is done with one marriage and ready to move on, one with experience, one with a talented female best friend. Coming-of-age stories are common, but mid-life stories about women are surprisingly rare.

All the characters are great. They also belong very specifically to their place and time. The humans are mostly the kind of people who live on the artistic fringes, some of them more successfully than others—I know a lot of people like them. One of the central things this book is doing is showing a variety of relationships between romantic partners who have their own artistic work, and different ways of supporting that within a relationship. There's art and life and the balance between them, and then there's magic getting into it—we have magical creatures as literal muses, and the story explored what becomes of that.

Windling is best known as the editor of some of the best fantasy and fantasy anthologies of the last few decades. She's one of the most influential editors in the genre—and still I wish she'd find more time for her own writing because this book is just marvellous.

413

As well as a precise place, time and social context it's also set in a localised mythological context. It's the book I always point to as doing this thing right, of showing a mythological context in which there were people and their magical neighbours living in the region and then there were Europeans and their magic coming in to that. Too many fantasies set in the New World use European mythology as if the European settlers brought it into a continent that was empty of any magical context beforehand. Windling doesn't do that. Nor does she deal with the mythology of the Native Americans as if it were a familiar European mythology. This story feels as if it came out of the bones of the land.

Best of all Windling goes at all this directly, aware of what she's doing. The story is about two generations of painters and poets who come from elsewhere to the Rincons, and cope with living in and artistically rendering the land in their own way. First there's the English poet Davis Cooper and his partner the Mexican painter Anna Naverra, who we see in memory and in letters that run through the text, grounding it in twentieth-century art and literary history. Then there's Maggie, also a poet, and the painter Juan del Rio. This is Maggie:

> "I've studied Davis Cooper as an English poet. Born and raised in the West Country. So when I read his poems I see English woods, I see the moor, and hedgerows, and walls of stone. And then I drive up here," she waved her hand at the dry land around them, "and I realise that these are the woods he's been talking about all along. These hills. This sky. Now I'm reading a whole different set of poems when I look at Cooper's work."

And Davis, whose life and letters run through the book:

> I need a land where sun and wind will strip a man down to

414

the soul and bleach his dying bones. I want to speak the language of stones.

Anna and Davis and Maggie and Juan all interact with the spirits of the land directly, and are changed in their different ways. There are people who can transform into trees or coyotes, there's the fascinating mystery of the spiral path, and the whole thing ties together beautifully. It feels real.

And it's in print, for once, so absolutely nothing stops you from buying it this moment and reading it for yourself.

118. A great castle made of sea: Why hasn't Susanna Clarke's Jonathan Strange & Mr Norrell been more influential?

Jonathan Strange & Mr Norrell was published in 2004. When I first read it in February 2005 I wrote a review on my LiveJournal which I shall quote because it is still my substantive reaction:

> It's set at the beginning of the nineteenth century, in an England that is the same but distorted by the operation of magic on history, and it concerns the bringing back of practical English magic. What it's about is the tension between the numinous and the known. The helical plot, which ascends slowly upwards, constantly circles a space in which the numinous and the known balance and shift and elements move between them. It's a truly astonishing feat and I've never seen anything like it.

I've just read it again, and I could pretty much write that post again. In summary—this is terrific, it reads like something written in an alternate history in which *Lud in the Mist* was the significant book of twentieth-century fantasy, and it goes directly at the movement between magical and the mundane.

I wasn't the only person to think this book was brilliant. It won the World Fantasy Award, it won the Hugo and the Mythopoeic Awards, it was *Time*'s number one book of the year, a *New York Times* notable book, it was in the top ten of almost every publication in Britain and the US and it was a huge international mega-bestseller. It did about as well as any book can do.

But five years later, it doesn't seem to have had any impact. I said it was as if the rest of us had been building sand castles on the beach and she had raised up a great castle made of sea, but five years on, sand castle fantasy is being published all around as if Clarke had never put finger to keyboard. I wonder why that is?

It may be that it's just too soon. Publishing is astonishingly slow. Books being published now were written several years ago. Influence does take time to permeate through. But wouldn't you think that in five years you'd start to see some influence? But even without publishing speed, it could take longer than that for Clarke's influence to be assimilated and reacted to. I shouldn't be so impatient. Ten years might be a better measure. If I'd looked for things influenced by Tolkien after five years I'd have assumed he'd had no effect.

Maybe it will take a generation, maybe the people who read Clarke when they were teenagers will grow up to write fantasy influenced by her, but it's not going to happen with people already grown up and publishing and set in their ways?

Perhaps it's just sui generis, so wonderful and unique that it can't really be an influence except as a spur to excellence?

Or maybe, in the same way it doesn't appear to have much in the way of immediate ancestors, it can't produce descendants? It's wonderful, but it's not what fantasy is, it isn't in dialogue with fantasy and it's hard for fantasy to engage with it?

After all, what do I mean by influence? There's plenty of fantasy set in Regency England—there's Novik's *Temeraire* for a start. I don't think we should have a sudden rash of books about

Napoleonic magic or books with charming footnotes containing short stories. I don't even want more books directly using faerie magic. (We have had some of those too.)

What I would have thought I'd have seen by now is stories that acknowledge the shadow *Jonathan Strange & Mr Norrell* cast across the possibilities, things that attempt to engage with the numinous in the way it does. Fantasy is all about ways of approaching the numinous—and everything I read is still using the traditional approaches. That's what I keep hoping for and not seeing.

Perhaps it will happen, given time.

Meanwhile, *Jonathan Strange & Mr Norrell* is there, it's incredible, and one can always read it again.

119. Gulp or sip:
How do you read?

I was chatting to a friend about Vikram Seth's *A Suitable Boy* and she mentioned that because it was so long she'd had trouble setting aside enough time to read it. It is long, but I hadn't had that problem, because I don't think of reading as something I have to stop to do. I read in the interstices of my day. I feel I have to clear time to write—I need free time that's also psychologically free time to write, if I have to go to the bank later that hangs over me and gets in the way. But I don't feel like that about reading at all. I read all the time I'm not actively doing anything else—and even sometimes when I am.

Actually, I read all the time. I carry my book around with me and read on the bus, on the metro, or if I'm waiting for someone. If I'm going out, I check that I have enough to read to last me. I generally read one book at a time, but occasionally I'll read a big heavy hardback at home and take a little light paperback out with me. If I'm really enjoying the hardback I'll lug it along—I'll always remember reading *Anathem* while going round IKEA with my mother-in-law. I always read if I'm eating alone. I have in fact perfected the art of eating with either a fork or chopsticks in my right hand with my book open in my left hand. I can turn pages one handed with no problem. This is one of the reasons I prefer paperbacks.

I read in cafes and tea houses. I don't think of this as going there especially to read, any more than I think of going there to breathe. I will be reading and breathing while I am there drinking tea, that goes without saying. I won't read if I'm there with somebody else, or if I'm having a meal with somebody else. But if it's just me, or if you're meeting me, you'll find me inside the book—and if I'm there with you, I'll get my book out for the two minutes while you're in the bathroom.

I read in the bath—and this is why I vastly prefer baths to showers. I haven't figured out a way to read in the shower yet. I used to read only in-print paperbacks and current SF magazines in the bath, but since I moved here where I have a huge old bath and very hot summers, I have given in and now even read hardbacks, as long as they belong to me. (I have never dropped a book in the bath, though I know the story about the person who dropped in *The Fires of Heaven* and *schlurp* suddenly found the book had sucked up all the water and they were high and dry.)

I mostly don't read when I'm sitting on the loo, but when I worked in an office I used to, and I'd finish my chapter, too.

I always read in bed, even if I haven't had time to read anything all day. I don't do this for any reason other than that I know no other way to fall asleep—I read until I am asleep, then I put the book down and take my glasses off and switch the light off. So even on the busiest, tiredest day, I read a couple of pages.

Now, I can if I want to sit down and read for an extended period of time, and I often do. Some books I have literally read without putting them down. If I am stuck in bed I'll lie there with a pile of books, reading directly from one to the next. It's the same when I'm on a long train journey on Amtrak—I'll just read and look out of the window for days. (It's great. You have such comfortable trains in the US, and so cheap. Wonderful way to get around.) There are some books that seem to repay more sustained attention, especially when I'm just starting them.

Conversely, there are others that I enjoy in little bits but that get wearying when I sit down and read them for hours. I have nothing against reading in great gulps—it's just that I don't find it necessary for enjoyment. Reading in little sips works too.

So I was wondering—how odd am I? How many people are like me, reading as they go about their day, and how many like my friend, needing clear chunks of free time to get into a book? Does it matter if it's a new book or a re-read? Do some books require more sustained attention than others? Are you a sipper or a gulper?*

---

* The responses on this were all over the place—there seem to be plenty of both kinds of people.

120. Quincentennial: Arthur C. Clarke's Imperial Earth

Arthur C. Clarke's great strength as a writer was the way his vision merged the poetic and the scientific. His great weakness was that he was too nice—he always had a terrible time envisaging conflict, which gave him a hard time with plot.

I know something about *Imperial Earth* (1975) that most of you don't, except theoretically. It was once a new book. It's obvious really, everything was new once. People bought shiny copies of *The Fellowship of the Ring* in the fifties and waited for the other volumes to come out. But I remember *Imperial Earth* being new, because I bought the paperback from one of those rotating wire racks of books they used to have in newsagents in the days when dinosaurs roamed the earth and everybody smoked and you could buy a new Arthur C. Clarke paperback and a quarter of Cadbury's mini eggs and still have change from a pound. I vividly remember taking both the book and the eggs up into the park and sitting on a bench in watery sunlight reading the book and eating the eggs until book and eggs were finished. I still have the book, and I can still taste the eggs when I read it, which must make that one of the best value-for-money pounds I ever spent. It was the Easter holidays of 1977 and I was twelve. I thought *Imperial Earth* was one of the best books Clarke had ever written.

Reading it now, it gets astonishing points for all the things old books usually have to get a pass on. It has gay characters, bisexuality is considered normal, there are poly relationships, the main character is a person of color and so are large numbers of the other characters, it contains an older female character, it passes the Bechdel test, the president of the US is female. I'm sure I didn't notice any of this when I first read it except the nifty blackness of Duncan Makenzie. There's not much in the way of ethnicity—this is pretty much a post-ethnic world, but as far as skin color goes, darker is considered more aesthetically pleasing. There is one minor character who is a Muslim and a haji. He's a cloning specialist. There's one fat bald character—these things are considered to be unusual aesthetic choices because they're both fixable.

It's an interesting vision of the universe. It's utopian—this is a solar system in which all the problems have been solved and everything is nice. There's no personal wealth, rulers (on Earth anyway) are chosen by lot from those qualified, capitalism has withered away, Earth has been reforested, the planets are being settled, everybody is happy except the odd psychopath. The quincentennial of the USA is being celebrated to calm delight. This is really an unusually positive future even for Clarke— Earth has a population of half a billion, the excesses of the twentieth century have been cleaned up, there aren't actually any problems as such.

Duncan Makenzie is the second clone of Malcolm Makenzie, the ruler of Titan. Malcolm definitely wasn't chosen by lot, he was the intrepid engineer who figured out a way to make colonizing Titan pay. He nevertheless runs the place benevolently, and not even the opposition have a real problem with him, or his clone Colin, or Colin's clone Duncan. Duncan goes to Earth to celebrate the quincentennial and, while he's there, to get a clone of himself made for the next generation of Makenzies. While he's there he runs into his old girlfriend Calindy and his old best friend Karl. In a different book, Karl would be a mad scientist and an antagonist. Here he's a slightly secretive and mildly deranged scientist.

The science is odd at this distance. There's what appears to be an iPhone, described in detail. There are "comsoles" which are home computers—they contain no moving parts and haven't changed at all in hundreds of years, but they have monitors and keyboards and they're networked, so pretty good. The spaceships buzzing between the planets are using new mini black hole propulsion drives, which might make Titan's lucrative hydrogen business obsolete and cause economic problems. We have learned a lot more about Titan since this book was written—all the Titan stuff is obsolete, but still nifty. We've also discovered the Kuiper belt since this was written, which again makes some of it obsolete. But, oh well, it was the state of knowledge when he wrote it.

When I was twelve I thought the (so incredibly mild as to be hardly there at all) sex and the relationship between Duncan, Calindy, and Karl were at the heart of the book. I also really liked the spaceship trip from Titan to Earth, and the stuff about SETI was all totally new to me. I was also very impressed by the stuff about cloning—again, totally new. I also credit the pentominoes with my subsequent obsession with Tetris.

Now I think the best bit of the book is the descriptions of exotic Titan, which seem perfectly normal to Duncan, and of perfectly normal Earth, which he sees as exotic and weird. The reversals here are still lovely—Duncan thinks a jet of oxygen burning off in the methane atmosphere is pretty normal but finds a horse alien and doesn't know what a butterfly is. I also like the terse conversations between the clones who understand each other too well to need to say things in full—but I don't for a minute believe that they would really be like that. I think cloned parents and children would have just as many problems as the normal kind. But the emotional feel of the cloning works.

It's hard to say how much of my enjoyment of this book is nostalgia (like the remembered taste of chocolate) and how much I actually enjoyed reading it. If I read it for the first time now nothing in it would be new and the only thing that would be odd would be how nice everything is. No conflict! The plot really is, "What I did on my summer holiday," and that plot has been done better than this. I notice it isn't in print, while Clarke's real classics still are. But I enjoyed reading it again, in the copy I bought new when Pan could still say, "His great new novel" on the cover. It's not his best, but even minor Clarke has charm.

121. Do you skim?

This is kind of a follow-up post to "Gulp or Sip," and like that post it arises from a conversation with a friend. (A different friend. I have a lot of friends who like to read.) This friend said that if she was getting bored with something in a book she'd skip ahead until it got interesting. "How do you know?" I asked. "I skim," she replied. "If there's a boring action sequence, or a boring sex scene, I'll skim until we get back to something interesting." To clarify—she doesn't read all the words. She stops reading and just casts her eyes over the text, speed reading occasional phrases until she has missed the bit she doesn't like. It's as if she's re-reading and she decides to skip a thread she didn't enjoy, except without having ever read it in the first place. Or it's like the way you might look for a particular bit on a page to quote without getting sucked in to reading the whole thing, except without having read it before. It's not like the way you can keep reading in your sleep and suddenly realise you didn't take in the last few pages. It's a deliberate action—the way in a non-fiction book you might decide not to read a chapter that covers a topic you don't need. Except, of course, that she does it with fiction, and not to a clearly marked endpoint, but to where the text gets interesting again.

I never do this. I've never even thought of it. It seems really weird to me.

So what I want to know is, do other people do this?

Ugol's Law states that if you ask, "Am I the only one who . . . ?" the answer is always no. There are things absolutely nobody does, but if any one person does something, then there are others who also do it. So it seems very likely that it's not just my friend, and other people do this.

What I want to know is, don't you miss things? I mean it might look like a boring sex scene, but who knows that the protagonists aren't going to break off foreplay to discuss the way neutron stars work? (Real example.) Or who knows what clever things the author might be doing in a boring battle scene? Patrick O'Brian uses them for characterisation. If a book is really too dull for me to care what happens, I might put it down altogether, but if it's interesting enough to keep reading, I can't imagine just skipping a chunk—nor have I really got a handle on where you'd start reading again. How can you tell? And how do you know you didn't miss something vital that might have made the whole book make more sense?

I'm talking about reading for pleasure here. I understand how it's possible to read boring non-fiction for information, and skip the sections labeled as containing no useful information. And I'm mostly talking about reading SF and fantasy, though goodness knows I don't skim when I'm reading mainstream novels either.

I read in hopes of little sparkling moments that are going to turn my head inside out. I increase my chances of getting them by reading the kind of writers who have done that to me before: (Vinge, Delany, Dean, Le Guin, Wilson, Schroeder, Cherryh . . .) where really skipping even a paragraph might leave you lost and confused at the end. I can see that there are other writers I enjoy whose work isn't that dense, but I still don't want to miss anything. Who knows where that moment might be hidden? It's either worth reading or it isn't, I can't see the point of half-reading it.

I can't understand how that could be fun. If it hasn't sucked me in so that I want to keep reading it then I might as well be eating broccoli. Or reading something else.

Are there books that have good bits and bad bits so clearly defined that this makes sense as a reading strategy? Why have I never read any of them? (Hypothesis: They're all about vampires and pirates.) How widespread is this anyway? If you do it, what do you get out of it? And if you've done it, do you feel as if you've really read the book and can talk about it afterwards?*

(Health warning: If you do this skimming thing with my books, please don't mention it. You might send me into a decline.)

---

* It turns out that a remarkable number of people skim. I still don't understand it.

122. A merrier world:
J. R. R. Tolkien's The Hobbit

The Hobbit isn't as good a book as *The Lord of the Rings*. It's a children's book, for one thing, and it talks down to the reader. It's not quite set in Middle Earth—or if it is, then it isn't quite set in the Third Age. It isn't pegged down to history and geography the way *The Lord of the Rings* is. Most of all, it's a first work by an immature writer; journeyman work and not the masterpiece he would later produce. But it's still an excellent book. After all, it's not much of a complaint to say that something isn't as good as the best book in the world.

If you are fortunate enough to share a house with a bright six-year-old, or a seven- or eight-year-old who still likes bedtime stories, I strongly recommend reading them a chapter of *The Hobbit* aloud every night before bed. It reads aloud brilliantly, and when you do this it's quite clear that Tolkien intended it that way. I've read not only *The Hobbit* but *The Lord of the Rings* aloud twice as well, and had it read to me once. The sentences form the rhythms of speech, the pauses are in the right place, they fall well on the ear. This isn't the case with a lot of books, even books I like. Many books were made to be read silently and fast. The other advantage of reading it aloud is that it allows you to read it even after you have it memorised and normal reading is difficult. It will also have the advantage that the child will encounter this early, so they won't get the pap first and think that's normal.

I first read *The Hobbit* when I was eight. I went on to read *The Lord of the Rings* immediately afterwards, with the words, "Isn't there another one of those around here?" What I liked about *The Hobbit* that first time through was the roster of adventures. It seemed to me a very good example of a kind of children's book with which I was familiar—Narnia, of course, but also the whole set of children's books in which children have magical adventures and come home safely. It didn't occur to me that it had been written before a lot of them—I had no concept as a child that things were written in order and could influence each other. *The Hobbit* fit into a category with *At the Back of the North Wind* and *The Lion, the Witch and the Wardrobe* and half of E. Nesbit and Enid Blyton.

The unusual thing about *The Hobbit* for me was that Bilbo Baggins was a hobbit and a grown-up. He had his own charming and unusual house and he indulged in grown-up pleasures like smoking and drinking. He didn't have to evade his parents to go off on an adventure. He lived in a world where there were not only dwarves and elves and wizards but also signs that said "Expert treasure hunter wants a good job, plenty of excitement and reasonable reward." He lived a life a child could see as independent, with people coming to tea unexpectedly and with dishes to be done afterwards (this happened in our house all the time), but without any of the complicated adult disadvantages of jobs and romance. Bilbo didn't want an adventure, but an adventure came and took him anyway. And it is "There and Back Again," at the end he returns home with treasure and the gift of poetry.

Of course, *The Lord of the Rings* isn't "another one of those." Reading *The Lord of the Rings* immediately afterwards was like being thrown into deep magical water which I fortunately learned to breathe, but from which I have never truly emerged.

Reading *The Hobbit* now is odd. I can see all the patronizing asides, which were the sort of thing I found so familiar in children's books that I'm sure they were quite invisible to me. I've read it many times between now and then, of course, including twice aloud, but while I know it extremely well I've never read it quite so obsessively that the words are carved in my DNA. I can find a paragraph I'd forgotten was there and think new thoughts when I'm reading it. That's why I picked it up, though it wasn't what I really wanted—but what I really wanted, I can't read anymore.

I notice all the differences between this world and the *LOTR* version of Middle Earth. I noticed how reluctant Tolkien is to name anything here—the Hill, the Water, the Great River, the Forest River, Lake Town, Dale—and this from the master namer. His names creep in around the edges—Gondolin, Moria, Esgaroth—but it's as if he's making a real effort to keep it linguistically simple. I find his using Anglo-Saxon runes instead of his own runes on the map unutterably sweet—he thought they'd be easier for children to read. (At eight, I couldn't read either. At forty-five, I can read both.) Now, my favourite part is the end, when things become morally complex. Then I don't think I understood that properly. I understood Thorin's greed for dragon gold—I'd read *The Voyage of the Dawn Treader* and I knew how that worked. What puzzled me was Bilbo's use of the Arkenstone, which seemed treacherous, especially as it didn't even work. Bilbo didn't kill the dragon, and the introduction of Bard at that point in the story seemed unprecedentedly abrupt—I wonder why Tolkien didn't introduce him earlier, in the Long Lake chapter? But it's Bilbo's information that allows the dragon to be killed, and that's good enough for me, then or now.

Tolkien is wonderful at writing that hardest of all things to write well, the journey. It really feels as if he understands time and distance and landscape. Adventures come at just the right moments. Mirkwood remains atmospheric and marvellous. The geography comes in order that's useful for the story, but it feels like real geography. Noticing world differences, I'm appalled at how casually Bilbo uses the Ring, and surprised how little notice everyone else pays to it—as if such things are normal. Then it was just a magic ring, like the one in *The Enchanted Castle*. The stone giants—were they ents? They don't seem quite ent-ish to me. What's up with that? And Beorn doesn't quite seem to fit anywhere either, with his performing animals and were-bearness.

The oddest thing about reading *The Hobbit* now is how (much more than *The Lord of the Rings*) it seems to be set in the fantasyland of role-playing games. It's a little quest, and the dwarves would have taken a hero if they could have found one, they make do with a burglar. There's that sign. The encounters come just as they're needed. Weapons and armour and magic items get picked up along the way. Kill the trolls, find a sword. Kill the dragon, find armour. Finish the adventure, get chests of gold and silver.

One more odd thing I noticed this time for the first time. Bilbo does his own washing up. He doesn't have servants. Frodo has Sam, and Gaffer Gamgee, too. But while Bilbo is clearly comfortably off, he does his own cooking and baking and cleaning. This would have been unprecedentedly eccentric for someone of his class in 1938. It's also against gender stereotypes—Bilbo had made his own seedcakes, as why shouldn't he, but in 1938 it was very unusual indeed for a man to bake. Bilbo isn't a man, of course, he isn't a middle-class Englishman who would have had a housekeeper, he is a respectable hobbit. But I think because the world has changed to make not having servants and men cooking seem relatively normal we don't notice that these choices must have been deliberate.

People often talk about how few women there are in *LOTR*. *The Hobbit* has none, absolutely none. I think the only mentions of women are Belladonna Took, Bilbo's mother (dead before the story starts), Thorin's sister, mother of Fili and Kili, and then Bilbo's eventual nieces. We see no women on the page, elf, dwarf, human, or hobbit. But I didn't miss them when I was eight and I don't miss them now. I had no trouble identifying with Bilbo. This is a world without sex, except for misty reproductive purposes, and entirely without romance. Bilbo is such a bachelor that it doesn't even need mentioning that he is—because Bilbo is in many ways a nominally adult child.

I think Bilbo is ambiguously gendered. He's always referred to as "he," but he keeps house and cooks, he isn't brave except at a pinch—he's brave without being at all macho, nor is his lack of machismo deprecated by the text, even when contrasted with the martial dwarves. Bilbo's allowed to be afraid. He has whole rooms full of clothes. There's a lot of the conventionally feminine in Bilbo, and there's a reading here in which Bilbo is a timid house-proud cooking hostess who discovers more facets on an adventure. (I'm sure I could do something with the buttons popping off too if I tried hard enough.) Unlike most heroes, it really wouldn't change Bilbo at all if you changed his pronoun. Now, isn't that an interesting thought to go rushing off behind without even a pocket handkerchief?

123. Monuments from the future: Robert Charles Wilson's The Chronoliths

Robert Charles Wilson has the best "what if" ideas of anybody writing today—well, maybe he's equal first with Schroeder and Egan. When people complain about science fiction these days lacking originality, he's one of the first people I mention as a counterexample. He thinks of wonderful "what if" questions and then tells stories about realistic characters living in the futures those questions lead them to. Sometimes he makes this work, and other times he asks a terrific question and gives it a less satisfying answer. (I'm looking at you, *Darwinia*.) He's never less than really really interesting, and when he pulls it off he's quite astoundingly good. *The Chronoliths* (2001) is one of my favourites. It was my very favourite until *Spin* overtook it.

The premise of *The Chronoliths* is that one day in 2021 a huge glassy monument commemorating a victory in 2041 comes crashing down in Thailand. Other monuments follow in other cities across Asia, many of them doing huge damage to life and property when they appear out of the future. They are made by a new kind of physics, and are definitely being sent back in time. Their monumental existence starts to shape the future they celebrate. Meanwhile people get caught up in their fields of weird probability, and their lives get even more distorted than the rest of history. This is the first-person close-up story of Scott and his family and what happened in the twenty years between the first message from the future arriving and being sent.

Our first-person narrator Scott is the typical modern everyman—he's a divorced father with problems with his own parents. He's divorced because he wasn't there for his wife and child when the first chronolith touched down and his daughter had an ear infection. The story covers twenty years—the daughter grows up and has agency, representing the next generation, the generation shaped by the inevitablity of the coming victories. The heart of the book is about being there for your family as opposed to finding out what the heck is going on with the huge mysterious world-changing thing that's happening—and Wilson does remarkably well with focusing on a dilemma that most SF doesn't even spend time blinking at.

There are enough cool ideas here for anyone. The speculation about time and probability and the implications of the technology that's sending the chronoliths back through time are fascinating. Then there's the human level—the motivation for doing it. They say they celebrate the victory of a mysterious Kuin—and before very long there are a lot of people claiming to be Kuin, everywhere. Kuin doesn't state positions, so Kuin stands for anything people want him to. Kuin's victory is inevitable. Everybody's responding to Kuin in some way, whether to welcome him or oppose him—but he isn't here yet.

There's also a mad scientist—she's called Sulamith Chopra, a Tamil who immigrated to the US when she was three. She's gay, too. (She's one of the good guys. But she is definitely a little mad.) There's a whole planet, though the hero and his family are American and most of the actual book takes place in the US. But really I think Wilson gets points for starting in Thailand and

435

having excursions to Jerusalem and Mexico—so many books set in the near future barely footnote the rest of the world. There's a fanatic and a love interest and a whole set of complicated people in the kind of complicated shapes of relationships people get into. There's a really good story—a really good human story and a really good science fiction story.

There's a particularly odd issue with reading a book that's ten years old and set ten years in the future—it seems simultaneously ahead and behind where it ought to be. There's a comment in the very beginning about the wats of Thailand, and the character says you can see pictures of them in any encyclopaedia—and that seems so old-fashioned! Google image search will show you pictures of them without getting out of your chair! Something weird seems to have happened to the Internet, because it's sort of there and sort of isn't—there's something more like satellite TV, and people print things out all the time and have printouts lying around. Maybe that's what people did in 1999, which is probably when this was written? It feels weird, it feels retro, and I didn't notice this when I first read it in 2002. There are also people going to airports and catching planes with only the most farcical levels of security—pre-9/11 U.S. norms, but how odd they seem! This doesn't make the book less enjoyable, and it certainly isn't the kind of problem Wilson could have done anything about, it's just odd. Twenty years ahead is one of the most difficult times to write.

The Chronoliths is a character story that also gives us a lot to think about—exactly what science fiction ought to do.

I read this in one gulp, barely setting it down at all, and I think I remember doing the same the first time I read it. So you might want to clear some time in your schedule for this one.

124. The Suck Fairy

I believe I've mentioned the Suck Fairy a few times here but without ever discussing her in depth. I first heard of her in a panel on re-reading at Anticipation, when Naomi Libicki explained her to the rest of us. Naomi has since said she heard of her from her friend Camwyn. Wherever she came from she's a very useful concept. This post is directly related to that panel, and also one at Boskone this year.

The Suck Fairy is an artefact of re-reading. If you read a book for the first time and it sucks, that's nothing to do with her. It just sucks. Some books do. The Suck Fairy comes in when you come back to a book that you liked when you read it before, and on re-reading—well, it sucks. You can say that you have changed, you can hit your forehead dramatically and ask yourself how you could possibly have missed the suckiness the first time—or you can say that the Suck Fairy has been through while the book was sitting on the shelf and inserted the suck. The longer the book has been on the shelf unread, the more time she's had to get into it. The advantage of this is exactly the same as the advantage of thinking of one's once-beloved ex as having been eaten by a zombie, who is now shambling around using the name and body of the former person. It lets one keep one's original love clear of the later betrayals.

Of course, there isn't really a Suck Fairy (also, there isn't really a zombie) but it's a useful way of remembering what's good while not dismissing the newly visible bad. Without the Suck Fairy, it's all too easy for the present suck to wipe out the good memories. And it's much better than doing the whole "hate myself for loving you" thing and beating yourself up. The name is genius, because it's always helpful when something isn't real but is a useful model to have names that make this clear. Nobody really believes in an actual literal Suck Fairy, but that doesn't stop her being very handy to know. She's wonderful shorthand for a whole complicated process.

In her simplest form, the Suck Fairy is just pure suckitude. You read a book you used to love, and—something's happened to it! The prose is terrible, the characters are thin, the plot is ridiculous. Worst of all, that wonderful bit you always remembered, the bit where they swim into the captured city under the water gate at dawn, and when they come out of the water in the first light and stand dripping on the quay, it all smells different because the enemy's campfires are cooking their different food—it turns out to be half a line. "Next morning we went in by the water gate." This most typically happens with re-reading children's books. It's like the moral opposite of skimming, where you've dreamed in extra details the book never mentioned. The thin thing you're re-reading can't possibly be what you remember, because what you remember mostly happened in your head. The Suck Fairy has sucked all the juice out of it.

Suck Fairies travel in battalions. Her biggest siblings are the Racism Fairy, the Sexism Fairy, and the Homophobia Fairy. Here, the thing you have to ask yourself is, "How could I have missed that!" and the real answer is you were younger, more naive, less conscious of issues that now loom larger. It's sometimes the "it was 1961" defence—very few people were thinking about these issues, and they went right over your head, too.

These are ones that frequently attack my shelves. Sometimes I can justify them with "the author was ahead of their own time on this issue, if behind ours." Heinlein gets far more hassle for his female characters than Clarke or Asimov, because Heinlein was actually thinking about women and having female characters widely visible. Other times, not so much—I just have to shudder and move on.

Then there's the Message Fairy. The lovely story you remember as being a bit like *The Phantom Tollbooth* has been replaced by a heavy-handed Christian allegory! Again, this most often happens with children's books or books read when you were a kid. Kids are really good at ignoring the heavy-handed message and getting with the fun parts. It's good they are, because adults have devoted a lot of effort writing them messages thinly disguised as stories and clubbing children over the head with them. I read a lot of older children's books when I was a kid, and you wouldn't believe how many sugar-coated tracts I sucked the sugar off and cheerfully ran off, spitting out the message undigested. (Despite going to church several times every Sunday for my whole childhood, I never figured out that Aslan was Jesus until told later.) The Message Fairy also attacked some YA books to insert messages telling teenagers not to do drugs and/or sex. Political messages also abound.

Closely related to the Message Fairy is the Trope Fairy. This isn't a case where the author's trying to disguise a message that you should love God, or the Free Market. It's more a case of buying into a message that there's One Person for Everyone, or Love Always Has Three Corners, or People Who Have Sex Die, or Torture Gets Results. These things are very common in narrative, and it's possible to read past them lots of times, and then when you do become aware of them, they're everywhere and make you want to scream. Once you've noticed The Black Guy Always Dies you can't but groan when it happens.

I find it very hard to re-read books once I've found the Suck Fairies have been at them. If I don't pick up the book I can try to keep the memory of the good times, but re-reading brings me face-to-face with the Suck Fairy.

125. Trains on the moon: John M. Ford's Growing Up Weightless

At the heart of John M. Ford's *Growing Up Weightless* (1993) is a train trip by a group of teenaged role-players across the far side of the moon. It's also the story of how thirteen-year-old Matt Ronay discovers what growing up means, and how his father, Albin, writes a symphony about water on the moon. It's set four generations after Luna became independent—and that's pronounced "lunna," not "loona," and absolutely never call it "the Moon," as if it were something Earth owned. This is a future with complex history that feels real. There's a story going on in the background about water and sacrifice and power politics. In fact there's a lot going on here—of course there is, it's a John M. Ford novel—but most of all it's about Matt Ronay and his role-playing group making a trip from Copernicus to Tsiolkovsky Observatory on the train, two days there and two days back, without asking permission or telling their parents where they're going. It's wonderful.

This is a solid science fiction future that feels absolutely real and worked out in every detail. We see a whole complex universe as it spreads out from Matt; Matt is our stone dropped into the puddle of this universe. He lives in Copernicus and hates Earth, resents his father, resents the constant surveillance he lives under, and is caught up with his group of friends and their computer-mediated role-playing game. He wants to go to the stars. His family have been important since his great-grandfather was one of the signatories to the Declaration of Independence. His father, Albin, is trying to solve the problem of water, in an antagonistic relationship with the Earth company Vaccor. His mother, Sonia, is a surgeon fitting people up with the enhancements they will need for space. She doesn't communicate well. Ships come in from the New Worlds, worlds around other stars, and Matt watches the ships land and longs passionately to be on one. Meanwhile he and his friends are getting old enough to accept jobs—Matt has offers, from Transport, from a theatre company, but none of them will let him leave home. He feels oppressed by the fact of Earth hanging in the sky above him. The secret trip to Tsiolkovsky is important because it's something they are doing unobserved and in the last moment before they have to take up responsibility.

As with Delany's *Triton, Growing Up Weightless* shows us a utopia from the point of view of people who aren't aware it's a utopia. They have faster-than-light travel and New Worlds out there, government is by consensus and committees meet in VR. Matt percieves his father and his world as oppressive, but he's thirteen—I've never seen both sides of a parent/teenager relationship done as well as they are done here. This is a better world—moon—for teenagers than anything else I can think of. And they have trains. (The appendices on the trains, for people really very interested in trains on the moon—that would be me—can be found in the NESFA collection *From the End of the Twentieth Century*.)

If John M. Ford had a flaw as a writer it was assuming too much. He never talked down to the reader. This is a book where

442

every word has to be read with full focused attention, or it absolutely will not make sense. Even with full attention I know I didn't understand everything that was going on the first time I read it. It's a book I enjoyed the first time with a side order of "huh?" and that I have liked more and more as I have re-read it and seen more and more in it. This is definitely a book that rewards re-reading, that blossoms and flowers on re-reading, a book I plan to re-read every few years for the rest of my life and see more in every time. I also think I'd have loved it when I was thirteen.

Growing Up Weightless is set very firmly within the points of view of the Ronay family, and they know what they know and don't think about it more than they naturally would. The point of view moves between Matt and Albin and (more rarely) Sonia as their paths cross. There's the central story to do with Matt growing up, and the background story to do with Albin and the water, and they coincide in the way father and thirteen-year-old sons usually do, rockily. There's also a sub-plot to do with Avakian, co-discoverer of the FTL drive. There's the relationship between Earth and Luna, there's the relationship between the solar system and the rest of the universe, there's the group of role-players and the dynamics within them. All of this, and the future in which they are all embedded, is written with the full fractal complexity of reality.

It's not surprising that Ford got the role-playing right—he was a major RPG writer and designer, winning three Origins Awards. But role-playing, and gaming in general, is usually so badly done in books that I want to put up a sign ten feet tall with blinking lights saying, "Look, he got the RPG right!" The kids are playing a Robin Hood–style game, within a VR interface in which the GM has programmed NPCs and situations for them. This prefigures World of Warcraft (the book is 1993!) but it's also got the feel of a real gaming group, which is social

443

interaction as much as anything. They're using VR to see what the characters see, but they're doing the dialogue from their own hearts. When the tech gets to the point where you can design your own worlds, this is what we will have. The computers too don't feel clunky—they might in another ten years, but for now the slates feel like future iPhones. Shall I say 1993 again? There's nothing here that makes you feel the book wasn't written yesterday. And it's full of the little details that make it feel solid—for instance, after so much about Matt hating the Earth and the Earth tourists ("Slammers") and defining Luna in opposition to Earth, we get a traveler from another solar system casually referring to "the Terralune."

Most books are in dialogue with other books, and this one speaks especially to Heinlein—to *The Moon Is a Harsh Mistress* and its Lunar revolution, and to *Space Family Stone* and its happy family leaving the post-revolutionary moon.

This is one of Ford's best books, written at the top of his powers, and I recommend it very highly.

126. Overloading the senses: Samuel Delany's Nova

I can't think of any other book that's anything like as old as *Nova* (1968!) that feels as modern. There's nothing here to apologize for or to smile ruefully over—there's one mention that by the end of the twentieth century humanity was on more than one planet, and that's it. This book was written the year before the moon landing, and it could have been written tomorrow without changing a word.

Not only is it not dated, but it feels exciting, it feels cutting edge, it feels like something I want to get my friends to read and talk about and get their heads blown off by. I'm so enthusiastic about how terrific this is that I want to jump up and down, saying, "*Nova!* Read *Nova!* Do you know how good it is?" Of course, since it came out in 1968 everybody has read it already—or have you? If it's sitting there looking like something you ought to get around to one day—pick it up! You'll be so glad you did.

I reviewed it here before. But I was itching to read it again, and I've thought of some new things to say about it.

Thematic spoilers but no plot spoilers:

The theme of *Nova* is sensory stimulus. There's Dan, who had his senses burned out observing a nova, so now he sees and hears and smells and touches everything through the brightness of that overload. There's Mouse, who has a sensory syrynx, an instrument that makes music, scents, images. The songs of the syrynx run through that story, and it can also be used as a weapon. There's the universe itself, complex, brightly layered, divided into three political groupings, with fashions and art forms and museums and jobs (everything from manufacturing to controlling spaceships) that are done by people jacked in to computers. There are lost aliens and new elements and levels of sophistication and revenge and superstition and desire. Delany succeeds in making this a fully realised and kaleidoscopic future. He tells us some things and shows us some things and implies other things and it all overlaps and keeps moving. It seems fractally complex like real human societies and yet it's comprehensible.

Nova is a book with layers of mythological reference—grail quest especially, but also other quests, Golden Fleece, the Flying Dutchman. I think I've figured out what it's doing with them, which is what confused the heck out of me originally and put me off the book. You know how sometimes people write something that's supposed to be the origin of a legend—the true story that inspired the myths? This is that only backwards, it's what the myths prefigure, so none of it maps directly, the myths are foreshadowings. Or, better, you know how figures from different myth cycles all come together on the Argo, or at Camelot? This accretion has happened here, and the legend of Lorq von Ray has attached to itself all these other trailing bits of quests. What that does is gives it resonance, echoes, facets, rather than establishing parallels the way these things normally do.

Delany's writing is often poetic and never more than here, where every metaphor is in service to the whole. This is the first page, Dan tells Mouse his story, as he tells everyone, ancient mariner that he is:

"We were moving out, boy, with the three hundred suns of the Pleiades glittering like a puddle of jewelled milk on our left, and all blackness wrapped around our right. The ship was me; I was the ship. With these sockets?" he tapped the insets on his wrists against the table, click—"I was plugged into my vane-projector. Then"—the stubble on his jaw rose and fell with the words—"centered on the dark, a light! It reached out, grabbed our eyes as we lay in the projection chambers and wouldn't let them go. It was like the universe was torn and all day raging through. I wouldn't go off sensory input. I wouldn't look away. All the colours you could think of were there, blotting the night. And finally the shock waves; the walls sang. Magnetic inductance oscillated over our ship, nearly rattled us apart. But then it was too late. I was blind."

I mentioned last time that the book has surprisingly interesting economics. This is a universe with rich people and poor people and people in the middle. You don't usually expect to see a grail-type quest set up with rational economics that make sense, but here we have that. There's a theory of labour, too, along with theories about art and revenge and love. There are also changing fashions in music and clothes, which is notable. There's a style of music just coming in, edgy, and ten years later it's nostalgia. This is what really happens, but it's rare to see it in science fiction, where you so often have things that define a planet and continue to define it.

We start seeing Lorq von Ray as the Flying Dutchman, and then we go back along his life and how he has grown to the point where we first see him. It's a portait of a man and a society. Something I noticed this time is that our point-of-view characters are this one rich man, Katin, who is educated middle class, and Mouse, who is a gypsy, who grew up without insets, poor around the Mediterranean. He's from Earth, Katin is from the moon, and Lorq is from the Pleiades. The three of them triangulate on the story, on the universe, and on the way it is told. What Mouse sees, what Katin sees, and what Lorq sees are different facets, which is part of what gives us such a faceted universe.

They're all men and so is the villain, Prince—the book is short of women. Those there are are iconic—Ruby Red, and Tyy, and Yana. Ruby is Prince's sister, who is a love interest for Lorq and her brother's helper. She's a character and she has agency but she's more icon than person. Tyy reads the cards, she's one of the crew, but she's very minor except as soothsayer. Yana is more a piece of background than a person. She's a terrific piece of background—but that's all she is. She's Lorq's aunt, she's the curator of a museum. Her politician husband was assassinated years before. And it's a great example of our angles on the world. To Lorq it was the heartbreaking death of a family member. To Katin it's a huge political event, he has seen it through the media, one of those epoch-changing things. Mouse has vaguely heard of it, he wasn't paying attention, he can't remember if Morgan killed Underwood or if Underwood killed Morgan.

This is a short book, but there's a lot in it, and I can see myself coming back to it over and over and finding more in it every time. Maybe in a few years' time I'll write you a calm coherent post about *Nova*. For now: wow.

127. Aliens and Jesuits: James Blish's A Case of Conscience

James Blish's *A Case of Conscience* is a very peculiar book indeed. I first read it years ago as part of the After Such Knowledge series. The other books in the series are explicitly fantasy or horror, this is science fiction set in a universe in which Christian theology as Blish imagines it is explicitly true. It's written in two distinct halves. In the first half, a four-man expedition to the planet Lithia, discovering it to be inhabited by aliens, discusses what recommendations they will make to their superiors. In the second half, a Lithian grows up on a decadent and dystopic Earth and causes chaos there.

It's like shooting fish in a barrel to point out all the things that are wrong with this book, from errors of theology and science to question begging and jumping to conclusions. But it's also very good. It's written in a quiet but compelling style that's thoroughly absorbing. It's easy to swallow the absurdities as I go along, it's only on reflection that they leap out. It has genuinely alien aliens, and we see one of them grow up from inside. It's very unusual and quite unforgettable. It won the 1959 Hugo, and it's good to see it going to a philosophic adventure story like this.

449

Four men were sent to Lithia: the Jesuit Father Ramon, a biologist; Cleaver, a physicist; Agronski, a geologist; and Michaelis, a chemist. Almost the whole first half of the book is taken up with them squabbling over what is to become of Lithia. Cleaver wants to make it into a sealed atomic research planet, Michaelis wants to open it up to trade and contact, Agronski will go along with whoever makes a good argument and Father Ramon at first wants alien contact and then wants the entire planet sealed off as he thinks it's a temptation created by Satan. The weirdest thing about this is that Lithia is the first planet inhabited by aliens that humanity has found. This is the first alien biology, the first alien language, the first alien civilisation. It's amazing that humanity would leave a decision about how to deal with that to one four-man team, or that anybody, no matter how obsessed a physicist, could even think that the potential for making bombs was more valuable than the actual living aliens.

The second half of the book is back on Earth—a horrible overpopulated and decadent Earth in which everybody is living underground for fear of a nuclear attack that never happened, and frantically having decadent parties or watching TV. This could be considered satire, except that it's too odd. Egtverchi, the Lithian who grows up among humans, does not instinctively follow the calm reasonable and utterly Christian-avant-le-dieu morality of the Lithians, but instead joins in the decadence and tries his best to destroy Earth in rioting once he has his own talk show. (No, really.) The very best part of the book describes his coming to consciousness from his own point of view. There's not much science fiction about becoming conscious and self-aware, only this chapter and Egan's "Orphanogenesis," yet it's a very interesting idea.

The book ends with Father Ramon exorcising the planet Lithia by FTL radio as the planet is simultaneously destroyed in a nuclear explosion as part of one of Cleaver's experiments.

Father Ramon seems to me to jump to conclusions about the demonic nature of Lithia, and the pope is no less hasty in his conclusions. Their reasons are very odd. Firstly, the Lithian process of growing up recapitulates evolution—they are born as fish, come out of the water and evolve through all the intervening stages up to sentience. The idea is that because this utterly proves evolution, people won't believe in creation. This doesn't seem like a Catholic position to me. Secondly, once they're sentient they are reasoning and reasonable and without any religious instruction they naturally seem to follow the Christian code as laid down by the Catholic Church. Father Ramon believes the devil made them and nobody could resist the temptation of seeing them and ceasing to believe in God—despite the fact that creation by the devil is the Manichean heresy, and he knows it is. The pope believes they're a demonic illusion that can be exorcised, and the text seems to go along with that.

I think what Blish was trying to do here was to come up with something that a Jesuit couldn't explain away. I decided to try this on a real Jesuit, my friend Brother Guy Consolmagno, SJ, an astronomer and keeper of the pope's meteorites. (He also has the world's coolest rosary.) I asked him first about evolution and then about the other stuff. Brother Guy:

Well, to start with, that's not and has never been any kind of traditional Catholic teaching about evolution. Certainly around the time of Pius X (say 1905) when the right wing of the Church was in the ascendency (following Leo XIII who was something of a liberal) there were those in the hierarchy who were very suspicious of evolution, but even then, there was never any official word against it.

As an example of what an educated layperson at that time thought about evolution, may I quote G. K. Chesterton, who in *Orthodoxy* (published in 1908) wrote:

451

If evolution simply means that a positive thing called an ape turned very slowly into a positive thing called a man, then it is stingless for the most orthodox; for a personal God might just as well do things slowly as quickly, especially if, like the Christian God, he were outside time. But if it means anything more, it means that there is no such thing as an ape to change, and no such thing as a man for him to change into. It means that there is no such thing as a thing. At best, there is only one thing, and that is a flux of everything and anything. This is an attack not upon the faith, but upon the mind; you cannot think if there are no things to think about. You cannot think if you are not separate from the subject of thought. Descartes said, "I think; therefore I am." The philosophic evolutionist reverses and negatives the epigram. He says, "I am not; therefore I cannot think." (from chapter 3, "The Suicide of Thought")

In other words, it's not the science that was considered wrong, but the philosophical implications that some people read into evolution. (In the case Chesterton was referring to, he was attacking the strict materialism that saw no differentiation between a man, an ape, and a pile of carbon and oxygen and other various atoms.)

Granted, this was written about 15 years before Chesterton formally entered the Church, but you can find similar statements in his later books. (I don't have them in electronic form so I can't search quickly.) And no one would call Chesterton a wooly liberal by any means!

A classic, specific endorsement of evolution in Catholic teaching came in 1950 with Pius XII's encyclical *Humani*

Generis, which basically makes the same point as Chesterton about accepting the possibility of the physical process of evolution while being wary of possible philo-sophical implications that could be drawn from it.

So, point one: even by the time that Blish wrote his book, this description of Catholic teaching of evolution was not only inaccurate, it was specifically contradicted by a papal encyclical.

Point two: as you point out, the attitude described is Manichean, which is not only not Catholic but even moreso not Jesuit. The whole nature of Jesuit spirituality, the way that we pray, how we think about the world, is one that specifically embraces the physical universe. "Find God in all things" is the sound-bite mantra. That's why we're scientists. If the world, or any part of it, is a creation of the devil (that idea itself is contrary to traditional Christianity since only God can create, and the devil is merely a shorthand way of referring to the absence of good, not a positive entity in itself) then why would you want to wallow around in it, studying it as a physical scientist?

Likewise it was the Jesuits who were the strongest (and still are) for "inculturation" and accepting alien cultures, be they Chinese or techies, for who they are, and adapting religious practices into a form and a language that can be accepted. Our best records of non-European cultures comes from Jesuit missionaries who were the strongest at protecting those cultures from the bad effects of Western influence ... often at great expense to the Jesuits them-selves (for examples, look up the Reductions of Paraguay, or the Chinese Rites controversy).

But I guess I am confused here about what Blish is trying to do. Is the main character becoming something of a Jansenist? It was the Jesuits who most forcefully attacked Jansenism (which is, after all, where the phrase "Case of Conscience" first comes from), and which can be taken as a kind extreme version of Manicheism. (And they accused the Dominicans of being too friendly to that point of view. Maybe the main character should have been a Dominican?)

Point three: every scientist is used to holding two or three (or six) contradictory thoughts in their heads at the same time. That's what science is all about—trying to make sense of stuff that at first glance doesn't make sense, that seems to contradict what you thought you understood, and thus come to a better understanding. So any scientist (not just a Jesuit) would be excited by encountering contradictions, and would be horrified at trying to destroy the evidence that doesn't fit.

Point four: what does it mean to have a "soul"? The classic definition is "intellect and free will"—in other words, self-awareness and the awareness of others; and the freedom to make choices based on that awareness. Freedom immediately demands the possibility of making the wrong choice, and indeed of making a choice you know is morally wrong. So how would you know that a race of creatures that didn't sin was even capable of sinning? If they are utterly incapable of sin, they are not free.

Point five, and somewhat more subtle . . . Even official church teachings like encyclicals are not normative rules that demand a lock-step rigid adherence; they're teachings, not rules, and meant to be applied within a context, or even debated and adapted. For example, there's a lot of Pius XII's encyclical which says, in effect, "I don't know how you could reconcile x, y, or

454

z with church teaching"—but that kind of formulation leaves open the possibility that someone else, coming along later on with more x's and z's to deal with, will indeed figure out the way to reconcile them. There's a big difference between saying "you can't believe this" and "I don't see how you can believe this" since the latter keeps the door open. Indeed, it is not the idea of sin that is hard to swallow in Christianity (just read the daily paper if you don't believe in the existence of evil) but the concept that it can be forgiven, constantly and continually.

As for creatures who have no sin . . . what's so hard about accepting the existence of such creatures? Aren't angels supposed to be exactly that?

Jo again: So, if Brother Guy had been on Lithia, we'd be in contact with cool aliens and finding out as much as we could about them.

Meanwhile *A Case of Conscience* remains a readable and thought-provoking book.

128. Swiftly goes the swordplay: Poul Anderson's The Broken Sword

The Broken Sword was first published in 1954, the same year as the original publication of *The Fellowship of the Ring,* so it's a pre-Tolkien fantasy, and certainly a pre-fantasy-boom fantasy. Lin Carter, who is one of the people who created fantasy as a marketing genre, feels the need to go on about this at great length in the introduction to the 1971 revised edition, because Anderson used the same list of dwarves in the Eddas that Tolkien did and has a Durin—this would be more convincing if Durin hadn't been mentioned in *The Hobbit* (1938) but it really doesn't matter. *The Broken Sword* is indeed entirely uninfluenced by Tolkien, or indeed anything else. It has been influential, but the most interesting thing about it is how unique it still is.

First, this book is grim. No, it's grimmer than that. Grim for Norse levels of grim. The truly unique thing Tolkien came up with was the eucatastrophe—where the forces of evil are all lined up to win and then the heroes pull off a last-minute wonder and everything is all right. He took the looming inevitability of Ragnarok and gave it a Catholic redemptive spin. Anderson stuck with Ragnarok. There hasn't been anything this grim in heroic fantasy since. There's kinslaughter and incest and rape and torture and betrayal . . . and yet it isn't depressing or gloomy. It's also very fast moving, not to mention short. My 1973 Sphere edition, which I've had since 1973, is barely over 200 pages long.

No actual plot spoilers anywhere!

The second deeply unusual thing is that it takes place on a whole planet.

The story is set in Britain, with excursions to other bits of Northern Europe, at the end of the tenth century. It's also set in Alfheim and other parts of faerie that lie contingent to our geography. So far so normal for fantasy set in our history, oh look, Europe. But unlike pretty much everything else I've ever read that does this, Anderson makes it all real. Faerie has countries too, and while the elves and trolls are at war here, there's a country over there with Chinese demons who can move only in straight lines, and one with djinni, and there's a faun homesick for Greece. I am always deeply uncomfortable with fantasy that takes European mythology and treats it as true and universal. What Anderson does is have mentions of other parts of the real world and other parts of the faerie world. He knows it's a planet, or a planet with a shadow-planet, and he makes that work as part of the deep background and the way things work. He's constantly alluding to the wider context. Similarly, all the gods are real, and while what we get is a lot of Odin meddling, Mananan also appears and Jesus is quite explicitly real and increasingly powerful. I loved this book when I was eleven, and I still love it, and it's hard to disentangle my old love from the actual text in front of me to have mature judgment. This was a deeply influential book on me—I don't mean my writing so much as me as a person. The Northern Thing is not my thing, but this struck really deep. I probably read it once a year for twenty years, and the only reason I don't read it often now is that when I do that, I start to memorise the words and I can't read it anymore. I can certainly recite all the poetry in it without hesitation.

The story is about a changeling—both halves. Imric the elf takes Scafloc, the son of Orm, and leaves in his place Valgard. Scafloc is a human who grows up with the elves, and Valgard is half-elf and half-troll, and he grows up with Scafloc's human family. Doom follows, and tragedy, especially when they cross paths. The book is about what happens to both of them. The elves and trolls are at war, though some suspect the Aesir and the Jotuns are behind it. There's a broken sword that must be reforged, there's doomed love, there's Odin being tricksy. There's a witch. There are great big battles. There's skin changing and betrayal and magic. Even the worst people are just a tiny bit sympathetic, and even the best people have flaws. This isn't good against evil, it's fighting for what seems to be the lighter shade of grey, and people trying to snatch what they can while huge complicated forces are doing things they can't understand.

Fantasy often simplifies politics to caricature. Anderson not only understood history and the way people were, but he made up the politics of faerie and of the gods and got them as complex as real history too. I read this now and it's all spare prose and saga style and he does so much in the little hints and I think, "Damn, he was good! What an incredible writer he was!"

If you haven't read it, you should pick it up now while there's such a pretty edition available. If you have read it, it's well worth reading again.

129. The work of disenchantment never ends: Kim Stanley Robinson's Icehenge

Icehenge (1984) is my favourite Kim Stanley Robinson novel, at least when I've just finished reading it. I first read it in 1985 as soon as it was published in Britain, picking it up because I'd been blown away by some of his short stories. *Icehenge* is incredibly ambitious and it really works, but its ambitions are very unlike what we usually see done in science fiction.

It's set on Mars and Pluto between 2248 and 2610. It's written in three sections, and all three are autobiographies—autobiography has become a popular genre in this future because with modern medicine everybody confidently expects to live about a thousand years. Unfortunately, memory is finite, so people only really remember about eighty years, with just occasional flashes of the time before that. Writing diaries and autobiographies for your future self saves them looking things up in the public records, and there might be things you want yourself to know about yourself that you don't want to get into those records.

It's not possible to discuss the weird cool things *Icehenge* does without some odd spoilers—to be specific, I can't talk about the

459

second and third parts of the book without spoiling the first part, and there's also a spoiler for some odd things it's doing.

The first section is the diary/memoir of Emma Weil. She's a lovely person to spend time with, direct, conflicted, an engineer. Her speciality is hydroponics and life-support. She's aboard a mining spaceship in the asteroids when a mutiny breaks out—the mutineers are part of a planned revolution and their spaceship is part of a planned jury-rigged starship. They want her to go with them to the stars. She chooses instead to return to Mars and get involved with the revolution there.

Reading this section is such a joy that it doesn't matter at all if you know what happens in it. This is also the most conventionally science-fictional section—Emma's an engineer, there's a starship and a revolution, there are technical details about closed systems and they all have long life, you think you know what kind of book you're getting into. You couldn't be more wrong.

The second section is set in 2547 and is the memoir of Hjalmar Nederland, who is a Martian archaeologist literally digging up the remnants of his own life. (He knows he lived in the dome he is excavating, though he doesn't remember it.) He finds Emma's diary and it vindicates his theories. This whole section is both structured around and atmospherically charged by T. S. Eliot's *The Waste Land*. Robinson directly references it from time to time: "We fragment these ruins against our shore," the unreal city of Alexandria, the vision of Emma as another climber. More than that, the spirit of the poem is the spirit of Nederland. He reads Cavafy, but he breathes Eliot. This is very hard to do, and even harder to do subtly, but Robinson manages it. It's a strange dance of despair. Nederland knows that we can't really know what happened in history, that we constantly revise and reimagine it, even our own history, even when we do remember it.

In this section we see Mars much more terraformed, but still caught in the strange political limbo. The Cold War is still going on on Earth, and Mars has the worst of both systems, the corporations squeezing and the five-year plans. It's interesting that they don't have an Internet and the Cold War has resolved itself in such a different way, when they have colonised the solar system and do have computers. I find this odder than older science fiction in some ways. This doesn't make me ask where is my Martian terraforming project and thousand-year lifespan. Perhaps because I first read it when it was shiny and new it still feels like the future, just one that's subtly skewed.

When a huge circle of standing liths is found on the north pole of Pluto, Nederland realises that a hint in Emma's journal explains that this amazing monument was left by the expedition she didn't join.

At about this point in my re-read, I realised that it is my love for *Icehenge* that prevents me from warming to Robinson's *Red Mars*. I like this version of long life and forgetting and this version of slow-changing Mars so much better than his later reimagining of them that I felt put off and then bored. Maybe I should give them another chance.

The third section, set in 2610, involves a debunking of Nederland's theory by Nederland's great-grandson, though Nederland is still alive on Mars and defending himself. And this is where Robinson provides the greatest meta-reading experience I've ever had. The whole thrust of this section makes me, the reader, want to defend the first part of the book from the charge of being a forgery. I love Emma Weil, I want her words to be real, I can't believe they're forged, that they're not real—but of course, at the same time, I totally know they're not real, Robinson wrote them, didn't he? I know they're not real and yet I passionately want to defend their reality within the frame of the story. I can't think of a comparable whiplash aesthetic experience. And it happens to me every single time. Emma's narrative must be authentically written by Emma and true—except that I already know it isn't, so I know nothing and I feel . . . strange. It's a fugue in text.

This is a book that asks questions and provides poetic experiences rather than a book that answers questions. It has a Gene Wolfe quote on the cover, and I'm not at all surprised that Gene Wolfe likes this. (I just wish T. S. Eliot could have lived to read it.) It's odd but it's also wonderful.

130. Literary criticism vs talking about books

I always resist when people call me a critic. I resist because my degree is in Classics and Ancient History, not in English. I never studied this stuff. I'm not qualified to be a critic. Literary criticism is a conversation, and it's a conversation I've never been part of—critics are in dialogue with the text but also in dialogue with each other. I'm talking about books as part of a different conversation, one with its roots much more in fan-zines and Usenet than in periodicals. Beyond that, I resist the term because critics are supposed to be impersonal and detached, they're not supposed to burble about how much they love books and how they cried on the train. Most of all I resist because I hate the way that necessary detachment and objectivity seem to suck the life and the joy of reading out of the books critics talk about.

As I was editing these posts into this volume, I kept noticing my spoiler warnings and wondering whether I should take them out. Critics don't use spoiler warnings. Spoiler warnings are fannish and embarrassing. But the *reason* real critics don't use spoiler warnings is because nobody reading real criticism is supposed to mind having the books spoiled, even though "spoilers" are well named—it does spoil a book to know what happens. Re-reading is forever, but you can only have the experience of reading a book for the first time once.

In the Penguin Classics edition of Elizabeth Gaskell's *North and South,* there's a footnote a third of the way through that gives away the ending. The enterprise of reading for pleasure was so far from the mind of Patricia Ingham, when writing the critical apparatus for that book, that she couldn't imagine that anybody on page 110 might prefer to read the next two hundred pages without knowing that X and Y will end up together. She clearly thinks that the only purpose for which anyone might pick up the book is to study it.

I don't want to be like her. I want to talk about books and turn people on to them, I don't want to spoil them. Many people don't mind spoilers, and that's just fine, they can read on past the warning. There are things you can't say about books without discussing the plot and the characters.

I'm talking about books I re-read, but the reason I am re-reading them is for the sheer joy of it. I want to share that, and that includes the joy of discovery. I left my spoiler warnings in so you could decide for yourself whether to keep reading. You know yourself and how you read. I gave you the warnings and trusted you to make an informed decision.

You may also have noticed a lack of critical detachment. I am talking about books because I love books. I'm not standing on a mountain peak holding them at arm's length and issuing Olympian pronouncements about them. I'm reading them in the bath and shouting with excitement because I have noticed something that is really *really* cool.

There's another odd thing, to do with what it's possible to take seriously. For a long time all of SF was, to use Delany's term, "paraliterature" and none of it was taken seriously. But for decades now there have been SF authors who are treated respectfully, who are studied, who have books written about them by

464

academics. But aside from that, within SF, some writers are given serious consideration and others aren't. There's canon formation. Le Guin is someone who can be taken seriously. So is Delany. But nobody takes Bujold seriously, or Brust, though they're both popular. C. J. Cherryh and William Gibson arrived in SF at much the same time in the 1980s. (Cherryh won her first Hugo in 1982, and Gibson in 1984.) Almost immediately Gibson became somebody to be respected, while people smile patronizingly when Cherryh is mentioned. There's a divide within SF between literary and popular and I think it's a line drawn in a very strange way, a line that doesn't have much to do with either the importance of the concerns or the literary quality of the work. Nor does it have to do with commercial potential—Gibson sells very well. But why is it only possible to write fannishly about Bujold, and seriously about Delany? It frustrates me equally that I'm not supposed to have fun with Gaskell and I am *only* allowed to have fun with Bujold. I want to consider them all together and look at them all from the same angle.

There's another thing I'm doing here that isn't part of the normal field of criticism, and that's talking about the practice of reading. Posts like "Why I re-read" and "Do you skim?" had huge responses as people talked about the way they approach reading, how it fits into their lives. I find this fascinating. But if I'd been putting together a volume of criticism, there would be more pieces on books and less of this kind of thing.

It's funny. I'm a real writer. But when it comes to this I feel as if I'm not really a grown-up critic. And I don't want to be. It's too much of a responsibility and not enough fun.

Thanks

These essays originally appeared on Tor.com. I'd like to thank Torie Atkinson, Pablo Defendini, Bridget McGovern, and the rest of the team at Tor.com for all their hard work that has made the site possible. I'd also like to thank Macmillan for being so innovative and having the imagination to agree to do something like this. Patrick Nielsen Hayden originally asked me to contribute and gave me my brief. Patrick and Teresa Nielsen Hayden also deserve huge thanks for coming up to Montreal and spending a weekend working on putting together this collection—it was both tremendous fun and very illuminating as a process. My husband, Emmet O'Brien, provided technical help as well as love and support. I'd also like to thank Alter Reiss, Rene Walling, Sasha Walton and Alison Sinclair for specific discussions that made some of these essays stronger.